MASTERING WORLD REGIONS AND CIVILIZATIONS

MARK JARRETT

Ph.D., Stanford University

STUART ZIMMER

JAMES KILLORAN

JARRETT PUBLISHING COMPANY

EAST COAST OFFICE
P.O. Box 1460
Ronkonkoma, NY 11779
631-981-4248

SOUTHERN OFFICE
50 Nettles Boulevard
Jensen Beach, FL 34957
800-859-7679

WEST COAST OFFICE
10 Folin Lane
Lafayette, CA 94549
925-906-9742

www.jarrettpub.com
1-800-859-7679   Fax: 631-588-4722

ISBN 1-935022-02-4   [978-1-935022-02-2]
Printed in the United States of America
First Edition
10 9 8 7 6 5 4 3 2 1   10 09 08

ACKNOWLEDGMENTS

The authors would like to thank the following Ohio educators who helped review the manuscript. Their respective comments, suggestions, and recommendations have proved invaluable in preparing this book.

Joetta Gregory
Middle School Social Studies
Curriculum Coordinator
Columbus City Schools
Columbus, Ohio

Russell F. Maruna
Supervisor of Academic Services
Educational Service Center of
Lorain County
Elyria, Ohio

Adam Motter
Learning Specialist,
Social Studies, K–12
Akron Public Schools
Akron, Ohio

The authors would like to extend a special thanks to the following educator for his efforts in designing and reviewing practice assessment items in this book:

Corbin Moore
Instructional Specialist,
Social Studies
Hamilton City Schools
Hamilton, Ohio

Layout, graphics, and typesetting: Burmar Technical Corporation, Sea Cliff, N.Y.
Maps: C.F. Enterprises, Inc., Huntington, N.Y.

This book is dedicated…

to my son Alex on starting his new college life — *Mark Jarrett*

to my wife Joan, my children Todd and Ronald, and my grandchildren Jared and Katie Rose — *Stuart Zimmer*

to my wife Donna, my children Christian, Carrie, and Jesse, and my grandchildren Aiden, Christian, and Olivia — *James Killoran*

TABLE OF CONTENTS

INTRODUCTION

In the sixth grade, you learned about world regions. You learned about the geography of the seven continents and how the earliest people in each region interacted with their environment. This year, you will learn about the history of the world, from the rise of civilizations to the European encounter with the Americas. You will also learn about economics, citizenship and government.

The purpose of this book is to improve your mastery of world regions and civilizations. The first part of the book will help you to improve your study skills, especially your social studies skills. You will learn techniques to help you remember important information. You will also learn other important skills — how to read maps and graphs, how to answer test questions, how to write essays, how to conduct research, and how to work effectively in a group.

In the rest of this book, you will learn and review major concepts from Ohio's social studies benchmarks for grades 6 and 7. These are the same concepts that will be tested in eighth grade by the **Ohio Achievement Test (OAT)**.

THE ORGANIZATION OF CONTENT CHAPTERS

Each content chapter of this book has the following features, designed to help you learn and recall important concepts and facts more easily:

MAJOR IDEAS

Each chapter is introduced by a "Major Ideas" section. This is an advanced organizer that summarizes the main ideas and concepts you will learn in that chapter.

APPLYING WHAT YOU HAVE LEARNED

Following the "Major Ideas" section, you will find several sections of text. Each section will discuss related events or ideas, and will include one or more "Applying What You Have Learned" activities. These activities will ask you to *describe*, *explain*, or *analyze* information and encourage you to think about what you have read. You will be asked to complete these activities, either alone or in small groups, as your teacher directs.

WHAT YOU SHOULD KNOW

Each chapter will conclude with a "What You Should Know" summary. This summary will repeat the most important concepts and facts from the chapter.

STUDY CARDS

The "What You Should Know" summary is followed by "Study Cards." These study cards identify the major ideas and facts in the chapter. They present this information in a different way. You can use these study cards on your own to quiz yourself, or with a group of classmates. You may wish to expand the number of "Study Cards" in the book by creating additional cards of your own.

CHECKING YOUR UNDERSTANDING

Each content chapter ends with practice test questions. These questions are designed to be just like those on the **Grade 8 Ohio Achievement Test**, which you will take next year. The answer to the first question in these sections is fully explained. Later questions provide you with independent practice in answering OAT-style questions.

THE ORGANIZATION OF EACH UNIT

All the content chapters on a standard, such as geography, form a separate unit. Each unit includes some further special features of its own to improve your learning.

UNIT OPENER

A "Unit Opener" provides a brief overview of the chapters in the unit. In addition, there is a "Word Wall" with the most important terms and concepts used in the unit.

CONCEPT MAP

A "Concept Map" at the end of the unit shows how all the information in the unit is related.

TESTING YOUR UNDERSTANDING

Lastly, there are additional test questions. This section provides a variety of multiple-choice, short-answer, and extended-response questions drawn from all of the chapters of the unit. These questions will challenge your ability to perform well on test questions from several subjects at the same time.

UNIT 1

SOCIAL STUDIES SKILLS AND METHODS

In this unit, you will learn about some of the most important social studies skills, such as how to interpret different types of data, conduct research, and work effectively in a group.

◆ **Chapter 1. Important Tools for Remembering Information.** In this chapter, you will learn a new technique for remembering information. You will also learn how to create your own study cards and what information to include on each card.

◆ **Chapter 2. How to Answer Multiple-Choice Questions.** In this chapter, you will learn about different kinds of multiple-choice questions. You will also learn the "E-R-A" approach — a unique method for answering every type of multiple-choice question you may face on a social studies test.

◆ **Chapter 3. Interpreting Different Types of Data.** Here, you will learn how to interpret various types of data, such as maps, graphs, tables, and flowcharts.

◆ **Chapter 4. How to Answer Short and Extended-Response Questions.** In this chapter, you will learn how to answer short and extended-response questions. You will learn about the "action words" used in these questions, and how to plan and write your answer. You will also evaluate sample student responses.

◆ **Chapter 5. Conducting a Research Project.** In this chapter, you will learn how to conduct research, analyze information, and organize your report or presentation. You will also learn how to list your sources in a bibliography.

◆ **Chapter 6. Working Effectively in a Group.** Here, you will learn how to work effectively in a group. You will learn to define group goals, assume various roles in the group, and evaluate the contribution of each member in the group.

KEY TERMS YOU WILL LEARN ABOUT IN THIS UNIT

- Term / Concept
- Study Card
- Map / Table
- Line Graph / Bar Graph
- Flow Charts / Diagrams
- Pictograph

- Rubric
- Generalization
- Almanac
- Gazetteer
- Periodical
- Internet

- Search Engine
- Primary Source
- Secondary Source
- Outline
- Bibliography
- Constructive Feedback

CHAPTER 1

IMPORTANT TOOLS FOR REMEMBERING INFORMATION

Social studies looks at how people in societies relate both to their physical environment and to each other. It includes the study of geography, history, economics, and government. In social studies, you will learn many new *terms*, *concepts*, and *people*. With so much information, it is sometimes hard to identify exactly what is and what is not important. This chapter will help you to do that.

IMPORTANT TERMS

Terms refer to specific things that actually happened or existed, such as particular events, places, groups or documents. When you learn a new term, think about its main features:

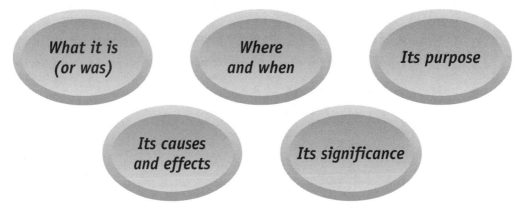

KEY CONCEPTS

Concepts are words or phrases that refer to categories of information. They allow us to organize large amounts of information. For example, Judaism, Christianity, and Islam share certain common characteristics. The concept *religion* acts as an umbrella, grouping these specific examples together by identifying what they have in common. Questions about concepts usually ask for a definition or an example of the concept. Thus, when you study a concept, you should pay careful attention to:

FAMOUS PEOPLE

In social studies, you will also learn about many famous people. When you learn about a person, focus on the person's background and upbringing, what the person accomplished, and why this was important.

background, upbringing, or position

accomplishments and impact

STUDY CARDS

To remember key *terms*, *concepts*, and *people*, it often helps to jot down the most important information and to draw a simple illustration on a separate study card. You can make these on index cards or by cutting up your notebook paper. For example, suppose you wanted to make a study card about your favorite sport. What information would you need? What terms would be included?

Every time you read about a key term, concept, or person, make a study card like the one on the right. Remember, you are not being judged for your artistic talent.

You can use these cards in many ways. You can cover part of the card to see if you can remember the covered

MONARCHY

Definition: In a monarchy, the ruler inherits his or her power. When the ruler — king, queen, emperor or empress — dies, power automatically passes to one of the monarch's children. This is usually the monarch's eldest son.

Example: King John of England, the monarch who signed the Magna Carta.

information. You can also work with the cards in groups. Show a classmate the picture on the card or the name of the term or concept. See if he or she can describe or explain it. Or see if you can create your own sample test questions based on information on the cards.

As you work your way through the pages of this book, you will find at least two **study cards** at the end of each content chapter They will identify the most important *terms*, *concepts*, and *people* in the chapter. You are encouraged to make a copy of these cards by photocopying that page. Then cut out the cards or copy the information onto an index card. If you consistently do this for each chapter, by the end of this school year you will have a large number of **study cards** to help you prepare for a final review or final test.

HOW TO ANSWER MULTIPLE-CHOICE QUESTIONS

In this chapter, you will learn how to answer multiple-choice questions. A **multiple-choice question** is one in which there is a question followed by several possible answers. Your job is to choose the **best** answer to the question.

Sometimes you may be presented with information in the form of a graph, quotation, or map as part of the question. You will then be asked a question about this information.

Let's take a look at some of the forms that multiple-choice questions can take:

RECALL OF IMPORTANT INFORMATION

Multiple-choice questions often test your knowledge of important terms, concepts, and people. Here is an example of how such questions may be asked:

---

1. Which **best** describes the Renaissance in Europe?

    A. a period of major achievements in art, architecture and literature
    B. a social system in which knights received land for service to their lord
    C. a system of beliefs about God and the afterlife
    D. a struggle between Christians and Muslims for control of the Holy Land

---

As you can see, this question tests your ability to recall information describing a specific period in European history — the Renaissance.

UNLOCKING THE ANSWER

What do you think is the answer to **Question 1**? _____

Explain why you selected that answer. _____

_____

_____

_____

_____

UNLAWFUL TO PHOTOCOPY

HOW TO USE THE "E-R-A" APPROACH

Whatever type of multiple-choice question you are asked, we suggest you follow the same three-step approach to answer it. Think of this as the **"E-R-A"** approach:

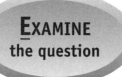
EXAMINE
the question

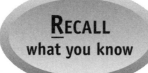
RECALL
what you know

APPLY
what you know

Let's take a closer look at each of these steps to see how they can help you select the right answer.

STEP 1: EXAMINE THE QUESTION

Start by carefully reading the question. Be sure you understand any information the question provides. Then make sure you understand what the question is asking for.

*This question asks you to select the **best description** of the Renaissance. Which answer choice correctly describes the Renaissance?*

STEP 2: RECALL WHAT YOU KNOW

Next, you should identify the topic that the question asks about. Take a moment to think about what you know about that topic. Mentally review all the important concepts, facts, and relationships you can remember.

In this case, you should think about what you can remember from your study of history. You may recall that the Renaissance was the name for the rebirth of culture that began in Italy in the 1400s. It soon spread to the rest of Europe. The Renaissance brought about achievements in art, literature, and architecture. Artists like Michelangelo and Leonardo da Vinci painted in a new, more realistic style. Renaissance scholars re-discovered Greek and Roman works of literature and philosophy. Architects studied classical examples to develop a new style of building.

STEP 3: APPLY WHAT YOU KNOW

Finally, take what you can recall about the topic and apply your knowledge to answer the question. Sometimes it helps to try to answer the question on your own **before** you look at the four answer choices. Then look to see if any of the answer choices are what you think the answer should be.

Review all the answer choices to make sure you have identified the best one. Eliminate any answer choices that do not make sense or that are obviously wrong. Then select your final answer.

Here, the question asks you to describe the Renaissance. To answer this question, you need to remember what the Renaissance was. Then you have to apply this information by selecting the best description of the Renaissance from the four answer choices.

- *Choice B describes feudalism, the system that existed in Europe during the Middle Ages. This was not the Renaissance.*
- *Choice C defines religion. This answer choice also does not describe the Renaissance.*
- *Choice D describes the Crusades. This answer choice is obviously wrong. It does not tell anything about the Renaissance.*
- ⭐ *Choice A is the best answer. It is the only answer choice that correctly describes what happened during the Renaissance.*

GENERALIZATIONS

A **generalization** identifies characteristics that several specific facts share. In order to understand generalizations better, look at these three statements about ancient civilizations:

Egyptian civilization developed along the Nile River.	Mesopotamian civilization developed along the Tigris and Euphrates Rivers.	Chinese civilization first arose along the Huang Ho.

What do these three specific facts show in general? They show that the world's first civilizations arose along major rivers. This statement is a **generalization**.

Some questions will test your ability to see the relationship between specific examples and generalizations about them. Here is how these questions may appear:

---

2. The city-states of ancient Greece grew rich from trade. The West African Kingdom of Ghana became wealthy by taxing the gold and salt trade.

Which general statements do these examples **best** support?

A. Trade usually leads to conflict and war between nations.
B. Trade between countries often leads to wealth and prosperity.
C. Merchants in ancient Greece and West Africa traded with each other.
D. Strong rulers often conquer neighboring peoples.

UNLOCKING THE ANSWER

🔑 What do you think is the answer to **Question 2**? _____

🔑 Explain why you selected that answer. _____

_____

_____

_____

_____

As you can see, this question asks you to make a generalization based on two examples. To answer questions about generalizations, you should again try the "E-R-A" approach. Let's see how this approach can be used to answer this question.

USING THE "E-R-A" APPROACH

◆ **Step 1: EXAMINE the Question**

First, read the question carefully. Be sure you understand what it is asking for. Does it ask you to make a generalization from examples? Or does it ask you to apply a generalization to a specific situation? In this case, the question gives two specific examples: trade in ancient Greece and trade in West Africa. Study these two examples to be sure you fully understand what they show.

USING THE "E-R-A" APPROACH *(continued)*

◆ **Step 2: Recall What You Know**

Now think about what you have learned about generalizations and about trade in Greece and West Africa. What do the two examples have in common? Notice that in both cases, societies grew rich from trade. This is an important generalization.

◆ **Step 3: APPLY What You Know**

Finally, apply what you know to find the correct answer. Look over the answer choices. Eliminate any answers that are not general statements or that do not apply to both examples. Then choose the best general statement from the remaining choices. In this example, all of the answer choices are generalizations. But only one of these generalizations applies to both of the examples in the question.

- ● *Choice A is wrong. There is nothing in the two examples that relates war to trade.*
- ● *Choice C is wrong. The two examples do not provide any information that tells us that ancient Greece and West Africa traded with each other.*
- ● *Choice D is also wrong. The examples do not tell about strong rulers or their conquests.*
- ✪ *Choice B is correct. The first example states that the ancient Greeks prospered from trade. The second example states Ghana prospered by taxing trade. The generalization that trade leads to wealth could be drawn from these examples.*

Now try answering a *generalization question* on your own.

Look at the information in the boxes below to answer **Question 3**.

Humans first appeared in East Africa. Thousands of years ago, humans spread from Africa to Asia and Europe in search of food.	Ancient peoples crossed from Asia to North America following the animal herds that provided their food.

3. What conclusion can **best** be drawn from these two examples?

    A. People migrated less often in the past than they do today.
    B. People sometimes migrate to meet their needs for survival.
    C. People often migrate in search of religious freedom.
    D. People who migrate are usually ruled by strong leaders.

To answer this question, try using the **"E-R-A"** approach.

APPLYING THE "E-R-A" APPROACH

◆ **Step 1: <u>E</u>XAMINE the Question**

What do both examples show? _____

_____

What does the question ask you to do? _____

_____

◆ **Step 2: <u>R</u>ECALL What You Know**

What do you recall about this topic? _____

_____

What do you recall about drawing conclusions? _____

_____

◆ **Step 3: <u>A</u>PPLY What You Know**

Based on what you know, which is the best answer? _____

Another type of *generalization question* starts with a general statement or concept, and then asks you to select the best example of it. Here is an example of such a question:

4. Which statement provides the **best** example of migration?

A. Ancient Greeks moved to Italy, where they set up colonies.
B. Christians and Muslims fought for control of the Holy Land.
C. Native Americans died from the introduction of European diseases.
D. Luther challenged the Pope's authority in religious matters.

CAUSE-AND-EFFECT QUESTIONS

Much of history consists of events leading to still other events. The explanation of *why* an event came about gives history much of its meaning. *Cause-and-effect questions* test your understanding of the relationship between a condition or event, its causes and its effects.

CAUSES. A **cause** is what made something happen. For example, if you turn the switch of a light, you *cause* the light to go on. Often, important developments in history have more than one cause. For example, the Renaissance was caused by the increasing wealth of Italian cities. The Renaissance was also caused by the discovery of new ideas from the study of ancient texts.

EFFECTS. An **effect** is what happens because of something. An effect is the result of an event, action or development. For example, when you turn the switch, the **effect** of that action is that the light goes on. Important historical developments often have several effects. The Renaissance gave birth to new forms of painting, music, literature and architecture. It also led to the invention of movable type, the exploration of the oceans, the questioning of Church teachings, and the birth of modern science. These were all important effects of the Renaissance.

CAUSE
Someone turned on the switch.

EFFECT
The light went on.

Many questions on social studies tests ask about cause-and-effect relationships. In answering these questions, be careful to understand what the question is asking for — the *cause* or the *effect*. Then think about the causes or effects of the event you are asked about.

5.   Which event helped lead to the end of serfdom in Western Europe?

    A.   Columbus' voyages to the Americas
    B.   the spread of the Black Death
    C.   the start of the Atlantic slave trade
    D.   the fall of Constantinople

To answer this question, you should again attempt to use the **"E-R-A"** approach.

USING THE "E-R-A" APPROACH

◆ **Step 1: EXAMINE the Question**

Read the question carefully. The question asks you to identify a cause. Your task is to identify one of the causes that led to the end of serfdom in Western Europe.

◆ **Step 2: Recall What You Know**

Mentally step back and think of everything you can remember about the end of serfdom in Western Europe. You should recall that **serfdom** *was a system established in the Middle Ages. Under this system, peasants, called serfs, worked on the lord's lands in exchange for his protection. This system lasted in Western Europe until the 1350s. Gradually, the system broke down. Lords wanted payments of rent instead of service. The spread of the Black Death also contributed to the end of serfdom. Many ordinary people died from the plague. Lords and towns needed workers. To attract workers, town officials ignored whether someone was a runaway serf.*

USING THE "E-R-A" APPROACH *(continued)*

◆ **Step 3: <u>A</u>PPLY What You Know**

Now you should apply what you know to find the correct answer.

● *In this example, **Choice A** is wrong. The encounter with the Americas in 1492 did not help end serfdom.*

● ***Choice C** is wrong because the rise of the Atlantic slave trade occurred after the end of serfdom.*

● ***Choice D** is also wrong. The fall of Constantinople in 1453 brought scholars to Italy and other places in Europe, but this did not help end serfdom.*

✪ *Answer **Choice B**, the spread of the Black Death, did contribute to the end of serfdom. Therefore, it is the best answer choice. The Black Death created conditions where serfs were needed by other landlords and towns. The shortage of labor allowed serfs to bargain for better conditions. This contributed to the end of serfdom.*

Now try answering another *cause-and-effect question* on your own by applying the "E-R-A" approach. Circle the letter of the correct answer choice.

---

6. Which development contributed to the rise of civilization in ancient Mesopotamia?

    A. the introduction of democratic government
    B. the growth of food surpluses from planting crops
    C. the settlement of religious differences
    D. the beginning of free public education

APPLYING THE "E-R-A" APPROACH

◆ **Step 1: <u>E</u>XAMINE the Question**

What does the question ask you to do? Does it ask you to identify a cause or an effect?

_____

_____

◆ **Step 2: <u>R</u>ECALL What You Know**

What do you recall about this topic? What do you remember about the rise of civilization in Mesopotamia? _____

_____

◆ **Step 3: <u>A</u>PPLY What You Know**

Applying what you know, which answer is best? Explain why the other choices are wrong. _____

_____

COMPARE AND CONTRAST QUESTIONS

We often compare two or more things to understand them better. To **compare**, we look at similarities and differences. Items are similar when they have characteristics in common. Items are different when they have features that are not shared. In addition to *"compare and contrast,"* such questions might use words such as *"similarities"* or *"differences."* A *compare-and-contrast question* might appear as follows:

---

7.   How were the Code of Hammurabi and the Roman Twelve Tables similar?

    A.   They proclaimed a belief in one God.
    B.   They established a written set of laws.
    C.   They provided records of economic activity.
    D.   They created new forms of government.

Again, use the **"E-R-A"** approach to narrow down choices and find the correct answer:

USING THE "E-R-A" APPROACH

◆ **Step 1: <u>E</u>XAMINE the Question**

*Read the question carefully. The question asks you to identify a **similarity**. Your task is to select the answer choice that identifies a similarity between the Code of Hammurabi and the Twelve Tables.*

◆ **Step 2: <u>R</u>ecall What You Know**

What do you know about the Code of Hammurabi and the Twelve Tables? Recall that the Code of Hammurabi was a written code. It was established by the ruler of ancient Babylonia. It specified what punishments Babylonians faced for each crime. For example, it called for "an eye for an eye, and a tooth for a tooth." The Twelve Tables were a group of laws set up by the Romans. Commoners (plebeians) demanded these laws be written so that nobles could not abuse them by changing the laws.

USING THE "E-R-A" APPROACH *(continued)*

◆ **Step 3: <u>A</u>PPLY What You Know**

Based on what you recall, which answer identifies a similarity between these two items?

● *Choice A is wrong. Neither document proclaimed a belief in one God.*

● *Choices C and D are also wrong. Neither the Code of Hammurabi nor the Twelve Tables recorded economic activity or established a new form of government.*

✪ *Choice B is the best answer. Both the Code of Hammurabi and the Twelve Tables established written laws.*

Now try answering a compare-and-contrast question on your own by applying the "**E-R-A**" approach.

---

8. What was an important difference between the ancient city-states of Sparta and Athens?

    A. Sparta allowed slavery.
    B. Sparta placed greater importance on the family.
    C. Sparta protected human rights.
    D. Sparta placed more emphasis on military service.

APPLYING THE "E-R-A" APPROACH

◆ **Step 1: <u>E</u>XAMINE the Question**

What does the question ask you to do? _____

_____

_____

_____

◆ **Step 2: <u>R</u>ECALL What You Know**

What do you recall about this topic? _____

_____

_____

_____

_____

APPLYING THE "E-R-A" APPROACH *(continued)*

◆ **Step 3: <u>A</u>PPLY What You Know**

Applying what you know, which is the best answer? Explain your answer.

_____

_____

_____

FACT-AND-OPINION QUESTIONS

Some social studies questions ask you to distinguish between *facts* and *opinions*.

◆ A **fact** is a statement that can be proven to be true. For example, the following is a factual statement: "Charlemagne was crowned in 800 A.D." We often check the accuracy of a factual statement by looking at several different sources.

◆ An **opinion** is an expression of someone's belief. It cannot be checked for accuracy. Often, opinions have words expressing feelings, such as *happy*, *satisfied*, or *brave*. An example of an opinion would be: "Spartan warriors were braver than Athenians." There is no way for us to check which group was really "braver."

Questions that ask you to distinguish facts from opinions might be phrased as:

9.   Which statement about the "Columbian Exchange" is a fact rather than an opinion?

A. The "Columbian Exchange" had a positive effect on the Americas.
B. The "Columbian Exchange" benefited England more than Spain.
C. The "Columbian Exchange" brought new foods and products to Europe and the Americas.
D. The "Columbian Exchange" was one of the great turning points in history.

UNLOCKING THE ANSWER

🗝 What do you think is the answer to **Question 9**? _____

🗝 Explain why you selected that answer. _____

_____

_____

Now try answering one more *fact-and-opinion question*. Apply what you have learned by using the "E-R-A" approach. Circle the letter of the correct answer.

---

10. Which statement about ancient Rome is an opinion rather than a fact?

A. The Roman Empire lasted more than 400 years.
B. Julius Caesar never became king or emperor of Rome.
C. Roman architecture was never as beautiful as Greek architecture.
D. The Pax Romana was a period of widespread peace from 27 B.C. to 395 A.D.

In this chapter, you learned how to answer different types of multiple-choice questions by applying the "E-R-A" approach. As you work your way through this book, you will notice a number of tools that will help you to practice what you have learned. These tools include:

◆ **Identification of Each Question.** Every question in this book is clearly identified by its *standard* and *benchmark*. This will help you to see which benchmarks you are having difficulty in mastering. You should focus your efforts on studying those benchmarks.

◆ **Checking Your Understanding.** Each chapter concludes with a *Checking Your Understanding* section composed of various OAT-style questions. The answer to the first of these questions will **always** be fully explained. It will show you how to find the correct answer by using the "E-R-A" approach. Additional questions will provide independent practice.

◆ **Testing Your Understanding.** At the end of each unit, you will find additional practice questions. These questions will assess your mastery of concepts and facts from all the chapters of the unit.

◆ **A Practice Test.** A final unit contains a complete practice test. This will help you bring all of your knowledge together. You will see how well you perform when you are asked to answer questions about everything you have learned in social studies in both sixth and seventh grade.

INTERPRETING DIFFERENT TYPES OF DATA

Social studies often requires us to interpret different types of information, or "**data.**" Historians look at old pictures, documents, and artifacts. Geographers study maps. Sociologists rely on tables and graphs to communicate their ideas.

You will also find that data-based questions are an important type of question on many social studies tests, including the **Ohio Achievement Test**. Data-based questions test your ability:

◆ to understand data   ◆ to draw conclusions from data

In this chapter, you will examine some of the major types of data used by social scientists on social studies tests:

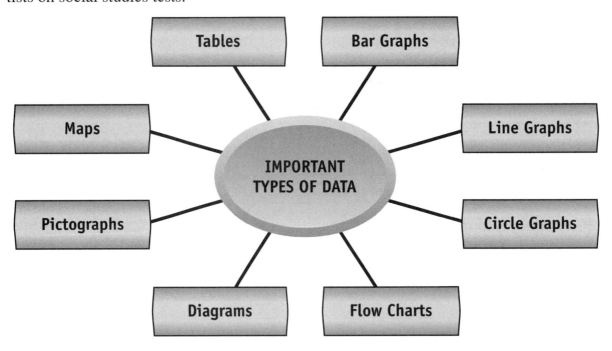

Tables · Bar Graphs · Maps · Line Graphs · **IMPORTANT TYPES OF DATA** · Pictographs · Circle Graphs · Diagrams · Flow Charts

MAPS

A **map** is a drawing of a geographic area. There are many kinds of maps. Most maps show the political divisions between countries or the major geographic features of an area. Historical maps often show political boundaries that existed in the past. There is almost no limit to the kinds of information that can be shown on a map.

STEPS TO UNDERSTANDING A MAP

1. **Look at the Title.** The title of the map usually describes the kind of information presented. For example, the title of the map below indicates that it is about the expansion of the early Roman Republic in Italy.

2. **Examine the Legend.** The legend lists the symbols used. It identifies what each symbol represents. In this map there are three symbols used:

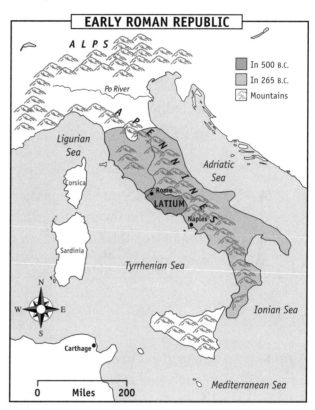

the dark gray-shaded box shows the area of the Roman Republic in 500 B.C.

the light gray-shaded box shows the area of the Roman Republic in 265 B.C.

this symbol is used to represent mountains.

3. **Check the Compass Rose.** The compass rose shows the four basic directions — north, south, east, and west. If there is no compass rose, you can usually assume north is at the top.

4. **View the Scale.** A map would be impossible to use if it were the same size as the area it shows. Mapmakers reduce the size so the map can fit onto a page. The scale is used to show the real distance between places on a map. Map scales are often shown as a line marked: **Miles** or **Scale of Miles**. For example, on this map slightly less than one inch equals about 200 miles.

FINDING SPECIFIC INFORMATION

To find specific information, you often have to use the legend and other map features. For example, if you wanted to find a mountain range to the east of Rome, here is what you must do:

◆ Carefully examine the map to find where Rome is located. Once you have found the location of Rome, look at the compass rose to determine which direction is east.

◆ Locate the mountains on the map that are east of Rome. Here, the Apennines lie just east of Rome.

ANSWERING MAP-BASED QUESTIONS

Look at the map on page 19 to answer the following questions:

1. What is the distance between Naples and Rome?

   A. about 100 miles
   B. exactly 150 miles
   C. 200 miles
   D. more than 200 miles

2. Which is a physical feature that might be added to this map of Rome?

   A. latitude and longitude
   B. population density
   C. types of vegetation
   D. a longer scale of miles

3. Which statement can be concluded from the map?

   A. By 500 B.C., the Roman Republic was the largest country in Western Europe.
   B. The Roman Republic greatly expanded in size between 500 B.C. and 265 B.C.
   C. The Roman Republic declined in size between 500 B.C. and 265 B.C.
   D. Romans were safe from invasion by sea.

TABLES

A **table** is an arrangement of information in columns and rows. A table is used to organize large amounts of information so that individual facts can be easily found and compared. Examine the table to the right:

WORLD POPULATION, 1650–1750 (in millions)

REGION	1650	1750
Africa	100	100
Asia	250	406
Americas	13	12
Europe	100	140

STEPS TO UNDERSTANDING A TABLE

1. **Look at the Title.** The title of the table tells you what it shows. As you can see from its title, this table provides information about the population of four regions in 1650 and 1750.

2. **Examine the Categories.** Each column represents a category in the headings across the top. In this table, there are three categories named in the headings: *Region*, *1650*, and *1750*. Each row represents the population of a different region during these two periods of time.

3. **Drawing Conclusions from the Data.** By examining a table, it is often possible to identify a trend or draw a conclusion. For example, historians believe the population of the Americas decreased slightly from 1650 to 1750. Can you think of a reason why the population of the Americas might have declined?

FINDING SPECIFIC INFORMATION

In order to find specific information, you need to see where the columns and rows meet or intersect. For example, suppose you wanted to find the population of Asia in 1750:

◆ First, put your finger on the column marked *Region*. Now slide your finger down the column until you reach the row for *Asia* — the continent that you are interested in.

◆ Next, move your finger across the row until it reaches the column for *1750*. You can see that in 1750, there were about 406 million people living in Asia.

ANSWERING TABLE-BASED QUESTIONS

Look at the table on page 20 to answer the following questions:

4. In which region did the size of the population remain unchanged between 1650 and 1750?

    A. Africa
    B. Asia
    C. Americas
    D. Europe

5. Which statement **best** explains why the population of the Americas declined from 1650 to 1750?

    A. Slave traders shipped slaves from the Americas to Africa.
    B. The native population of the Americas continued to be reduced by diseases introduced by Europeans.
    C. European invaders caused Native Americans to migrate to Europe.
    D. Europeans introduced Christianity to the Native Americans.

BAR GRAPHS

A **bar graph** is a chart made of parallel bars with different lengths. A bar graph is often used to show a comparison of two or more things. Sometimes a bar graph shows how one thing has changed over time.

STEPS TO UNDERSTANDING A BAR GRAPH

1. **Look at the Title.** The title tells you what the bar graph shows. For example, the title of this bar graph tells you that the graph shows the population of the world in 1650. In fact, this bar graph shows some of the same information as the table on page 20, but in a different format.

2. **Examine the Bars or Legend.** Usually the bars of the graph will be labeled. If not, then a legend will tell you what each bar represents. In this graph, a legend is not necessary: each bar represents a different region.

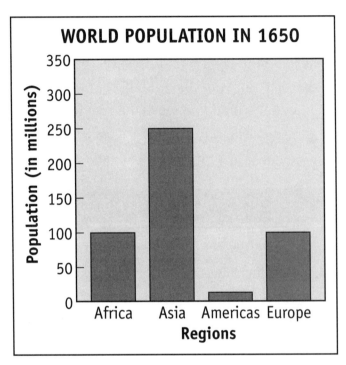

3. **Look at the Vertical and Horizontal Axes.**

   ◆ The **horizontal axis** runs along the bottom of the bar graph. It usually identifies the bars. Here, the horizontal axis indicates the four different regions that are being compared — Africa, Asia, the Americas, and Europe.

   ◆ The **vertical axis** runs along the left-hand side of the graph. It measures the length of the bars. In this graph, it measures population in millions of people.

FINDING SPECIFIC INFORMATION

To find specific information, you need to examine carefully the different bars. For example, suppose you wanted to find the population of Europe in 1650. Here is what you must do:

◆ On the horizontal axis, locate the region that you are seeking information about. In this case, you would need to select the bar that represents *Europe*.

◆ Then, run your finger to the top of the bar marked *Europe* and slide it straight across to the left.

◆ When your finger reaches the vertical axis, it should be at 100. This means that the population of Europe in 1650 was about "100" — or 100 million people.

ANSWERING BAR GRAPH-BASED QUESTIONS

Look at the bar graph on page 22 to answer the following questions:

6. What was the population of Africa in 1650?

    A. less than 25 million
    B. 50 million
    C. 100 million
    D. 250 million

7. Which statement is supported by information from the graph?

    A. There was little difference in population size between these regions.
    B. Asia was the least populated continent.
    C. There were more people living in Africa than in Europe.
    D. The Asian population was greater than all of the other regions combined.

LINE GRAPHS

A **line graph** is a chart composed of a series of points connected in a line. A line graph is often used to show how something has changed over time.

STEPS TO UNDERSTANDING A LINE GRAPH

1. **Look at the Title.** The title identifies its topic. For example, the title of this graph is *World Population in Prehistory*. As its title indicates, the graph shows the changes that have occurred in the world's population from 25,000 years ago to now.

2. **Legend.** A line graph may have several lines. A legend often identifies each line. In this graph, a legend is not necessary. Here, the title indicates what the line shows — the world's estimated population from 25,000 years ago to now.

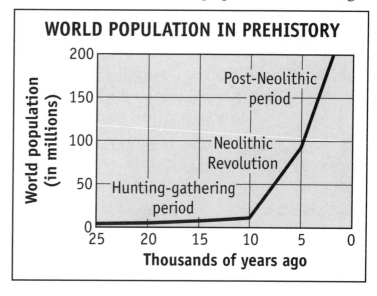

3. **Look over the Vertical and Horizontal Axis.**

   ◆ **Horizontal Axis.** The horizontal axis runs along the bottom of the line graph. In this line graph, the horizontal axis shows *Thousands of Years Ago*. The graph begins at 25,000 years ago. The axis is marked in five-thousand year intervals.

   ◆ **Vertical Axis.** The vertical axis runs along the left side of the graph. It usually measures an amount. As you move up the vertical axis, the numbers increase. In this line graph, world population is shown in millions. Therefore, the number "50" represents a world population of *50 million* people.

4. **Check for Trends.** Sometimes a line graph will reveal a trend. A **trend** is the general direction in which things are moving. We can often see a trend by examining the movement or direction of a line.

APPLYING WHAT YOU HAVE LEARNED

▼ What trends do you see in this line graph of world population? _____

_____

_____

_____

_____

FINDING SPECIFIC INFORMATION

To find specific information, you must closely examine the movement of the line on the graph. For example, if you wanted to know the population of the world 10,000 years ago, here is what you must do:

◆ Begin by sliding your finger along the horizontal axis marked *Thousands of Years Ago* till you reach the number *10*. This number 10 represents 10,000 years ago. Then move your finger up until you reach the line.

◆ Next, check the vertical axis. You are looking to see the amount reached at this point. The point where "10" meets the line is between "0" and "50" million people. However, the line is much closer to "0" than "50." Thus, the population of the entire world ten thousand years ago was only about 7 or 8 million people, the same as the population of New York City today. Remember, this is not an exact number but an estimate of the number of people who lived at that time.

ANSWERING LINE GRAPH-BASED QUESTIONS

Look at the line graph on page 23 to answer the following questions:

8. Which period on the graph shows the greatest increase in world population?

   A. from 20,000 to 15,000 years ago
   B. from 15,000 to 10,000 years ago

   C. from 10,000 to 5,000 years ago
   D. from 5,000 to 2,500 years ago

9. Which **best** describes the general trend of world population growth after the Neolithic Revolution?

   A. World population has continued to increase, but not as rapidly as before the Neolithic Revolution.
   B. The greatest growth in world population occurred during the hunting and gathering period.
   C. World population has generally decreased since the Neolithic Revolution.
   D. World population has increased dramatically since the Neolithic Revolution.

CIRCLE GRAPHS

A **circle graph**, sometimes referred to as a pie chart, is a circle divided into sections or slices of different sizes. A circle graph is used to show relationships between a whole and its parts.

STEPS TO UNDERSTANDING A CIRCLE GRAPH

1. **Look at the Title.** The title tells you what the graph is about. For example, this graph shows *Athenian Voting and Non-Voting Populations, 450 B.C.* The graph indicates the major groups in the ancient city-state of Athens that could and could not vote.

2. **Examine the Legend.** Sometimes a circle graph will have a legend to indicate what each slice represents. Often, as in this graph, the slices themselves are labeled to tell the reader what they represent. In this case, the legend explains the meaning of the dark and shaded areas. These show which part of the population was permitted to vote.

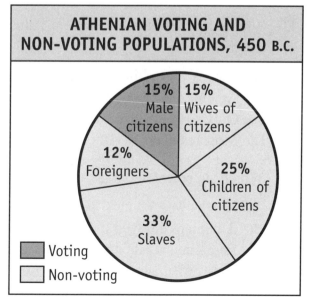

ATHENIAN VOTING AND
NON-VOTING POPULATIONS, 450 B.C.

15% Male citizens
15% Wives of citizens
12% Foreigners
25% Children of citizens
33% Slaves

Voting
Non-voting

3. **Look at the Slices.** Each slice shows the size of something in relation to the whole circle. Think of the circle as 100% of something. If you add all the slices together, they will total 100%. In this graph, the size of each slice tells you the relative size of a particular group in Athenian society. If you add all the slices representing these groups together, you will get 100% of the population of ancient Athens.

FINDING SPECIFIC INFORMATION

To find specific information, you need to examine each slice. For example, if you wanted to know the largest non-voting part of the Athenian population, here is what you would have to do:

◆ Look at the graph and determine according to the legend that you are interested in the shaded slices.

◆ Then you need to find which of these slices is the largest.

◆ In this circle graph, the slice marked *Slaves* represents 33% of the graph. It is the largest part of the non-voting Athenian population.

ANSWERING CIRCLE GRAPH-BASED QUESTIONS

Look at the circle graph on page 25 to answer the following questions:

10. Which group in ancient Athens was permitted to vote?

   A. foreigners
   B. wives of citizens
   C. children
   D. male citizens

11. Which conclusion about ancient Athens can **best** be drawn from information on the graph?

   A. Athens was mainly a military dictatorship.
   B. Athenians strongly believed in the ideal of social equality.
   C. Only some residents of Athens had the right to vote.
   D. Most residents of Athens voted in elections.

12. Which statement about ancient Athens is supported by the graph?

   A. Athens was the most populous city-state of ancient Greece.
   B. Athenians enjoyed living in their city-state.
   C. Foreigners made up the largest group in ancient Athens.
   D. Most Athenians were barred from voting in elections.

DIAGRAMS

A **diagram** is a simplified picture that shows how several things are related or how different parts of something work together. The purpose of a diagram is to help the reader visualize how something works or how it is organized. Each item in the diagram is usually identified. Arrows often indicate important relationships.

STEPS TO UNDERSTANDING A DIAGRAM

ORGANIZATION OF JAPANESE SOCIETY (1200–1700)

EMPEROR
Held highest rank in society but had no political power

Shogun
Actual ruler

Daimyo
Owners of large estates

Samurai
Warriors loyal to daimyo

Peasants
Three fourths of population

Artisans

Merchants
Low status but gradually gained influence

1. **Look at the Title.** The title tells you what the diagram is about. For example, this diagram is entitled *Organization of Japanese Society (1200–1700)*. The graph shows the major social groups that existed in Japan over a 500-year period.

2. **Examine the Legend.** Sometimes a diagram has a legend. The legend identifies what each symbol represents. In this diagram, each symbol is clearly marked, so there is no need for a separate legend.

3. **Understanding the Diagram.** This diagram shows the different ranks that once existed in Japanese society. As you study this diagram, you should notice that the highest ranking person in Japan was the Emperor. The horizontal lines in the diagram show how different social groups in Japan related to each other.

FINDING SPECIFIC INFORMATION

To find specific information, examine the diagram carefully. For example, if you wanted to find the position that peasants held in traditional Japanese society, you would:

◆ Locate the figure in the diagram representing the peasants. You then need to determine how this figure relates to the other members of society in the diagram.

◆ In this diagram, peasants do not have a high social ranking. Although peasants made up three-fourths of the population in Japan, they remained near the bottom of the social ladder.

ANSWERING DIAGRAM-BASED QUESTIONS

Look at the diagram on page 27 to answer the following questions:

13. Based on the information in the diagram, which statement is correct?

    A. Samurai were the main owners of large estates in Japan.
    B. Samurai were loyal to their daimyo.
    C. The Shogun had a higher social rank than the Emperor.
    D. Daimyos made up the most populous group in Japanese society.

14. Which type of political and social order is illustrated by the diagram?

    A. tribal   C. nomadic
    B. feudal   D. democratic

15. What conclusion can **best** be reached from the information in the diagram?

    A. The Shogun enjoyed a higher social rank than the Emperor.
    B. Merchants were the most respected social class in Japan.
    C. The Shogun actually ruled over Japan during this period.
    D. Social relations in Japan during this period were based on equality.

FLOW CHARTS

A **flow chart** is a special type of diagram. A flow chart is often used to describe a process, such as how laws are made. A flow chart can also be used to show the steps of a decision and the possible consequences of each step.

STEPS TO UNDERSTANDING A FLOW CHART

1. Look at the Title. Start by looking at the title. It tells you what the flow chart is all about. In this flow chart, the title is: *European Trade with their Colonies*. This flow chart shows the process that some European nations followed to accumulate wealth. You may recall that this system of trade existed between several European powers and their colonies from the sixteenth century to the eighteenth century.

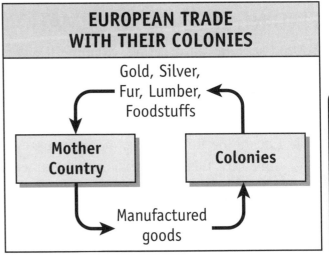

EUROPEAN TRADE WITH THEIR COLONIES

Gold, Silver, Fur, Lumber, Foodstuffs

Mother Country   Colonies

Manufactured goods

The flow chart shows that Europeans sold expensive manufactured goods to their colonies. The colonies, in turn, supplied their "mother countries" with cheaper raw materials.

2. **Examine the Arrows and Shapes.** In a flow chart, circles, squares, and other shapes are connected by arrows or lines. Each shape usually indicates a step in a process. Arrows indicate where each step leads — often to several choices or outcomes.

ANSWERING A FLOW CHART-BASED QUESTION

Look at the flow chart on page 28 to answer the following questions:

16. Which process is illustrated by the flow chart?

   A. colonialism
   B. revolution
   C. mercantalism
   D. feudalism

17. Based on the information in the flow chart, which statement is most accurate?

   A. Colonies mainly shipped manufactured goods to their "Mother Country."
   B. The "Mother Country" generally sent expensive manufactured goods to colonies in exchange for gold, silver and other raw materials.
   C. The center of world manufacturing was in the colonies.
   D. The Trans-Atlantic slave trade encouraged colonial manufacturing.

PICTOGRAPHS

A **pictograph** is a chart that uses symbols or pictures to represent a number or an idea. Pictographs can provide a quick and clear "picture" of the information. However, the data that pictographs provide is often approximated.

STEPS TO UNDERSTANDING A PICTOGRAPH

1. **Look at the Title.** Start by examining the title. It tells you that this pictograph shows the large number of people affected by plague in the 14th century.

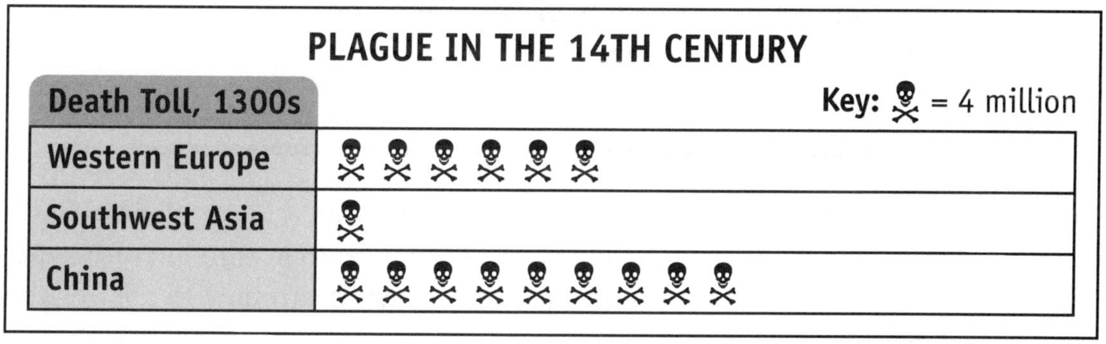

PLAGUE IN THE 14TH CENTURY	
Death Toll, 1300s	Key: ☠ = 4 million
Western Europe	☠ ☠ ☠ ☠ ☠ ☠
Southwest Asia	☠
China	☠ ☠ ☠ ☠ ☠ ☠ ☠ ☠ ☠ ☠

2. **Examine the Key.** A key or legend identifies what each picture represents. In this pictograph, each small picture of a skull represents four million deaths from plague. This pictograph shows the three areas that were most affected by plague (*also known as the "Black Death"*): Western Europe, Southwest Asia, and China.

FINDING SPECIFIC INFORMATION

To find specific information, you have to look at a region and count the number of symbols next to it. For example, if you wanted to find the number of people who died from plague in Western Europe, here is what you have to do:

◆ First, locate the region the question is asking about. The regions are listed on the left side of the pictograph.

◆ Now count the number of skulls that appear next to *Western Europe*. There are six skulls. Each one represents four million people. Six times four million equals 24 million.

◆ Thus, based on the information in this pictograph, we can conclude that about 24 million people died from plague in Western Europe during the 1300s.

ANSWERING PICTOGRAPH-BASED QUESTIONS

Look at the pictograph on page 29 to answer the following questions:

18. How many people died from plague in China in the 1300s?

   A. 4 million
   B. 28 million
   C. 36 million
   D. 48 million

19. What conclusion can **best** be drawn from the information in the pictograph?

   A. Plague was the most dangerous disease ever to affect the world.
   B. Plague killed most of the world's population.
   C. Almost a third of the population of Western Europe died from plague.
   D. Plague affected more than one region in the world.

In this chapter, you have learned how to interpret various types of data and how to answer questions about them. In future chapters, you will learn how to interpret other types of data — such as timelines. In the next chapter, you will learn how to answer short and extended-response questions.

CHAPTER 4

HOW TO ANSWER SHORT AND EXTENDED-RESPONSE QUESTIONS

Some questions on social studies tests will ask you to write an answer in your own words. Next year, on the **Grade 8 Ohio Achievement Test**, you will be required to answer two types of these: short-answer and extended-response questions.

SHORT AND EXTENDED-RESPONSE QUESTIONS

Although the OAT may seem far off, it is a good idea to start learning how to respond to these kinds of questions so you will be prepared when the test comes.

SHORT-ANSWER QUESTIONS

Short-answer questions require you to write a few sentences to answer the question. A short-answer question will usually require you to give **two** facts or pieces of information. Your answer will be worth up to two points. Although your answer should be short, the question itself may be long. It may even include a document, map or other piece of data as part of the question.

EXTENDED-RESPONSE QUESTIONS

An **extended-response question** may be similar to a short-answer question, except that more information is required in the answer. Typically, the question requires **four** pieces of information in your response. These could be four separate items. Or these might be two items that you are expected to describe. First, you might be asked to **identify** the item. Then you could be asked to describe or explain each item by adding additional details. These questions will be worth four points.

THE FOCUS OF MOST SHORT-ANSWER AND EXTENDED-RESPONSE QUESTIONS

Short-answer and extended-response questions test your knowledge of a wide-range of topics. These questions typically focus on the following:

Interpreting Data

You may be asked to explain a quotation, graph, or some other piece of data.

Explaining Cause-and-Effect Relationships

Many short-answer and extended-response questions ask about cause-and-effect relationships. Although there are many ways such questions can be asked, most often they will appear as:

◆ What were the **causes** of the decline of the native population of Mexico?

◆ What were the **effects** of the Crusades on European culture?

Explaining Different Sides of an Issue or Points of View

Some questions will ask you to compare points of view. For this reason, it is important to make sure that you always understand different points of view when you study an event or development. These questions might be phrased as:

◆ How did Christians and Muslims view the Crusades?

◆ How did Native Americans and Europeans view each other?

◆ How did Protestants and Catholics view the Reformation?

◆ What were the arguments for and against establishing overseas colonies?

Solving Practical Problems

You might be asked how citizens in your community should approach an important problem, such as pollution.

HOW TO RESPOND TO A SHORT-ANSWER OR EXTENDED-RESPONSE QUESTION

To write a good response to a short-answer or extended-response question, you need to do the following:

◆ Understand the language of the question. Be sure you understand exactly what is being asked for.

◆ Interpret any documents or other data in the question.

◆ Understand any critical thinking skill tested by the question (such as *cause-and-effect*, *compare and contrast*, *identify and describe*, or *evaluate*)

◆ Recall the factual information needed to answer the question.

◆ Organize this information into a meaningful response that answers the question.

◆ Take the time to write your answer.

◆ Review and revise your answer for errors.

CREATING YOUR RESPONSE

There are many ways of approaching short-answer or extended-response questions. One of the most common approaches is to use three main steps:

1 Analyze and Plan   **2** Write Your Answer   **3** Review and Revise Your Answer

STEP 1: ANALYZE AND PLAN

To answer either a short-answer or an extended-response question, you must first look carefully at the directions of the question. The exact instructions for what you are supposed to do in writing your answer will usually be found in the **"action words"** of the question. These action words will ask for particular information.

SOME OF THE MOST COMMON "ACTION WORDS"

Analyze	To explain the parts of something, or how it works.
Compare	To identify similarities and differences of two or more things.
Describe	To give the characteristics of something — the *who*, *what*, *where*, and *how*. A description can also tell how something changes over time.
Explain	• To *explain how* something happened, tell the way in which it took place. • To *explain why* something happened, give the reasons why it happened (or causes of the event). • To *explain the effects* of something, describe each effect and tell how it came about.
Identify	To name something or state what it is.
Support	To give facts or examples to justify a conclusion, generalization or point of view.

Identify and Describe

Many questions will ask you to *identify* and *describe* something. This means that you should first state what the thing is (*identify it*). Then you should provide further supporting details (*describe it*). For example, you might tell about the *who, what, where, when, how,* and *why* of the item you are describing or explaining.

IDENTIFY		DESCRIBE / EXPLAIN
State what the item is		Give further supporting details, such as — *who, what, when, where, how,* and *why.*

After you have studied the "action words" in the question, you must next identify **all** the parts of the question. Then take a few moments to plan your answer. It often helps to plan your answer with an **answer box**, showing the different parts of the question. Fill in the answer box with your ideas, or simply check off each part of the box as you complete that part of your response. Even if you decide not to write out an answer box, you should do this process mentally.

◆ **Short-answer questions** will have **two** parts. For example, a short-answer question might ask you to *identify* two effects of the European encounter with the Americas. An answer box for this question might appear as follows:

One effect of the European encounter with the Americans:	Your Response
A second effect of the European encounter with the Americans:	Your Response

◆ **Extended-response questions** usually have **four** parts. For example, an extended-response question might read as follows:

> European exploration and imperialism after 1400 had a major impact on the peoples of Africa, Asia, and the Americas.
>
> In your **Answer Document**, identify and describe two ways that European exploration and imperialism affected the peoples of Africa, Asia, or the Americas. (4 points)

Here is what an answer box might look like for answering this question:

First Way	Identify:	Describe:
	Decline of Native American populations	*Europeans brought new diseases like smallpox and measles to the "New World." Native American peoples had no immunity. Millions of Native Americans died from these new diseases.*
Another Way	Identify:	Describe:
	Trans-Atlantic Slave Trade	*Europeans wanted workers for mines and plantations in the Americas. They bargained for captured Africans on the coast of West Africa. Then they chained and shipped these captives across the Atlantic to the Americas as slaves. They were treated brutally and many died crossing the Atlantic.*

How Many Boxes Will You Need? Remember that a short-answer question usually has **two parts** to complete, while an extended-response question has **four parts**. Your answer box should therefore be made up of either two or four boxes to fill in. When you take the actual OAT next year, you will get a clue about each question from its point value. The number of points (**2** or **4**) will tell you if the question is a short-answer or an extended-response.

The Subject of the Question. After you have determined how many parts you need for your answer, think about the *subject* of the question. Does it ask about a cause-and-effect relationship, different viewpoints on a historical issue, ways that citizens can participate in government, or something else? Mentally step back and think about the subject matter of the question, just as you would for a multiple-choice question. **Recall** what you know. Then fill in your answer box using any relevant information you can recall that helps you to answer the question.

STEP 2: WRITE YOUR ANSWER

The next step in responding to a short-answer or extended-response question is to **write** your answer.

◆ **Echo the Question.** It may help to "echo" the question to introduce your answer. To echo the question, repeat it in the form of a positive statement. For the example, you could begin: *"Two important effects of European exploration and imperialism were the decline of Native American populations and the Trans-Atlantic Slave Trade."*

◆ **Rely on Your Notes.** Now use the notes you put in your answer box to help you write your answer. Turn each point in your notes or answer box into one or more complete sentences. Check off sections of your answer box each time you complete that part of your answer.

◆ **Use Only Accurate Information.** Be sure any information that you include is accurate. Even if you do not know all of the answer, put in as much *accurate information* as you can. This will allow you to earn partial credit. You may lose points for including inaccurate information.

STEP 3: REVIEW AND REVISE YOUR ANSWER

Once you have finished writing, read over your answer *before* you hand it in. Make sure you have provided all of the information required by the question. As you review your response, ask yourself these important questions:

Did I follow the directions and answer all parts of the question?	**Did I provide enough details and examples to support my answer?**	**Is all the information I have included accurate?**

HOW YOUR ANSWER WILL BE SCORED

Look again at the model question that appeared earlier in this chapter on page 34. On the following pages you will find four sample student responses to this question. Read each response. Then give it a score of **0** to **4** points and explain why you gave it that score.

RESPONSE 1:

European exploration and imperialism had a major impact. The people of Africa and Asia were very affected. Africans enjoyed increased trade. Asians ate new kinds of foods.

Your score: [   ] Explain why you gave that score. _____

_____

_____

_____

_____

RESPONSE 2:

European exploration had a major impact on the peoples of the Americas and Africa. In America, people were affected by the arrival of new diseases. European explorers brought diseases like measles and smallpox to the Americas. Native American Indians had no immunity to these European diseases. Millions of Native American Indians died from epidemics that spread rapidly through their population. On the island where Columbus first landed, the entire Native American population was wiped out. The Aztecs were weakened by smallpox. The great Aztec empire quickly fell to the Spanish conquest.

Africans were also greatly affected by European exploration and imperialism. Europeans in the "New World" turned to Africa for a new work force when the Native American Indians died from diseases. African tribes captured enemy tribes and sold them to European sea captains for European weapons. The captives were taken in slave ships and brutally treated on their voyage across the Atlantic Ocean. On arriving in the Americas, these enslaved Africans were forced to work under cruel and harsh conditions in mines and on plantations.

Your score: [   ] Explain why you gave that score. _____

_____

_____

_____

_____

_____

_____

_____

_____

_____

_____

_____

_____

_____

RESPONSE 3:

European exploration and imperialism had a major impact on Africans, Asians, and Americans. In North and South America, Spanish conquerors defeated local empires and turned these areas into colonies. Cortes defeated the Aztecs in Mexico, and Pizarro conquered the Incas of Peru. Spanish priests attempted to convert the natives to Catholicism. Some local peoples were enslaved and forced to work in mines or on plantations. Spain grew rich from the gold and silver that was shipped to Europe from the Americas.

Your score: ☐ Explain why you gave that score. _____

_____

_____

_____

_____

RESPONSE 4:

European exploration and imperialism affected the peoples of Asia and the Americas in many ways. Many Asians were affected by increasing trade. Europeans bought silk, spices, and tea from Asia. In exchange, Asians received gold and some goods from Europe. Americans were affected by the arrival of new diseases from Europe.

Your score: ☐ Explain why you gave that score. _____

_____

_____

_____

_____

HOW DID YOU SCORE EACH RESPONSE?

Compare how you scored these four responses with the scores given by your classmates. To score responses on the actual test, scorers will use a **rubric**.

The rubric tells a scorer what information an extended-response should include to receive a score of **0**, **1**, **2**, **3**, or **4**. Here is a sample rubric for scoring responses to the question you just examined:

4-POINT RUBRIC / ITEM-SPECIFIC SCORING GUIDE

4 Points   The student correctly identifies two ways that European exploration and imperialism affected the peoples of Africa, Asia or the Americas, and describes each way. Answers may include the following:

Some Ways European Exploration and Imperialism Affected the Americas, Africa, and Asia:

- *Effect:* Europeans brought a variety of new foods and animals to the Americas
- *Description:* Europeans brought the first horses, dogs, chickens, sheep, goats, grapes, oranges and wheat to the Americas.

- *Effect:* Europeans brought deadly new diseases to the Americas.
- *Description:* Europeans brought measles and smallpox; Indians had no immunity to these diseases; millions of Native Americans died.

- *Effect:* Introduction of the Trans-Atlantic Slave Trade to Africa.
- *Description:* Africans captured members of other tribes; sold captives to European slave traders; captives taken across Atlantic Ocean; many died; served as slaves in the Americas; West African population was reduced.

- *Effect:* Europeans established colonies in the Americas.
- *Description:* Spanish *conquistadores* conquered Native American empires like the Aztecs in Mexico and the Inca in Peru; many Native Americans were forced into virtual slavery; the Spanish king became ruler of the Americas; priests tried to convert Indians to Christianity; Europeans established farms, mines, and plantations.

3 Points   The student identifies two effects but only describes **ONE** effect.

2 Points   The student correctly identifies two effects, but does not describe either effect **OR** the student correctly identifies **ONE** effect and describes it, but does not identify a second effect.

1 Point   The student correctly identifies only **ONE** effect but does not describe that effect.

0 points   The student does not meet any of the above requirements.

Based on this rubric, the responses would most likely be scored as follows:

Response 1

This student does not specifically identify any of the ways that European exploration and imperialism affected either the Americas, Africa or Asia. Where information is provided, it is inaccurate. Since none of the required points are found in this response, it should receive a score of **0**.

Response 2

This student correctly identifies one way that European exploration affected the Americas and one way it affected Africa. Each of these ways is fully described with supporting details and examples that are accurate. Since all four of the required points are found in this response, it should receive a score of **4**.

Response 3

This student correctly identifies one effect of European exploration and describes it with supporting facts. However, the student has failed to identify a second way Americans, Africans or Asians were affected by European exploration. Since this response had only two of the required four points, it should receive a score of **2**.

Response 4

This student identifies one way that the Americas were affected and one way Asians were affected. However, the student neglected to describe either of these ways by giving additional supporting details. Since two of the four points are found in this answer, the response should receive a score of **2**.

As you can see from this scoring exercise, the most important part of answering any short-answer or extended-response question is:

◆ reading the question carefully

AND

◆ answering *all the parts* of the question with *accurate information.*

To do well in answering a short-answer or an extended-response question, you must provide accurate and detailed information that includes all the points that the question asks for. The number of words that you write is much less important than providing correct information that fully answers the question.

CHAPTER 5

CONDUCTING A RESEARCH PROJECT

Historians often conduct research to find solutions to a problem or to learn about a topic. In this chapter, you will learn how to find information, analyze different perspectives, present a position supported by evidence, and give credit to sources with a bibliography.

MAJOR IDEAS

SOCIAL STUDIES SKILLS AND METHODS, BENCHMARKS A, B AND C

A. There are many different types of resources you can use for research. These include **almanacs**, **gazetteers**, **trade books**, **periodicals**, **video tapes** and **electronic sources**.

B. Sources are generally divided into **primary** and **secondary sources**.

C. You should be able to **summarize**, make **generalizations**, and draw **conclusions** from the information you collect. Conclusions should be supported with evidence.

D. **Outlines** and **graphic organizers** can be used to organize information.

E. People often view the same event from different perspectives. In researching historical events, be sure to explore different points of view. Also, be sure not to evaluate the past in terms of today's values.

F. A complete research project always includes a **bibliography**.

STEPS IN CONDUCTING RESEARCH

There are several steps to every research project:

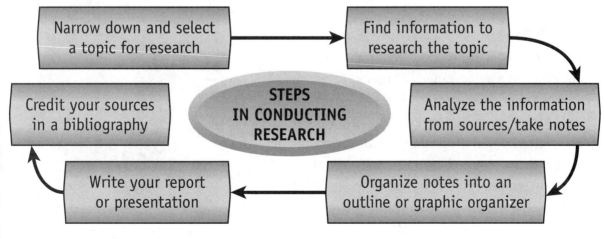

This chapter will review each of these steps in greater detail.

CHOOSING A TOPIC

The first step in any research project is to choose a topic. For example, you might be interested in writing a report about ancient Rome. However, it would be too difficult for you to research and report on everything about ancient Rome. There is simply too much information. Instead, you need to narrow down your topic. You need to select a specific aspect of ancient Rome for your report, such as Roman painting styles, Roman weapons, the role of women in ancient Rome, or the life of a Roman leader, such as Julius Caesar. On the other hand, your topic must not be so narrow that you cannot find enough information to write about it.

APPLYING WHAT YOU HAVE LEARNED

▼ Imagine you have been assigned to write a research report about ancient Rome. Select a topic that you think might be interesting to research:

_____

_____

_____

USING SOURCES TO FIND INFORMATION

Once you have chosen a topic for research, the next step is to find information. A **source** is something that provides information. There are many different kinds of sources. These include the following:

ALMANACS

An **almanac** is a book that contains up-to-date information on a wide range of topics. A new edition is published every year to keep its information current. Almanacs generally cover a wide variety of topics, such as population statistics, descriptions of countries, short biographies of famous people, and winners of Nobel Prizes and other awards. They are especially useful for researching statistics or the background to current events.

TRADE BOOKS

A **trade book** is any book written for a general audience. Trade books usually focus on a particular topic, such as Roman architecture or the Crusades. Most nonfiction books in your public and school library would be considered trade books.

GAZETTEERS

A **gazetteer** is a geographical dictionary. It lists places — countries, cities, rivers, mountains — with descriptions of their political or physical geography and related statistical information. Gazetteers also provide definitions of specific geographical terms.

PERIODICALS

A **periodical** is any newspaper, magazine, or journal. These are called periodicals because they are published at periodic intervals. Articles in magazines and journals usually focus on a particular topic and report the latest news or research. Daily newspapers are often used by researchers for their descriptions of events.

VIDEOTAPES / DVDS

Videotapes and **DVDs** include newsreels, recorded interviews, and documentaries. Researchers use these sources to discover views of actual events as they happened, to see interviews of leading figures, or to review documentary materials collected by the film-maker.

ELECTRONIC SOURCES

The **Internet**, the major electronic source of information today, has also become the most widely used source of information in general. Almost any kind of information can be found on the Internet. Search engines like **Google**, **Yahoo** or **AOL** are used to locate websites with information about a topic.

Searching the Internet. Each search engine has a blank box on the screen where you key in the **subject** or **keywords** you wish to search. When you click the search button, your computer will search the web and create a list of sites for you to explore. Click on each site on the list to see if it provides information to use in your report. If your search provides too many web sites, use a narrower subject or keyword. An advanced search feature often allows you to specify two or more keywords that the site you are searching for must have. This feature can help you to narrow down your search.

Remember that many web sites are created by organizations or individuals committed to a particular product or viewpoint. As with all sources, information appearing on the Internet may be biased or may even be incorrect. You have to use it cautiously.

APPLYING WHAT YOU HAVE LEARNED

▼ Let's suppose you are still writing a report about some aspect of ancient Rome. List two sources of information that you might consult:

* _____

* _____

▼ List two key words you would use to search the Internet for information for your report:

* _____   * _____

PRIMARY AND SECONDARY SOURCES

All sources, including those on the Internet, can be divided into two main categories — primary and secondary sources.

PRIMARY SOURCES

Primary sources are original records of an event under investigation. They include eye-witness reports, official records from the time of the event, letters sent by people involved in the event, diaries, photographs, oral histories and surviving artifacts (*objects*). Even a work of contemporary fiction, such as a story or poem, may be a primary source if it reveals how people felt about things at the time it was written. All historical knowledge about past events can be traced back to primary sources.

Glass handle jugs discovered at an ancient Roman settlement in Syria. Are these primary or secondary sources?

SECONDARY SOURCES

Secondary sources are the writings and interpretations of later writers who have reviewed the information in primary sources. Secondary sources such as textbooks, trade books, and encyclopedia articles often contain convenient summaries of information found in primary sources. These summaries also reveal the writer's interpretation or point of view.

APPLYING WHAT YOU HAVE LEARNED

Suppose you find a website on the Internet about ancient Rome. Which of the following materials on the website are primary and which are secondary sources?

Website Information	Type of Source?	Explain Your Answer
Pictures by a modern artist showing how Rome looked in ancient times.	☐ Primary ☐ Secondary	
Roman Republic coins in a museum in Rome.	☐ Primary ☐ Secondary	
Modern reproductions of Roman arrowheads being sold to tourists.	☐ Primary ☐ Secondary	
Pieces of ancient pottery unearthed near an old Roman settlement.	☐ Primary ☐ Secondary	

TAKING NOTES

After you locate your sources, you need to read them for information and to take notes. When taking notes for a research project, include only information you need. Do not take notes on information that does not relate to your topic, even if this information seems interesting to you. It is often helpful to use **index cards** when taking notes. The following is usually included on each note card:

◆ **Subject.** Use a key word or phrase to identify the subject of the note card. Later you will be able to organize the information you have collected by grouping your note cards together with these key words.

◆ **Notes.** Your notes should be brief. They should contain a short review of the main points you think you might use. You can always look back at your original source to find more details and factual information.

◆ **Source.** Identify the source where you found the information. Provide the author and name of the book. Write down the publisher, city of publication and copyright date of the source on at least one card. You will need this information for your bibliography.

Here is an example of information that might be included on a note card about the life of Julius Caesar. Notice that full sentences are not needed. Simply jot down facts briefly.

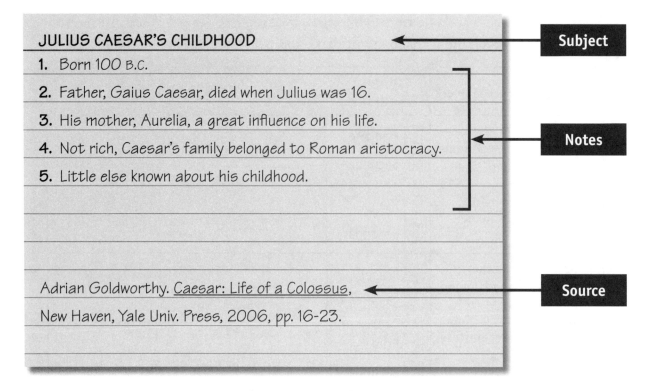

JULIUS CAESAR'S CHILDHOOD ← Subject

1. Born 100 B.C.
2. Father, Gaius Caesar, died when Julius was 16.
3. His mother, Aurelia, a great influence on his life.
4. Not rich, Caesar's family belonged to Roman aristocracy.
5. Little else known about his childhood.

← Notes

Adrian Goldworthy. <u>Caesar: Life of a Colossus</u>, ← Source
New Haven, Yale Univ. Press, 2006, pp. 16-23.

ANALYZING INFORMATION

When researching a topic, it is useful to look at multiple sources. This will help you to research the topic from more than one point of view. When reading a source, pay particular attention to the background and viewpoint of the author. Often, the author's background shapes his or her perspective — how the author views the event. Different people often view the same event very differently. By reading several points of view, you can come to your own conclusions about what actually happened and its significance.

Christopher Columbus

In 1992, the world marked the 500th anniversary of Columbus' first voyage across the Atlantic Ocean. Many people celebrated this event with exhibitions and festivities.

However, the anniversary awakened a debate as to whether Columbus was a hero or a villain. The following pages contain four statements from people who actually knew Columbus. Read these primary sources and form your own opinion. Then share your views with members of your class.

KING FERDINAND AND QUEEN ISABELLA OF SPAIN

"Columbus is the most beloved of our subjects. He first approached us in 1486 with a plan to sail west to reach the Indies. Columbus promised us wealth and power. After six years, we finally gave him what he needed. We agreed to give him one-tenth of all the riches he brought to us — but only if he made good on his word. Columbus did this and more. He obtained new lands for Spain. He spread our Christian religion in places where it was unknown. Because of him, Spain became the richest country in the world. We ate new foods and used new products. We now realize that the world is a larger place than we had imagined. Columbus has widened our horizons and is the creator of our modern world."

Christopher Columbus at the court of Ferdinand and Isabella, rulers of Spain.

PERALONSA NIÑO, MEMBER OF COLUMBUS' CREW

"Columbus was feared and respected by our crew. We set sail from Spain on August 3, 1492, sailing west. We had no idea what we would find or even if we would return. Many of the crew believed the world was flat, and that if you sailed far enough out on the ocean, you would fall off the edge. When we lost sight of land, many of us wept, fearing we might never see land again. We had enough water and supplies for 28 days. But after that, what? By early October, most of the crew were ready to kill Columbus and turn back. Luckily for Columbus, land was sighted just at this time."

Artist's drawing of the ship used by Columbus to cross the Atlantic Ocean.

FATHER MARCHENA, A SPANISH PRIEST

"Columbus was probably the greatest man who ever lived. His courage allowed him to reach land by sailing west. His discovery of the Western Hemisphere introduced its natives to our Christian teachings. These people were ignorant savages. Thanks to Columbus, these savages had an opportunity to learn our Christian faith. They now have a chance to enter the Heavenly gates and save their souls. Columbus has brought riches and power to our country. He has taught the natives to grow new crops, to speak new languages, and to lead civilized lives as Christians."

CHIEF CAONABO OF THE TAINO NATIVE AMERICANS

"Columbus was an arrogant man, without feelings for us. His arrival was a horrible event for our people. We were happy before he arrived. We greeted him with gifts, but he returned our friendship by claiming our homeland for his masters. When he sailed back to Spain, he left many of his men on our island. They bullied our people. I finally led an attack of our brave warriors against these cowards. We killed them and burnt down their settlement. But the next year, Columbus returned with 17 ships. He shipped many of our people to Spain as slaves. His soldiers and cannons defeated us in battle. Soon we were all enslaved. Meanwhile, thousands of my people died from mysterious diseases brought by these European invaders."

Chief Caonabo and his wife

APPLYING WHAT YOU HAVE LEARNED

▼ Select two of the statements above. For each statement selected, explain how the writer's position may have affected how he or she viewed Columbus.

- _____

_____

- _____

_____

▼ Why is it valuable to read several accounts with different viewpoints to understand a historical event? _____

_____

_____

_____

_____

_____

_____

As you can see, it is important to consider several points of view when researching a topic. By comparing these different points of view, you get a better understanding of what actually happened and why.

Using Note Cards to Compare Viewpoints. One way to compare different sources and viewpoints is to use note cards. You already know how to identify each card by its topic and the source where you found the information. You can group all the cards on the same topic together and compare what each source says about it. To write your report, you can summarize what these different sources say about the topic and then make your own generalizations or draw your own conclusions.

THE DANGER OF EVALUATING THE PAST IN TERMS OF TODAY

When using primary sources, it is especially important to understand the past on its own terms. It would be a serious mistake to evaluate the past in terms of the norms and values we accept today.

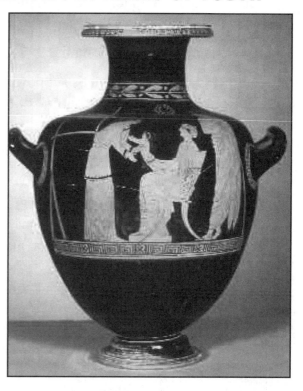

For example, almost all Americans would now condemn slavery. However, in ancient times almost all societies had some form of slavery. This does not mean that slavery was good. Many people objected to slavery, even in the past. But we cannot assume that all people who accepted slavery in the past were bad or immoral. They simply did not have the benefit of the ideas and experiences that contribute to the way we think today.

A slave taking a baby from its master, pictured on an Athenian vase, 450 B.C.

MAKING AN OUTLINE

When you have finished taking notes from your sources, you should review your note cards and organize your information into an outline. An **outline** is a brief plan in which each topic or major idea is divided into smaller units.

An outline gives you a blueprint to follow for writing your report. The purpose of the outline is to show how the different parts of your report are related. It may help to think of your outline as the "road map" for your research paper.

Outlining your project before you write will help you to stay focused on your topic and to see connections that you otherwise might not have seen. You can also use your outline to decide the best order to present your points. A good outline will reveal if you have gathered enough information to write your paper. Lastly, an outline helps you to see if some note cards should be discarded because they are not relevant to your paper.

Your outline can be written in many different ways. The most common form of outline begins with general topics and then provides additional details.

◆ **Roman Numerals.** The major topics of an outline are usually identified by Roman numerals (I, II, III, etc.).

◆ **Capital Letters.** If the topic listed by a Roman numeral needs to be divided further, its sub-topics are identified by capital letters (A, B, C, etc.).

◆ **Arabic Numerals.** If these sub-topics need to be divided even further, each smaller topic is given an Arabic numeral (1, 2, 3).

To illustrate this process, let's suppose you were writing a report about Julius Caesar in ancient Rome. Here is what an outline of this report might look like:

THE LIFE OF JULIUS CAESAR (100–44 B.C.)

I. Early Life
    A. Father was Gaius, mother was Aurelia
    B. Born to aristocratic family
    C. Becomes head of family at age 16
II. Early Political Career
    A. First steps
        1. Studies public speaking
        2. Kidnapped by pirates
            a. Ransom paid to pirates
            b. Caesar freed
            c. Caesar defeats and executes pirates
    B. Allies with Pompey
III. Conquest of Gaul
IV. Civil War
    A. Caesar quarrels with Pompey
    B. Caesar brings army to Rome
V. Dictatorship and Assassination of Caesar

GRAPHIC ORGANIZERS

The same information could be put in the form of a **graphic organizer**, such as a concept map. Here is how a concept map for this same report might look:

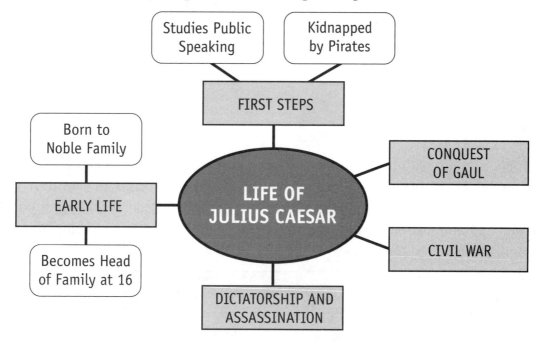

WRITING YOUR REPORT

After you complete your outline or graphic organizer, you are ready to write your report or oral presentation. Turn each major section of your outline into a separate paragraph or part of your presentation. Be sure to include facts and details from your note cards to support each of your main points. As you write, re-read your work several times to make sure that it is logical and flows smoothly. You should be sure to use transitions in your writing to indicate to your reader when you change times, locations, topics or ideas.

SUPPORTING A POSITION

In your project, you may present your own "**position**" — a special point of view, generalization or conclusion — based on the evidence. Some researchers present a general position on their topic in a **thesis statement** — a simple statement of the main point the researcher is trying to make.

You should try to persuade readers that any position or conclusion you present is correct by providing evidence. This evidence should consist of facts you have found in both primary and secondary sources. These facts should be clear, specific, and detailed. They should also be clearly related to what you are trying to show. The facts you present in your report should closely support the conclusions you have reached.

In order to show the reader that the information in a report is accurate, researchers identify their sources. These sources are listed in a bibliography.

CREDITING SOURCES IN A BIBLIOGRAPHY

When writing a report, it is important to give credit to your sources in a **bibliography**. This allows readers to check your sources and your use of facts. Usually, the bibliography is found at the end of your report.

BOOKS

For each book, begin with the author's last name, followed by the first name and a period. Then write the title of the book, which is underlined and followed by a period. If you are typing your report on a computer, you can *italicize* the title instead of underlining it. Next put the place of publication, a colon (:), the name of the publisher, a comma, the date of publication, and a period. Entries should be alphabetized by the author's last name.

> Abbot, Jacob. History of Julius Caesar. New York: F. M. Lupton, 1999.

PERIODICALS

For a magazine or newspaper article, put the author's last name, then first name, followed by a period. Next, put the title or headline of the article in quotation marks, followed by a comma. Then put the name of the periodical, which should be underlined (or *italicized*), followed by its date of publication, and the pages where the article can be found.

> Harigan, Bob. "Julius Caesar," National Geographic, May 2004, pp. 3-9.

ENCYCLOPEDIAS

For an encyclopedia article that is not signed, put the title of the article in quotation marks, followed by a comma. Then put the title of the encyclopedia, which is underlined. Next, put the copyright year, volume number, and page numbers. For an encyclopedia article that is signed, begin the entry with the name of the author of the article, followed by a period.

> "Julius Caesar," World Book Encyclopedia. 2000. Volume 8, p. 255.

WHAT YOU SHOULD KNOW

☑ You should know that there are many different types of resources you can use for research. These include almanacs, gazetteers, trade books, periodicals, video tapes and electronic sources.

☐ You should know that sources are generally divided into primary and secondary.

☐ You should be able to summarize, make generalizations, and draw conclusions from the information you collect. You should also know that conclusions should be supported with evidence.

☐ You should know that outlines can be used to organize information.

☐ You should know that people often view the same event from different perspectives. In researching historical events, be sure to explore different viewpoints. Also be sure not to evaluate the past in terms of today's values.

☐ You should know that a research project always includes a bibliography.

CHAPTER STUDY CARDS

Steps in Conducting Research
★ Choose a topic
★ Use sources to find information
★ Take notes
★ Analyze information
★ Make an outline or graphic organizer
★ Write your report
★ Support a position
★ Credit sources in a bibliography

Types of Sources
★ Almanac   ★ Periodicals
★ Gazetteer   ★ Videotapes / DVDs
★ Trade Books   ★ Internet

When Doing Research You Should:
★ Research several different perspectives.
★ Avoid evaluating the past in terms of today's values.

Primary and Secondary Sources
★ **Primary.** Original records of an event
  • Official records from the event
  • Diaries and letters
  • Oral histories
  • Artifacts
★ **Secondary.** Writings based on a review of information in primary sources
  • Textbooks
  • Encyclopedias

Advantages of Using an Outline
★ Stays focused.
★ Reveals connections.
★ Selects the best order.
★ Shows if you have enough information.
★ Allows you to see what is relevant.

Bibliography
★ Lists sources in alphabetical order.
★ Use the last name of author first.
★ Underline or italicize book titles, periodicals.

CHECKING YOUR UNDERSTANDING

1. Which heading best completes the partial outline below?

   A. Sources of information
   B. Published government documents
   C. Primary sources
   D. Bibliography

 SKILLS A

I. _____
   A. gazetteer
   B. trade books
   C. almanac
   D. periodicals

 HINT

*First, **examine** the question. You can see that it tests your knowledge of sources of information. **Recall** that all sub-topics in the outline—A through D are sources of information. They are not all primary sources or government documents, so Choices A and C can be eliminated. They are also not in the form of a bibliography, so eliminate Choice D. The best answer is **Choice A**.*

Now try answering some additional questions on your own.

2. Which document is an example of a primary source of information?

   A. a novel about life during the Neolithic Revolution
   B. a personal diary left by a Roman emperor
   C. a textbook with an article about ancient Greece
   D. an encyclopedia article on ancient Roman culture

   SKILLS A: 6.1

3. Which source would be **best** to find information about the land area and current population of China?

   A. almanac   C. diary
   B. novel   D. videotape

   SKILLS A: 6.1

4. Jared is writing a report about the conflict between the ancient Romans and Gauls. What should Jared avoid doing in writing his report?

   A. using multiple sources to get differing viewpoints
   B. evaluating past events in terms of today's values
   C. using visual as well as written sources
   D. describing events from the perspectives of various people

   SKILLS B: 7.1

5. Each year Mr. Sanchez assigns a report about the Protestant Reformation. He requires his students to find at least three different sources of information. These must include both primary and secondary sources.

Which resource is an example of a secondary source?

A. an entry from John Calvin's personal journal
B. a modern biography about the life of Martin Luther
C. letters from William Shakespeare to his friend
D. official church records from the Vatican

SKILLS
B: 6.2

6. Samantha has developed a position or thesis statement for her presentation on the exploration of the Americas. In her report to the class, she intends to prove that Christopher Columbus should not be remembered as a great explorer, but as a destroyer of Native American civilizations.

SKILLS
C: 6.6

Which statement best supports her position?

A. Through much of his life, Columbus believed he had landed in the East Indies.
B. During Columbus' first voyage, some of his crew wanted to turn back and considered mutiny.
C. Columbus brought wealth and prosperity to Spain and saved the souls of the savages that he encountered.
D. Columbus enslaved native peoples and after his voyage millions died from disease.

7. Maria is completing her research paper. Where should she identify the sources she has used to gather her information?

A. on the title page
B. before her table of contents

C. in her introduction
D. in the bibliography

SKILLS
C: 6.5

When you take the *Ohio Achievement Test* next year, you will be asked to write your short-answer and extended-responses in an "**Answer Document**." In this book, you can write your answer either on the lines that follow each question or on a separate sheet of paper. Your teacher may want to make a copy of the box for writing responses (*found on page 264*) for you to use.

8. Authors often cite their sources when they present an opinion or write a position paper.

In your **Answer Document**, identify one way in which authors can cite their sources and give one reason why it is important for them to do this. (2 points)

SKILLS
D: 6.7

_____

_____

CHAPTER 6

WORKING EFFECTIVELY IN A GROUP

In order for a society to survive, its members must be able to work in groups. In this chapter, you will learn how to work effectively in a group.

MAJOR IDEAS

SOCIAL STUDIES SKILLS AND METHODS, BENCHMARK D

A. To work effectively in a group, group members should set **guidelines**, **rules**, and **timelines** for group work.

B. To work effectively in a group, each member should be an active listener, provide **constructive feedback** to others, and help establish **group goals**.

C. To work effectively in a group, members should take different roles within the group and recognize the contributions of others.

WORKING IN A GROUP

By working together, people can often accomplish more than they could do by acting individually. A group of people can complete a project that is too large or complex for one individual. People acting in groups have built irrigation systems, planted crops, constructed large buildings, cured diseases, explored the oceans, settled new lands, and advanced learning.

The Amish often rely on working in groups.

APPLYING WHAT YOU HAVE LEARNED

▼ Give one example of a task you accomplished as the member of a group.

_____

_____

STRATEGIES FOR EFFECTIVE GROUP WORK

There are many strategies for working effectively in a group:

ESTABLISH GOALS, GUIDELINES, RULES AND TIMELINES

For a group to work effectively, it must set its goals at the start. Members should discuss the rules, guidelines and timelines they need. For example, if a group is preparing an oral presentation, it should decide which topics to cover, how to divide the work between them, and when members should report back to the group. The group should also establish rules, such as to take turns in speaking and not to interrupt one another. Some groups further engage in team-building activities, like playing a game. In this, way members become more familiar and comfortable with each other.

BE AN ACTIVE LISTENER AND PROVIDE FEEDBACK

It is important to listen to other members of the group and not just to think about what you are about to say. It helps to take notes and to ask questions of each speaker. When you comment on what another speaker has said — known as providing "feedback" — be friendly and constructive. **Constructive feedback** tells the speaker how to make the presentation better by doing something differently. It is always helpful to compliment something that another group member has said. Never attack a speaker's personality or appearance.

TAKE DIFFERENT ROLES WITHIN THE GROUP

Members should take turns at different roles within the group. This will help each member better appreciate the efforts of other members in the group. It will also give each member of the group a chance to see where he or she has the most talent.

APPLYING WHAT YOU HAVE LEARNED

▼ List two rules that you think are important for group work:

1. _____

2. _____

▼ Select one of these rules and explain why it is important. _____

_____

_____

The Role of the Group Leader. It is especially important to take turns leading the group discussion. Everyone should have a chance to act as group leader. The leader's responsibility is to recognize each speaker. The leader should let each person speak without interruption, and make sure everyone is listening. Sometimes the leader should summarize what a speaker has said before selecting the next person to speak.

RECOGNIZE OTHER MEMBERS' CONTRIBUTIONS

To maintain enthusiasm within the group, be sure to recognize the contributions of each member. Praise for something another member has said or done is often all that is needed for that member to feel important and appreciated.

MANAGE ANY CONFLICTS WITHIN THE GROUP

To manage conflicts within the group, members should decide in advance on a fair way of resolving any disputes that may arise. For example, for a group report on ancient Rome, two group members may want to research the same topic. Members might have decided in advance to flip a coin, pull a name from a hat, or take a vote. Deciding in advance makes the resolution of the conflict easier for all sides to accept.

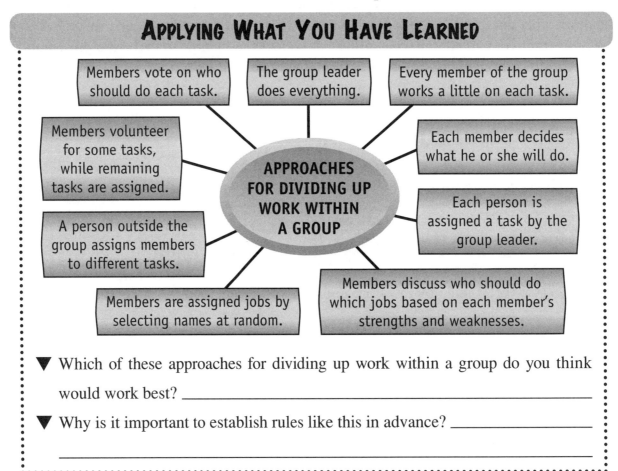

APPLYING WHAT YOU HAVE LEARNED

Members vote on who should do each task.

The group leader does everything.

Every member of the group works a little on each task.

Members volunteer for some tasks, while remaining tasks are assigned.

Each member decides what he or she will do.

APPROACHES FOR DIVIDING UP WORK WITHIN A GROUP

Each person is assigned a task by the group leader.

A person outside the group assigns members to different tasks.

Members are assigned jobs by selecting names at random.

Members discuss who should do which jobs based on each member's strengths and weaknesses.

▼ Which of these approaches for dividing up work within a group do you think would work best? _____

▼ Why is it important to establish rules like this in advance? _____

_____

REFLECT ON THE PERFORMANCE OF THE GROUP

After your group project is complete, members should reflect on what they have learned. This learning should not be limited to what was learned about the topic: students should also reflect on what they have learned from the experience of working in a group. Members should also think about how they might have made their project or working experience even better.

APPLYING WHAT YOU HAVE LEARNED

▼ Think of a time when you worked as part of a group. Explain how working together as a group made it possible to accomplish a task that would have been difficult to achieve through individual efforts.

_____

_____

_____

▼ What special problems, if any, did the members of your group have in acting

together? _____

_____

_____

▼ Which of the strategies in this chapter did the members of your group use to work more effectively?

_____

_____

_____

WHAT YOU SHOULD KNOW

☐ You should know that to work effectively in a group, members should set guidelines, rules, and timelines for group work.

☐ You should know that to work effectively in a group, each member should be an active listener; provide constructive feedback, and help establish group goals.

☐ You should know that to work effectively in a group, members should take different roles within the group and recognize the contributions of others.

CHAPTER STUDY CARDS

Methods of Working Effectively in a Group	Dealing with Other Members in a Group
★ Help to establish group goals. ★ Set guidelines, rules, and timelines. ★ Be an active listener. ★ Promote **constructive feedback** among members of the group. ★ Take different roles within the group. ★ Recognize the contributions made by other individuals in the group. ★ Group members should reflect on what they have learned.	★ Set manageable and realistic guidelines in advance. ★ Disputes should be resolved in a manner that is fair to all members of the group. ★ Decide in advance on ways to resolve disputes that may arise. ★ Everyone likes some praise. Recognize the contributions of other members of the group.

CHECKING YOUR UNDERSTANDING

1. What is the **best** reason for giving constructive feedback to others when working together in a group?

    A. Constructive feedback assures that the project is done on a time.
    B. Constructive feedback resolves conflicts in advance.
    C. Constructive feedback helps others to improve without hurting their feelings.
    D. Constructive feedback fairly divides work among group members.

    SKILLS
    D: 6.7

HINT

*First **examine** the question. It asks why constructive feedback is so important. You should **recall** that constructive feedback communicates to others how they might improve without attacking them or offending their feelings. Finally, **apply** this knowledge to choose the correct answer. **Choices A, B, and D** all mention important aspects of working together in groups. However, they do not explain the importance of providing constructive feedback. The best answer is **Choice C**.*

Now try answering some additional questions on your own.

2. What would be the **most** effective rule for resolving a conflict between two people in a group who want to perform the same task?

    A. Have the two members argue with each other.
    B. Have the group leader pick the member he or she likes best.
    C. Have the group decide in advance a fair way to decide such questions.
    D. Have members of the group choose the one who is most popular.

    SKILLS
    D: 7.3

Look at the outline below.

> I. _____
>   A. Focus on what the speaker is saying
>   B. Take notes and summarize key points
>   C. Ask clarifying questions

3. Which title best completes the outline?

    A. Constructive Feedback
    B. Active Listening
    C. Confict Management
    D. Recognition of Contributions

    SKILLS
    D: 6.7

4. Why is it important to reflect on the performance of a classroom group in which one has participated?

    A. It is a good way to manage conflict within the group.
    B. It is a good way to establish goals and roles within the group.
    C. It helps the group complete the project in an orderly and timely manner.
    D. It helps the group determine if its goals were met and identify ways it might improve.

    SKILLS
    D: 7.4

5. You have been put in a group with three other students to answer a series of questions about specific primary source documents. According to your teacher's instructions, each group member will have a turn as group discussion leader.

    In your **Answer Document**, identify two reasons why it is beneficial for students to take on various roles within a group. (2 points)

    SKILLS
    D: 6.7

    _____

    _____

    _____

    _____

UNIT 1: SKILLS AND METHODS CONCEPT MAP

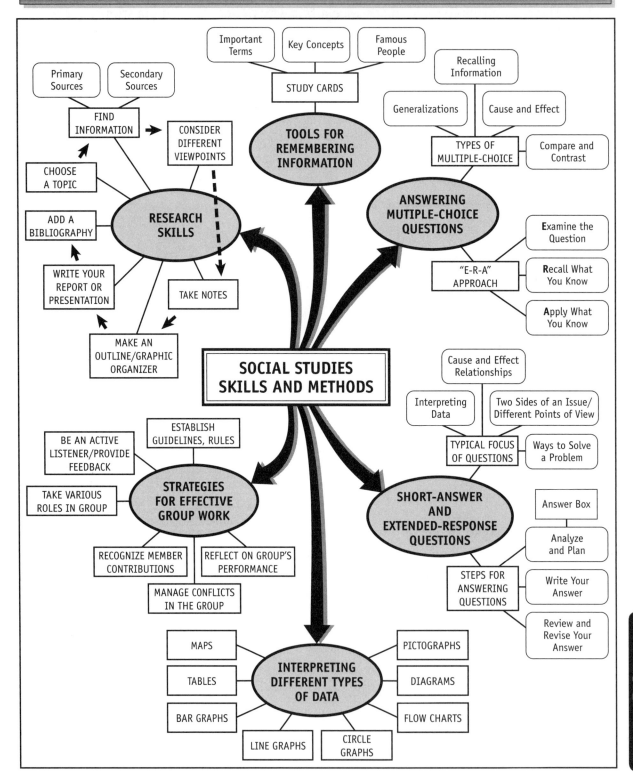

Primary Sources

Secondary Sources

Important Terms

Key Concepts

Famous People

STUDY CARDS

Recalling Information

FIND INFORMATION →

CONSIDER DIFFERENT VIEWPOINTS

TOOLS FOR REMEMBERING INFORMATION

Generalizations

Cause and Effect

CHOOSE A TOPIC

TYPES OF MULTIPLE-CHOICE

Compare and Contrast

ADD A BIBLIOGRAPHY

RESEARCH SKILLS

ANSWERING MUTIPLE-CHOICE QUESTIONS

Examine the Question

WRITE YOUR REPORT OR PRESENTATION

TAKE NOTES

"E-R-A" APPROACH

Recall What You Know

MAKE AN OUTLINE/GRAPHIC ORGANIZER

Apply What You Know

Cause and Effect Relationships

SOCIAL STUDIES SKILLS AND METHODS

Interpreting Data

Two Sides of an Issue/ Different Points of View

ESTABLISH GUIDELINES, RULES

TYPICAL FOCUS OF QUESTIONS

Ways to Solve a Problem

BE AN ACTIVE LISTENER/PROVIDE FEEDBACK

STRATEGIES FOR EFFECTIVE GROUP WORK

SHORT-ANSWER AND EXTENDED-RESPONSE QUESTIONS

Answer Box

TAKE VARIOUS ROLES IN GROUP

Analyze and Plan

RECOGNIZE MEMBER CONTRIBUTIONS

REFLECT ON GROUP'S PERFORMANCE

STEPS FOR ANSWERING QUESTIONS

Write Your Answer

MANAGE CONFLICTS IN THE GROUP

Review and Revise Your Answer

MAPS

PICTOGRAPHS

TABLES

INTERPRETING DIFFERENT TYPES OF DATA

DIAGRAMS

BAR GRAPHS

FLOW CHARTS

LINE GRAPHS

CIRCLE GRAPHS

TESTING YOUR UNDERSTANDING

1. Your teacher has assigned you the task of group leader for a presentation on Buddhism. What action should you and your fellow group members take first in order to work more effectively?

    A. Provide constructive feedback to group members.
    B. Establish group goals, guidelines, rules, roles, and timelines.
    C. Manage conflict within the group during the assigned activity.
    D. Actively listen to other group members as they perform their roles.

    SKILLS
    D: 7.3

Look at the graph below.

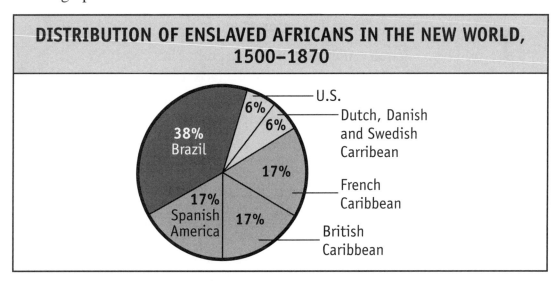

DISTRIBUTION OF ENSLAVED AFRICANS IN THE NEW WORLD, 1500–1870

- 38% Brazil
- 6% U.S.
- 6% Dutch, Danish and Swedish Carribean
- 17% French Caribbean
- 17% British Caribbean
- 17% Spanish America

2. Which statement is **best** supported by information in the graph?

    A. There was little trade in enslaved Africans before the 1500s.
    B. In Holland, Denmark, and Sweden, slavery was widely practiced.
    C. Slaves were better treated in Brazil than in the United States.
    D. Most enslaved Africans were sent to the Caribbean and Spanish America.

    SKILLS
    D: 6.4

3. Amy used a magazine article on the Crusades for her position paper.

    Which citation is the correct format to use for her bibliography?

    SKILLS
    D: 6.5

    A. Murphy, Thomas. <u>The Holy War</u>. Columbus: Ohio State University Press, 1976.
    B. Thomas Murphy. "The Holy War." <u>Newsweek</u>. January 2008. pp. 27–35.
    C. "Crusades," 2006. Volume 3, p. 405. <u>World Book Encyclopedia</u>.
    D. *The Last Crusade*. Lucas, Ira. p. 5. (Columbus: Ohio State University Press, 1988)

Look at the graph below.

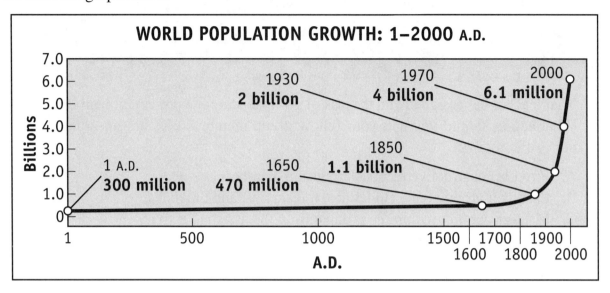

WORLD POPULATION GROWTH: 1–2000 A.D.

4.   Which statement is **best** supported by information in the graph?

A. The world's population remained unchanged from 1 A.D. to 1650.

B. The greatest world's population growth took place from 1000 to 1500.

C. The population growth rate decreased from 1650 to 1800.

D. The world's population more than tripled between 1930 and 2000.

5.   What conclusion about the Maurya and Gupta Empires is supported by information in the map?

A. The Maurya Empire extended farther than the Gupta did.

B. Trade between the Maurya and Gupta Empires led to frequent warfare.

C. An extensive and widespread road system helped to unify the people of ancient India.

D. The population of southern India grew at a faster rate than that of northern India.

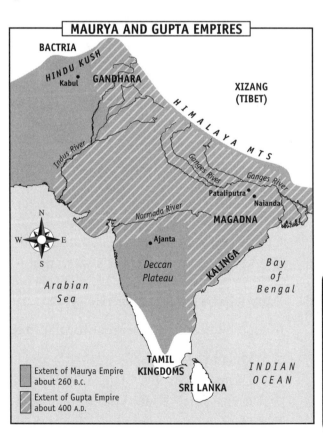

Look at the map below.

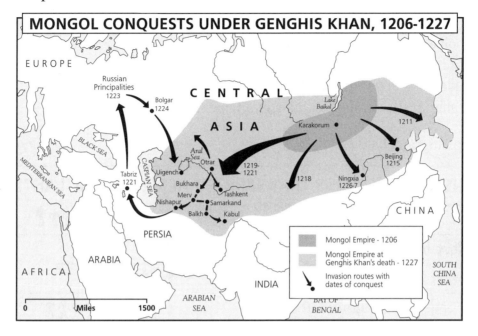

6.   Why did the boundaries of the Mongol Empire change between 1206 and 1227 A.D.?

A.   The Mongols expanded their empire into Europe and North Africa.

B.   The Mongols were forced back to their homelands in Central Asia.

C.   The Mongols expanded their empire across Central and East Asia.

D.   The Mongols established outposts in Southern China and Southeast Asia.

SKILLS
B: 6.2

Look at the map below.

7.   Which **best** describes where the largest Australian cities are located?

A.   interior areas with the least precipitation

B.   northern coastal regions with tropical climates

C.   interior areas with 20 to 40 centimeters of rain each year

D.   southern and eastern coastal areas with 40-60 centimeters of rain each year

SKILLS
B: 6.2

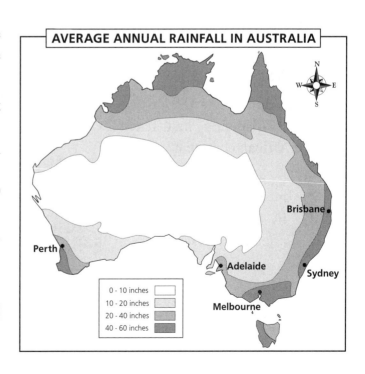

8. Which source would provide the most information for a research project dealing with the Neolithic Revolution?

    A. a book about the history of early humankind
    B. a gazetteer of important terms
    C. a trade book about the Roman Empire
    D. an Internet site dealing with ancient Greece

SKILLS
A: 6.1

Look at the pictograph below.

ENSLAVED PERSONS TRANSPORTED ACROSS THE ATLANTIC

From the 1520s through 1867, an estimated 10 to 15 million Africans were delivered to the New World.

Key: 🚶🚶🚶🚶 = 1 million

Dutch West Indies (including Surinam)	🚶🚶
French West Indies	🚶🚶🚶🚶🚶🚶
Spanish Empire (including Cuba)	🚶🚶🚶🚶🚶🚶🚶🚶🚶🚶
British West Indies, British N. America & U.S.	🚶🚶🚶🚶🚶🚶🚶🚶🚶🚶
Brazil	🚶🚶🚶🚶🚶🚶🚶🚶🚶🚶🚶🚶🚶🚶🚶🚶

9. Which statement is accurate based on the pictograph?

    A. About a million and a half enslaved persons were sent to the French West Indies.
    B. Each symbol represents one million enslaved persons.
    C. Most enslaved persons were sent to British North America.
    D. More slaves went to the Spanish Empire than to all other areas.

SKILLS
A: 6.4

Look at the map.

10. According to the map, when did Christianity first reach the African continent?

    A. by 400 A.D.
    B. by 800 A.D.
    C. by 1100 A.D.
    D. after 1100 A.D.

SKILLS
A: 6.1

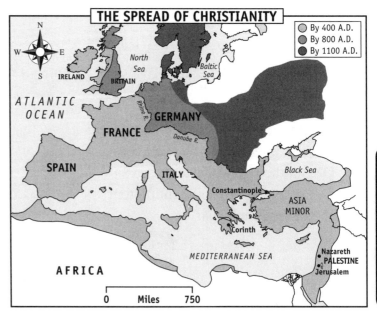

THE SPREAD OF CHRISTIANITY

By 400 A.D.
By 800 A.D.
By 1100 A.D.

11. Colin has gathered resources and made note cards for a research paper for his social studies class. What should he do next to make sure his paper is focused on his topic?

A. Go to the library to find more information.

B. Construct an outline or graphic organizer.

C. Type a title page and list of sources.

D. Begin writing his paper on his computer.

> SKILLS
> A: 6.1

12. What would be the **best** source to find the definition of a mountain range?

A. an almanac

B. a gazetteer

C. a trade book dealing with life oudoors

D. a *National Geographic* magazine

> SKILLS
> A: 6.1

13. When doing research for a report, it advisable to use a combination of primary and secondary sources.

In your **Answer Document**, explain how primary and secondary sources differ. (2 points)

> SKILLS
> B: 6.2

_____

_____

14. People often view the same historical event from different perspectives.

In your **Answer Document**, identify two reasons why it is important to use multiple viewpoints and frames of reference when doing research on a historical event. (2 points)

> SKILLS
> C: 7.2

_____

_____

15. Your social studies teacher has appointed you as the leader of a small group of your fellow classmates.

In your **Answer Document**, identify two strategies that you would use to lead the group in a constructive way. Then explain one reason for using each strategy. (4 points)

> SKILLS
> B: 6.7

_____

_____

_____

_____

_____

UNIT 2

GEOGRAPHY —
REGIONS AND PEOPLES
OF THE WORLD

In this unit, you will learn about **geography** — the study of Earth's surface features and how location, physical features and resources affect people and how they live.

◆ **Chapter 7. Exploring the Seven Continents.** In this chapter, you will learn the main physical and human features of Earth's seven continents. You will also learn how to identify any location on Earth by using its latitude and longitude coordinates.

◆ **Chapter 8. The World's Physical and Human Regions.** In this chapter, you will learn the difference between a physical and human region and the patterns of characteristics that help to define a region. You will also learn how regions change and how economic activities are distributed within a region.

◆ **Chapter 9. Movement.** In this chapter, you will learn how people, products, and ideas move from place to place. You will also learn how contacts between societies often lead to change.

◆ **Chapter 10. People and the Environment.** In this chapter, you will learn how the physical environment influences people living in a place, and how they, in turn, often modify their environment. You will also learn about the positive and negative consequences of such changes.

KEY TERMS YOU WILL LEARN ABOUT IN THIS UNIT

- Continent
- Absolute Location
- Relative Location
- Latitude
- Longitude
- Population Distribution
- Physical Region
- Human Region

- Cultural Region
- Subcontinent
- Migration
- Cultural Diffusion
- Amazon Rainforest
- Sahel Region
- "Push" Factors
- "Pull" Factors

- Movement
- Trade
- Landforms
- Vegetation
- Weathering
- Seismic Activity
- Agriculture
- Urban Growth

Each content unit in this book opens with a special "Looking At" feature. The purpose of these sections is to provide a foundation for understanding a major theme of the unit. In this unit, you will learn about the five themes of geography.

LOOKING AT THE FIVE THEMES OF GEOGRAPHY

The word "geography" comes from two ancient Greek words — the word for the *Earth* and the word for *writing*. Modern geography includes the study of Earth's surface features and how the location, climate, physical features and resources of a place affect the people who live there. Modern geographers have identified **five major themes** to help us understand how the world and its peoples are linked. Each theme highlights one part of the study of geography. These five major themes are *location*, *place*, *region*, *human-environment interaction*, and *movement*.

LOCATION

Location deals with where something can be found at any moment in time. Each object has its own unique "location." **Absolute location** is the exact position of a mountain, lake, city or other object on Earth's surface. For example, the absolute location of your school is its unique address. On a map, your school occupies a single place. On the other hand, **relative location** deals with the position of something on Earth's surface in relation to other things. Relative location uses such terms as "near by" or "at the corner of" to identify location.

PLACE

Place refers to the special features of a location that distinguish it from other locations. For example, what is Egypt like? Is it hot or cool? mountainous or flat? Geographers use special terms to describe the physical characteristics of a place. They look at its **topography** (*land surface features*) and **climate** (*weather conditions over a long period*). They also examine its **natural resources** (*such as minerals, fertile soil or fresh water*).

What can we determine from this photograph about the climate and topography of Egypt?

REGIONS

A **region** is an area that shares common features. The people in a region have more contacts with others within that region than with those outside it. The concept of region is flexible. Different regions, like that of the Roman Empire, may expand and contract over time. In studying any new region, ask yourself: What makes this area a region? What are its common features?

HUMAN-ENVIRONMENT INTERACTION

Human-environment interactions are the ways in which the physical setting of a place interacts with the people who live there. Since ancient times, people have affected their environment in many ways: cutting down forests, planting fields, irrigating the land, and building cities. The physical environment equally affects people. It shapes what people do. For example, the kind of society that develops in a desert will be quite different from one that emerges in a tropical rainforest.

MOVEMENT

Throughout history, some areas have been freer and more prosperous than others, encouraging migration. Some areas have the resources to make certain goods, while other areas have those same goods. These differences have stimulated trade and other contacts among peoples. Understanding the **movement** of goods, people and ideas from one place to another is a final important theme of geography.

APPLYING WHAT YOU HAVE LEARNED

Describe where you live, using the "five themes" of geography:

▼ What is the location of your community? _____

_____

▼ What are the characteristics of the place where you live? _____

_____

▼ Which region does your community belong to? _____

_____

▼ How have the people in your community been affected by their physical environment? How have they modified their environment?

_____

_____

CHAPTER 7

EXPLORING THE SEVEN CONTINENTS

In this chapter, you will learn about the major physical and human features of each of Earth's seven continents, including where those features are located. You will also learn how to locate points on a world map using latitude and longitude.

MAJOR IDEAS

GEOGRAPHY, BENCHMARKS A AND B

A. A **continent** is a large land mass. The seven continents are Africa, Antarctica, Asia, Australia, Europe, North America, and South America. Europe and Asia actually share the same landmass.

B. Each continent has its own distinct **physical features**, including mountain ranges, deserts, bodies of water, climate, plant and animal life, and natural resources.

C. Human activities have transformed Earth's surface by cutting down forests, making farmland, mining minerals, building roads, and creating cities. Each continent has been divided into **countries** and has its own major **cities**.

THE WORLD'S CONTINENTS AND OCEANS

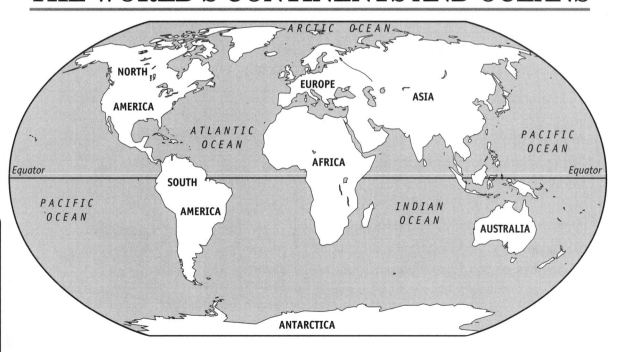

Geographers have identified seven **continents** — the major land masses of the world: **Asia**, **Africa**, **North America**, **South America**, **Antarctica**, **Europe**, and **Australia**.

Most of the Earth's surface is covered by four oceans: the (1) **Atlantic**, (2) **Pacific**, (3) **Indian**, and (4) **Arctic Ocean**.

APPLYING WHAT YOU HAVE LEARNED

▼ Make a photocopy of a map of the world or print an outline map from the Internet. On your map, identify the seven continents and the four oceans.

SKILL BUILDER: LATITUDE AND LONGITUDE

Geographers have created two sets of imaginary lines — called **latitude** and **longitude** — to locate places on Earth's surface. Together, a place's latitude and longitude identify its **absolute location**.

LATITUDE

Latitudes are imaginary horizontal lines that run across the Earth. One simple way to remember how latitudes run is to think of them as the steps of a <u>lad</u>der that run horizontally. Latitude lines run parallel to each other. As parallel lines, they never meet. Latitude lines show how far north or south a location is. The **equator** is the most important latitude line. It stretches around the middle of the Earth. Every point on the equator is the same distance from the North Pole as it is from the South Pole. All other latitude lines are identified by how far north or south of the equator they are.

Each latitude line is assigned a number in degrees to show its distance from the equator. The symbol for **degrees** is °. Going in either direction from the equator, we mark latitude lines from 1° to 90°. An "**N**" or "**S**" is added after the number of degrees to show if the line is **north** or **south** of the equator. For example, a latitude 37 degrees north of the equator would be written as 37°N. The North Pole is located at 90°N. Lines south of the equator have an "S" after the number of degrees.

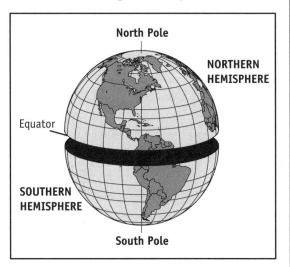

At sea level, the weather along the equator (*0° degrees latitude*) is usually hot. Higher latitudes experience seasonal changes. Earth's tilt as it revolves around the sun causes these seasons to change. When it is winter north of the equator, it is summer south of the equator.

LONGITUDE

Longitudes are imaginary lines that run up and down the Earth. Unlike latitude lines, they are not parallel. All the longitude lines meet at both the North and South Poles.

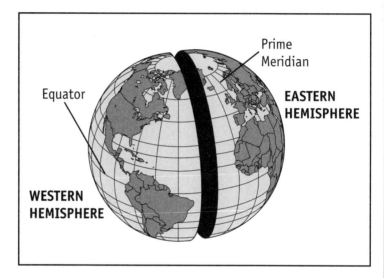

The **Prime Meridian** is the most important longitude line. Geographers use it to divide the Earth into two hemispheres. The half of the earth west of the Prime Meridian is known as the **Western Hemisphere**; the half to the east is known as the **Eastern Hemisphere**. Mapmakers often draw the division between the hemispheres slightly west of the Prime Meridian to show all of Europe and Africa in the Eastern Hemisphere. Like the equator, the Prime Meridian is identified as zero degrees (0°). Going in either direction from the Prime Meridian, longitude lines increase from 1° to 180°. Geographers add "**E**" or "**W**" to indicate if the line is east or west of the Prime Meridian.

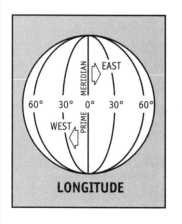

LONGITUDE

+

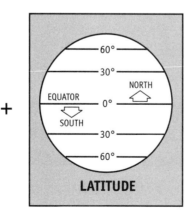

LATITUDE

=

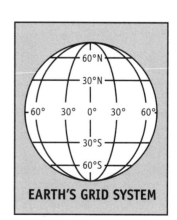

EARTH'S GRID SYSTEM

APPLYING WHAT YOU HAVE LEARNED

▼ Below is a map of the ancient Gupta Empire. What is the absolute location of Point A? Starting from the 80°E line, move your finger up until you reach the 30°N line. This point is identified by two coordinates: 80°E, 30°N. You can see that this point is located within the Himalayan Mountains.

Use this map to answer the questions below:

1. What are the latitude and longitude of Point B on the map?

_____

2. What are the coordinates for the Point C at the southern tip of India?

_____

3. Identify any point in Tibet by its coordinates.

_____

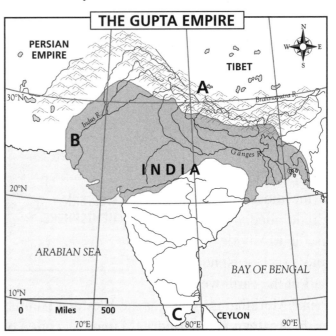

EARTH'S SEVEN CONTINENTS

Now that you are able to identify where the continents and oceans of the world are located, let's examine the main physical and human features of each continent.

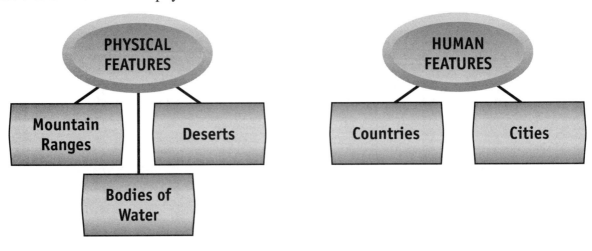

AFRICA

SIZE AND LOCATION

Africa is the second largest continent in area. It is almost three times the size of the United States. To the north, Africa is separated from Europe by the Mediterranean Sea. To the east lie the Red Sea and Indian Ocean. On the west, Africa is bordered by the Atlantic Ocean.

MAJOR PHYSICAL FEATURES

◆ **Deserts.** The **Sahara Desert**, which takes up most of North Africa, is the world's largest desert. It separates Africans north and south of it because this dry, sandy region is difficult to cross. For centuries, the Sahara isolated sub-Saharan Africa (*Africa south of the Sahara*) from the rest of the world. Farther south, Africa also has the **Kalahari Desert**.

◆ **Savannas.** Much of Africa is **savanna** — land where tall, wild grasses grow. Savannas are the best areas in Africa for growing crops and raising livestock. Most Africans live in the savanna region or along the coasts.

◆ **Tropical Rainforests.** In Central and West Africa, hot and humid rainforests get 60 to 100 inches of rainfall a year. This climate produces thick forest and jungle areas, making travel difficult. Rainforests are home to more plant and animal species than anywhere else on Earth.

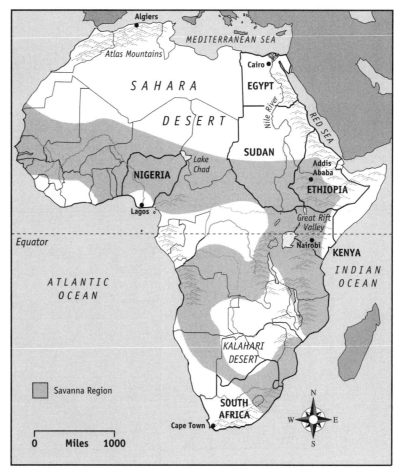

◆ **Mountains and Valleys.** The **Atlas Mountains** are found on the northwest edge of Africa. The **Great Rift Valley** runs through the highlands of Ethiopia and Kenya, to the east.

◆ **Bodies of Water.** Africa has several major rivers — the **Nile**, **Congo**, **Zambezi** and **Niger**. The Nile, the world's longest river, flows 4,150 miles from Central Africa through Egypt and into the Mediterranean. The banks of the Nile River provide some of Africa's richest farmland. Important lakes include **Lake Victoria** (*the largest freshwater lake in the world in surface area*) and **Lake Tanganyika**.

◆ **Climate.** Much of Africa is warm, with hot summers and mild winters. The amount of rainfall differs greatly; deserts receive too little water for farming, while some other areas receive too much rain.

HUMAN FEATURES: COUNTRIES AND CITIES

Today, almost 900 million people live in Africa, making Africa the second largest continent in population. There are more than 60 countries in Africa, including Sudan, Algeria, Libya, Egypt, Nigeria, Kenya, Ethiopia, and South Africa. Africa's major cities include Cairo (*Egypt*), Nairobi (*Kenya*), Addis Ababa (*Ethiopia*), Lagos (*Nigeria*), and Cape Town (*South Africa*).

APPLYING WHAT YOU HAVE LEARNED

Use the map below to complete the task:

▼ Select three major cities in Africa from the map. Then indicate each city's latitude and longitude coordinates.

• City (1): _____

   Coordinates:

   _____

• City (2): _____

   Coordinates:

   _____

• City (3): _____

   Coordinates:

   _____

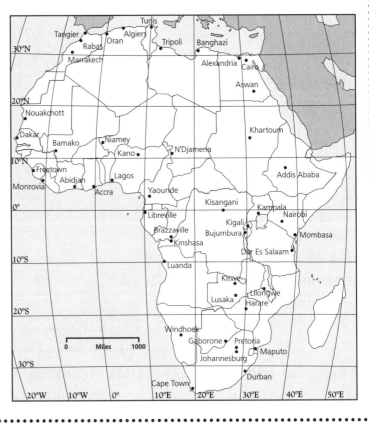

EUROPE

SIZE AND LOCATION

Europe is the second smallest continent in land area. It is bounded by the North Sea, the Atlantic Ocean, the Mediterranean Sea, the Black Sea and the Ural Mountains. Europe and Asia actually both share the same land mass. This land mass is so large that geographers have divided it into two continents. Great Britain, Ireland and Iceland are island nations in the Atlantic.

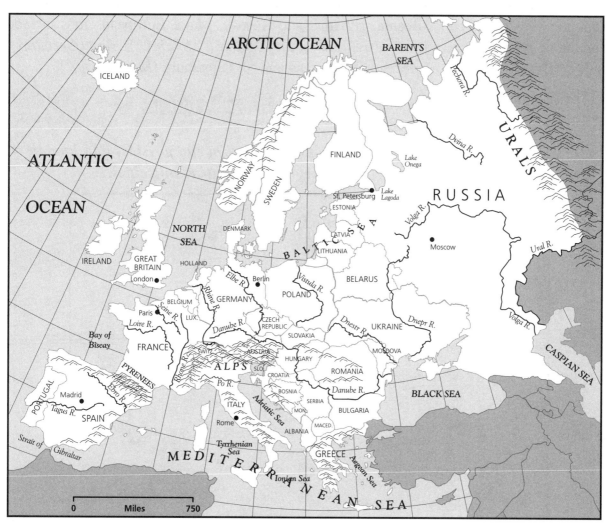

MAJOR PHYSICAL FEATURES

◆ **Mountains.** There are many mountain ranges in Europe. They include the **Alps**, **Pyrenees Apennines**, and **Balkans**. These mountains helped to create defensible borders between areas. They encouraged Europeans to develop many separate nationalities, each with its own language and customs.

◆ **Bodies of Water.** Europe includes several major bodies of water. In the north are the **Baltic** and **North Seas**. In the south, there are the **Mediterranean Sea** and **Black Sea**. Europe also has many major rivers, including the **Danube**, **Rhine**, **Loire**, **Rhone**, **Vistula** and **Volga**.

HUMAN FEATURES: COUNTRIES AND CITIES

In Europe, many different ethnic groups live close to one another. This gave rise to a large number of countries, including Ireland, Great Britain, France, Spain, Italy and Germany in Western Europe. Eastern Europe includes Russia, Poland, Ukraine, the Czech Republic, Slovakia, Serbia, Bosnia, Albania, and Kosovo. Major European cities include London (*England*), Paris (*France*), Rome (*Italy*), Madrid (*Spain*), Berlin (*Germany*), Dublin (*Ireland*), Athens (*Greece*), and Moscow and St. Petersburg (*Russia*).

APPLYING WHAT YOU HAVE LEARNED

On this map of Europe, show the location of each of the physical and human features identified below. Use the Internet to find countries and cities.

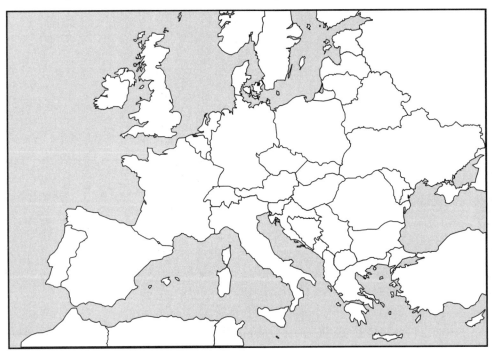

▼ **Seas:** Baltic, North Sea, Mediterranean, and Black Sea.

▼ **Mountain Ranges:** Alps, Pyrenees and Apennines

▼ **Countries:** Great Britain, Spain, France, Italy, Germany, Poland, and Russia.

▼ **Cities:** London, Madrid, Paris, Rome, and Berlin

ASIA

Asia is the world's largest continent. Today, it is home to two-thirds of the world's population. Because of its immense size and the diversity of its cultures, geographers often think of Asia as composed of several distinct regions.

THE MIDDLE EAST

SIZE AND LOCATION

The Middle East lies at the "crossroads" of three continents, connecting Africa, Asia and Europe. It borders one of the world's most important waterways, the **Suez Canal**, which shortens the traveling distance between Europe and Asia.

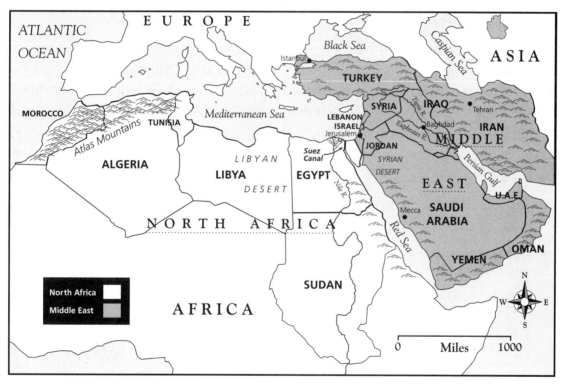

MAJOR PHYSICAL FEATURES

◆ **Deserts.** Much of the Middle East is desert. For example, most of the Arabian Peninsula is desert.

◆ **Bodies of Water.** There are several important rivers in the Middle East, including the **Jordan**, **Tigris** and **Euphrates Rivers**. The mild climate and good soil found along these rivers made them centers of some of the world's earliest civilizations. Other major bodies of water bordering the Middle East include the **Mediterranean Sea**, **Black Sea**, **Red Sea** and the **Persian Gulf**.

◆ **Climate.** Most of the Middle East is located near the **equator**. The area has warm winters and hot, dry summers. While lacking adequate water supplies, the Middle East has about half of the world's known oil reserves.

HUMAN FEATURES: COUNTRIES AND CITIES

Important countries in the Middle East include Israel, Syria, Turkey, Iraq, Saudi Arabia and Iran. Major cities are Jerusalem (*Israel*), Baghdad (*Iraq*), Tehran (*Iran*), Mecca (*Saudi Arabia*) and Istanbul (*Turkey*). Many geographers classify North Africa as part of the same cultural region as the Middle East.

NORTHERN AND CENTRAL ASIA

SIZE AND LOCATION

Northern Asia is occupied by the country of **Russia**, which stretches from Eastern Europe to the Pacific. Russia is the world's largest country in area. Although the majority of its population is located in Europe, most of Russia's land area is in Asia. **Siberia**, in northeastern Russia, is a cold region with forests. Northernmost Russia is **tundra**, where the ground is frozen much of the year. **Central Asia** consists of a vast corridor south of Russia, made up of mountains, deserts and **steppes** (*treeless grasslands*). The steppes provide excellent grazing land.

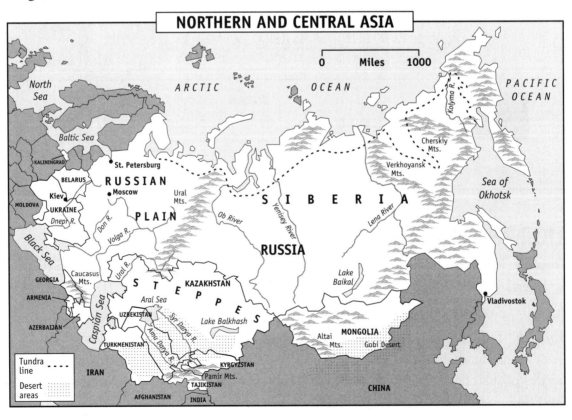

MAJOR PHYSICAL FEATURES

◆ **Bodies of Water.** The **Arctic Ocean**, north of Russia, is frozen for most of the year. Major rivers in Asian Russia are the **Ob** and **Lena**.

◆ **Mountains.** The **Ural Mountains** separate European and Asian Russia, while the **Pamir Mountains** separate Russia from China.

◆ **Climate.** Most of Russia has long, cold winters and short mild summers.

MAJOR HUMAN FEATURES

Important countries in Northern and Central Asia include Russia, Kazakhstan, Afghanistan, and Mongolia. Important cities include Vladivostock (*Russia*), and Kabul (*Afghanistan*).

EAST ASIA

SIZE AND LOCATION

East Asia includes three important countries: (1) China, (2) Korea, and (3) Japan. **China** is the world's third largest country in area: only Russia and Canada are larger. **Korea** is a peninsula extending from the northeastern coast of China. **Japan** consists of four main islands and a number of smaller islands, separated from the Asian mainland by the Sea of Japan.

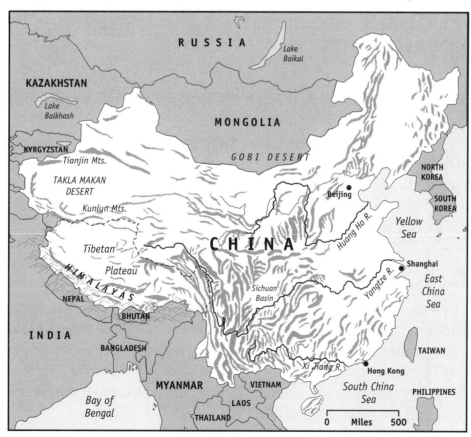

MAJOR PHYSICAL FEATURES

◆ **Bodies of Water.** Important rivers include the **Hwang Ho** (*Yellow River*) and the **Yangtze**. These river valleys were important centers of early civilizations.

◆ **Mountains.** China's southern and western borders are ringed by the **Himalayan**, **Kunlun**, and **Tianjin Mountains**. To the west is the mountainous area of **Tibet**. Much of Japan and Korea are also mountainous. About 85% of Japan is covered by mountains and hills. **Mount Fujiyama**, an extinct volcano, is the highest and most famous mountain in Japan.

◆ **Deserts.** The **Gobi Desert** is located to the north of China. For much of its past, mountains, deserts, and surrounding seas served to isolate East Asia from the rest of the world.

HUMAN FEATURES: COUNTRIES AND CITIES

China has been the world's most populous nation for most of its history. One out of every five people in the world today is Chinese. The eastern part of China consists of a vast plain with fertile valleys. Most of China's population lives in this area. China's major cities include Beijing, Shanghai, and Hong Kong. Although Japan's land area is small, it has a relatively large population — almost half that of the United States. Japan's major cities include Tokyo and Kyoto. Korea is divided in two. South Korea's largest city is Seoul.

SOUTH AND SOUTHEAST ASIA

SIZE AND LOCATION

Most of **South Asia** is a **subcontinent** — a large piece of land smaller than a continent. The Indian subcontinent, about the size of the United States, looks like a large triangle coming out of Asia, jutting into the Indian Ocean. Southeast Asia also consists of a **peninsula** — land surrounded by water on three sides — and a series of islands on the southeast corner of the Asian mainland. Surrounded by the Pacific and Indian Oceans, it provides the shortest water route between these two oceans.

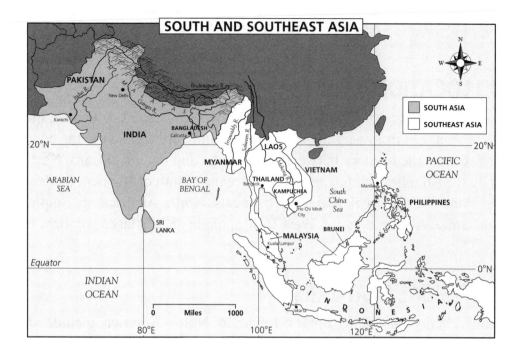

MAJOR PHYSICAL FEATURES

◆ **Mountains.** The **Himalayas**, north of India, are the highest mountains in the world. They separate the Indian subcontinent from the rest of Asia. Mountains also cut off Southeast Asia from the rest of the continent. Divided by mountains, the peoples of Vietnam, Laos and Cambodia developed their own languages, customs and cultures.

◆ **Bodies of Water.** The main rivers of the Indian subcontinent are the **Indus** and **Ganges**. Here, some of the world's earliest civilizations began. The Ganges is considered holy by Hindus, the largest religious group in India. According to Hindu belief, washing in the Ganges removes one's sins and gains rewards in the next life. The **Mekong**, **Salween** and **Irrawaddy Rivers** are major rivers in Southeast Asia.

◆ **Climate.** Both South and Southeast Asia have warm winters and hot summers. The most important climatic feature is the **monsoons** — winds that blow over the region and bring heavy rains in the summer. Monsoon rains provide water for crops and support life, but they also cause severe flooding, property damage and death.

HUMAN FEATURES: COUNTRIES AND CITIES

The main countries of South Asia are India, Pakistan and Bangladesh. India has the world's second largest population, almost equal to that of China. Southeast Asia consists of a peninsula that includes Thailand, Cambodia, Laos and Vietnam. Southeast Asia also includes several large island nations: Indonesia, Malaysia and the Philippines. Important cities are Mumbai (*Bombay*), Calcutta and New Delhi in India, Jakarta in Indonesia, and Manila in the Philippines.

NORTH AMERICA

SIZE AND LOCATION

North America is the world's third largest continent in area. Located in the Western Hemisphere, it stretches from near the North Pole southwards almost to the equator. From east to west, it covers the territory between the Atlantic and Pacific Oceans. North America is bordered by the Atlantic, Pacific, and Arctic Oceans. South of Mexico, the land narrows into Central America. **Central America** connects North America to South America. Northeast of Central America are the **West Indies**, made up of a large number of islands in the Caribbean Sea.

MAJOR PHYSICAL FEATURES

◆ **Mountains.** Major mountain ranges found in North America include the **Rocky Mountains** in the west and the **Appalachian Mountains** in the east.

◆ **Bodies of Water.** The **St. Lawrence River** separates the United States from eastern Canada. The **Mississippi River** drains much of the United States. The **Great Lakes** — Lake Superior, Lake Michigan, Lake Huron, Lake Erie, and Lake Ontario — form the largest system of fresh surface water on Earth. The **Rio Grande** separates the United States from Mexico. The **Panama Canal**, located in Central America, connects the Atlantic and the Pacific Oceans.

◆ **Plains.** West of the Mississippi River is a region known as the **Great Plains**, containing some of the world's most productive farmland.

MAJOR HUMAN FEATURES: COUNTRIES AND CITIES

There are several countries that make up North America. They have a combined population of more than 500 million people. The major cities of the United States include Boston, New York City, Houston, Philadelphia, Cleveland, Chicago, and Los Angeles. Washington, D.C. is the nation's capital. Canada's major cities include Toronto, Montreal and Quebec. Mexico City is the capital of Mexico. Central America is divided into seven smaller countries.

APPLYING WHAT YOU HAVE LEARNED

Use the map below to find the latitude and longitude for each of the following:

1. Ottawa: _____

2. Great Lakes: _____

3. Mexico City: _____

4. Mississippi River: _____

5. Panama Canal: _____

6. Rocky Mountains: _____

7. Costa Rica: _____

8. Jamaica: _____

SOUTH AMERICA

SIZE AND LOCATION

South America describes the lands in the Western Hemisphere south of Central America. South America is the fourth largest continent in size. Stretching over 7,000 miles, it covers territory between the Atlantic and Pacific Oceans.

MAJOR PHYSICAL FEATURES

◆ **Mountains.** The **Andes Mountains** are among the highest in the world. They stretch over 4,500 miles in the western part of South America. The Andes have separated people in some parts of South America from those in other parts. These mountains were once the home of the Inca Empire.

◆ **Grasslands and Plains.** Mountains and poor soils make much of the land in South America unproductive. One exception is the **pampas** of Argentina and Uruguay. The pampas provide large areas of fertile soil for growing crops and grazing cattle.

◆ **Rainforests.** Rainforests are located on the east coast of Central America and the northern part of South America. They tend to have warm, humid climates. The **Amazon Rainforest**, the world's largest rainforest, makes up a large part of Brazil.

◆ **Bodies of Water.** The **Amazon River** is the second longest river in the world. In addition, South America has the **Orinoco** and the **Rio de la Plata Rivers**. A large percentage of South America's population lives near these river systems. They form the basis for much of the continent's transportation.

◆ **Climate.** Much of South America is quite warm because it lies near the **equator**. However, because of its mountains and ocean winds, many places in South America have comfortable temperatures. Some of the greatest concentrations of people are in the higher elevations where temperatures are cooler.

HUMAN FEATURES: COUNTRIES AND CITIES

South America has a total population of more than 370 million people. Important countries in South America include Brazil, Argentina, Chile and Peru. Major cities in South America include Rio de Janeiro (*Brazil*), Buenos Aires (*Argentina*), Lima (*Peru*), and Santiago (*Chile*).

APPLYING WHAT YOU HAVE LEARNED

Using the map to the right, locate the following:

1. Andes Mountains

2. Pampas

3. Amazon River

4. Equator

5. Chile

6. Peru

7. Brazil

8. Argentina

9. Amazon Rainforest

10. Rio de Janeiro

11. São Paulo

12. Buenos Aires

13. Lima

AUSTRALIA

Surrounded by the Indian and Pacific Oceans, Australia is cut off from Asia by the Arafura and Timor Seas. The world's largest coral reef, the **Great Barrier Reef**, is found here. Australia is the only country that is an entire continent. Its largest cities are Melbourne and Sidney.

ANTARCTICA

Antarctica is the world's southernmost continent and covers the South Pole; about 98% of this continent is covered by ice.

APPLYING WHAT YOU HAVE LEARNED

This chart lists some of the major physical and human features for each of the seven continents. Use an outline map of the world to complete the following task.

▼ Select any *four physical features* and any *three cities* from the chart below.

▼ Locate and label each feature and city on your outline map.

Continent	Major Physical Features	MAJOR CITIES
Asia	Largest and most populous continent; Himalaya Mountains; Gobi Desert; Indian Subcontinent; Arabian Peninsula; Rivers: Tigris and Euphrates, Indus, Ganges, Mekong, Yangtze; Huang Ho; Island nations include: Japan, Indonesia, Philippines, Malaysia.	Beijing, Shanghai, Hong Kong, Tokyo, Mumbai, Manila, Mecca, Djakarta, Singapore, Seoul, Tehran, Istanbul, Baghdad, Jeruselem
Africa	Second largest continent; Atlas Mountains; Sahara Desert; Rivers: Nile, Congo, Niger; Great Rift Valley; Kalahari Desert; Tropical rainforests of Central and West Africa.	Cairo, Nairobi, Lagos, Capetown
North America	Third largest continent; Appalachian and Rocky Mountains; Great Lakes; Rivers: Mississippi, Rio Grande; West Indies; Central America.	Mexico City, New York, Los Angeles, Chicago, Boston, Montreal, Toronto, Miami, Havana
South America	Fourth largest continent; mostly in Southern Hemisphere; Andes Mountains; Amazon Rainforest; pampas.	Rio de Janeiro, Buenos Aires, Lima, Santiago
Europe	Shares its landmass with Asia; Mountains: Alps and Pyrenees; Rivers: Danube, Rhine, Rhone, Loire, Vistula, Volga; Mediterranean, Baltic, North and Black Seas.	London, Paris, Dublin, Berlin, Moscow, Madrid, Rome, Athens, St. Petersburg
Australia	Great Barrier Reef.	Melbourne, Sidney
Antarctica	Covers the South Pole; mainly frozen.	

WHAT YOU SHOULD KNOW

☐ You should know that a continent is a large land mass. The seven continents are Africa, Antarctica, Asia, Australia, Europe, North America, and South America.

☐ You should also know Europe and Asia share the same landmass.

☐ You should know that each continent has its own distinct physical features. These physical features include its mountain ranges, deserts, bodies of water, climate, plant and animal life, and natural resources.

☐ You should know that human activities have transformed Earth's surface by cutting down forests, making farmland, mining minerals, building roads, and creating cities. Each continent has its own countries and major cities.

CHAPTER STUDY CARDS

Earth's Seven Continents
★ **Africa.** Second largest continent in area.
★ **Antarctica.** Covers the South Pole.
★ **North America.** Consists mainly of Canada, the United States and Mexico; includes Central America.
★ **South America.** Located between the Atlantic and the Pacific Oceans.
★ **Europe.** Second smallest continent in area.
★ **Asia.** World's largest continent.
★ **Australia.** Surrounded by the Indian and Pacific Oceans.

Latitude and Longitude
★ **Latitude.** Imaginary horizontal lines that run across Earth. Measured in degrees to show how far north or south a location is. **Equator:** the most important latitude line.
★ **Longitude.** Imaginary lines that run up and down Earth. All longitude lines meet at the North and South Poles. The **Prime Meridian:** the most important longitude line.
★ Together, longitude and latitude define a place's absolute location.

Major Physical Features
★ **Oceans.** Atlantic, Pacific, Indian, Arctic.
★ **Seas.** Mediterranean Sea, Black Sea, Baltic Sea.
★ **Mountain Ranges.** Himalayas, Rockies, Appalachians, Alps, Pyrenees, Andes, Urals.
★ **Rivers.** Mississippi, Rio Grande, St. Lawrence, Amazon, Nile, Rhine, Danube, Tigris, Euphrates, Volga, Ganges, Indus, Yangtze, Huang Ho.
★ **Deserts.** Sahara, Gobi, Kalahari, Arabian.
★ **Rainforests.** Amazon Rainforest.

Humans Affect on the Land
Humans affect the land in a number of important ways:
★ They cut down forests.
★ They create farmland.
★ They build roads.
★ They create countries.
★ They create cities.

Major Cities
Beijing, Shanghai, Mexico City, Tokyo, London, Rome, Paris, Cairo, Mumbai, Mecca, and Jerusalem.

CHECKING YOUR UNDERSTANDING

Examine the map of the world below.

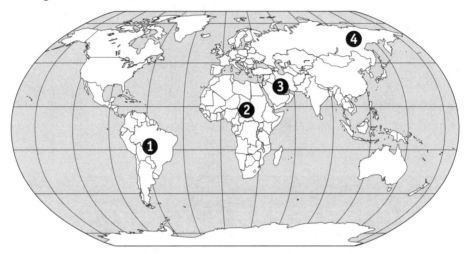

1.   Which number on the map shows the location of the Amazon Rainforest?

A. 1   C. 3

B. 2   D. 4

GEOG
A: 6.1

This question tests your understanding of where one of the world's major physical features is located. You should recall that the Amazon Rainforest is located in Brazil in South America. Rainforests are warm and quite moist. The Amazon Rainforest is located in Brazil, which is a part of South America. On the map, number 1 is located in South America. Thus, **Choice A** *is the correct answer.*

Now try answering some additional questions on your own.

2.   Which number on the map shows the continent where the Sahara Desert is located?

A. 1   C. 3

B. 2   D. 4

GEOG
A: 6.1

3.   Which two physical features are located on the continent of Africa?

A. Sahara Desert and the Nile River

B. Gobi Desert and the Himalayan Mountains

C. Andes Mountains and the Amazon River

D. Pyrenees Mountains and the Seine River

GEOG
A: 6.1

4. Part of which continent is shown in the map to the right?

A. South America
B. Africa
C. Asia
D. Australia

GEOG
A: 6.1

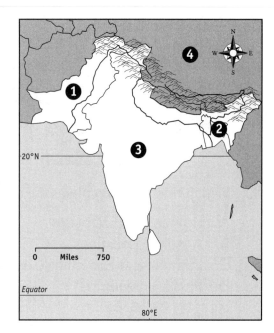

5. What is the name of the mountains that separate the countries marked as Number 3 and 4 on the map?

A. Rocky Mountains
B. Himalayan Mountains
C. Pyrenees Mountains
D. Andes Mountains

GEOG
A: 6.1

Look at the map below.

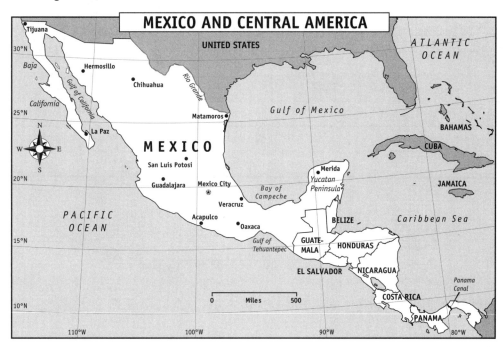

6. Which city is located at 21 degrees north latitude, 103 degrees west longitude?

A. Acapulco
B. Mexico City
C. Veracruz
D. Guadalajara

GEOG
A: 6.2

7. Which coordinates are located within the country of Nicaragua?

A. 15°N, 90°W
B. 15°N, 85°W
C. 13°N, 85°W
D. 10°N, 85°W

GEOG
A: 6.2

Look at the chart below.

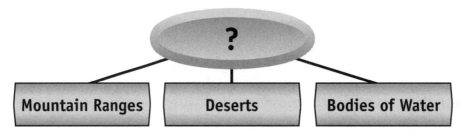

8. Which title **best** completes the chart?

A. Human Characteristics
B. Absolute Locations
C. Latitude and Longitude Coordinates
D. Physical Features

GEOG B:
6.1, 7.1

Look at the map of the world below.

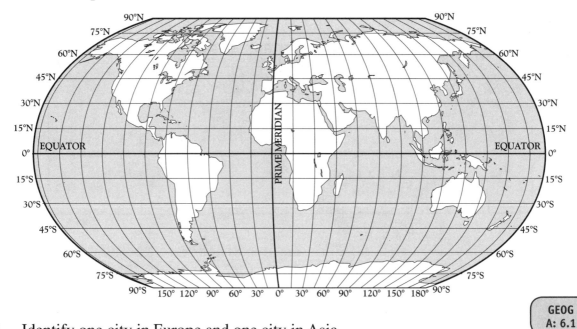

GEOG
A: 6.1

9. Identify one city in Europe and one city in Asia.

Europe: _____   Asia: _____

Then place each city in its proper location on the map above. (4 points)

10. Identify two continents through which the Prime Meridian passes (2 points).

GEOG
A: 6.2

_____

_____

CHAPTER 8

THE WORLD'S PHYSICAL AND HUMAN REGIONS

In this chapter, you will learn about one of the five themes of geography — regions. You will also learn about the differences between physical and human regions, how regions change over time, and how economic activities are distributed within a region.

MAJOR IDEAS

GEOGRAPHY, BENCHMARK B

A. A **region** is an area with common features.

B. A **physical region** is an area with common physical characteristics.

C. A **human region** is an area with characteristics shared by people living there. These shared characteristics may include language, religion, history and government.

D. The physical and human characteristics of a region can change over time. Regions themselves may expand, contract or even disappear.

E. Economic activities, such as farming, mining, fishing and manufacturing, are distributed within a region based on landforms, the location of resources, transportation and communication routes, and other factors.

F. Changes in technology, transportation, communications or resources can lead to changes in the distribution of economic activities in a region.

WHAT IS A REGION?

A **region** is an area that shares common features and characteristics. There are both physical regions and human regions.

PHYSICAL REGIONS

A **physical region** is an area that shares common physical characteristics — such as climate, plant and animal life, and land forms. Its characteristics are different from those of surrounding areas outside the region. The **Amazon Rainforest** in South America is an example of a physical region. Throughout this area, the climate is hot all year, with frequent rain showers. A variety of tropical trees grow in the Amazon. Their interlocking tops form a dense canopy (*umbrella*) over the rainforest.

The **Sahara Desert**, the world's largest desert, is another example of a physical region with its own characteristics. The climate is extremely hot and dry. Much of the Sahara is sand without plant life. The northern and southern ends of the Sahara have some rainfall, grasslands, and desert shrubs.

Much of the Sahara is covered by sand dunes and seas of sand.

HUMAN REGIONS

A **human region** is defined by the common characteristics of the people living there. The people in a human region may speak the same language, practice the same religion, share the same customs, or live under the same government.

A **country** is one form of human region. It is an area created by humans, with certain characteristics. Each country has its own borders, separating it from other countries. Each country also has its own government and laws. People in a country often speak the same language or group of languages. They usually also share a common history and have many common customs.

Cultural Regions. Cultural regions are also regions based on human characteristics. They are areas in which people share common cultural characteristics — such as religious beliefs, customs, and art forms. Often cultural regions correspond to physical regions. For example, the Middle East might be viewed as a physical region. This region has a warm, dry climate with many deserts and mountain areas. The Middle East also has several fertile river valleys and mild coastal areas.

Besides being a physical region, the Middle East is also a cultural region. A large number of people in the Middle East have a common history and heritage. Most people are Muslims. Most speak Arabic. At one time, almost all of this region was ruled by the Ottoman Empire.

Most of the people in the Middle East practice the Muslim religion.

Latin America. Latin America is another example of a cultural region. The name "Latin America" is applied to the Americas south of the United States. This large cultural region consists of four main areas — Mexico, Central America, the West Indies (Caribbean), and South America.

This region is called "Latin America" because the area was once colonized by Spain and Portugal, whose languages come from Latin. Many Latin Americans are of mixed Native American Indian, African, and European descent. Most speak Spanish or Portuguese, and the majority follow the Catholic religion.

APPLYING WHAT YOU HAVE LEARNED

	Example	Characteristics Making This a Physical or Human Region
Physical Region		
Human Region		

HOW REGIONS CHANGE OVER TIME

Both physical and human regions can change over time. It may take thousands or even millions of years for the climate, landforms or other physical characteristics of a region to change. However, human regions can change more quickly.

CHANGES TO PHYSICAL REGIONS

Change to a physical region often takes thousands of years. The Sahara Desert in North Africa provides such an example. Scientists believe it was once a jungle. As Earth's climate grew warmer, the Sahara grew drier. Over thousands of years, it became a desert.

The Siberian-Alaskan Land Bridge. Siberia and Alaska were once a single physical region. A land bridge connected them during the Ice Age. When the Earth became warmer, the ice melted, raising sea levels and burying the land bridge. Alaska and Siberia became separated by the sea and were no longer a single physical region.

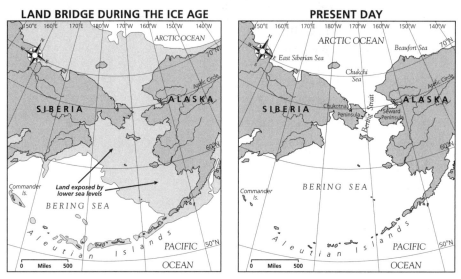

Alaska and Siberia during the last Ice Age (left) and today (right).

APPLYING WHAT YOU HAVE LEARNED

▼ Why do physical regions sometimes change over time? _____

_____

_____

_____

CHANGES TO HUMAN REGIONS

Human regions change more quickly than physical ones. They are affected by shifting trade routes, war, disease, or new contacts with other cultures. Human regions can expand, contract, or even disappear over time.

North and South America, for example, once consisted of many American Indian cultural groups. These groups divided the Americas into different regions — such as the Inca and Aztec empires, the tribal lands of the Iroquois Nations, and the Great Plains inhabited by such tribes as the Sioux. The arrival of Europeans greatly disrupted these American Indian tribes. They changed the Americas into new regions based on European exploration, conquest and colonization. Former American Indian lands became new human regions ruled by European powers — New Spain, New France, and the thirteen English colonies.

CASE STUDY: THE ROMAN EMPIRE

The ancient Roman Empire once formed a vast human region that changed over time and eventually disappeared. Ancient Rome began as a city-state near the west coast of central Italy. After conquering the rest of Italy, Rome defeated Carthage, its main rival in the Mediterranean. Next Rome conquered Spain, Gaul (*present-day France*), Greece, Egypt and Britain. This allowed Rome to extend its control throughout much of Europe and the Mediterranean world. After several centuries, Rome began to shrink under the impact of attacks by hostile barbarian tribes. Eventually, this human region divided into two separate empires and finally collapsed.

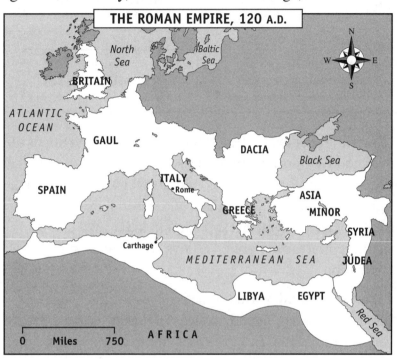

THE ROMAN EMPIRE, 120 A.D.

APPLYING WHAT YOU HAVE LEARNED

▼ Why do human regions often change faster than physical regions? _____

_____

_____

_____

HOW ECONOMIC ACTIVITIES ARE DISTRIBUTED IN A REGION

Economic activities are the things people do to meet their needs, such as *farming*, *fishing*, *keeping livestock*, *mining* and *manufacturing*. Many factors affect how these economic activities are distributed within a region.

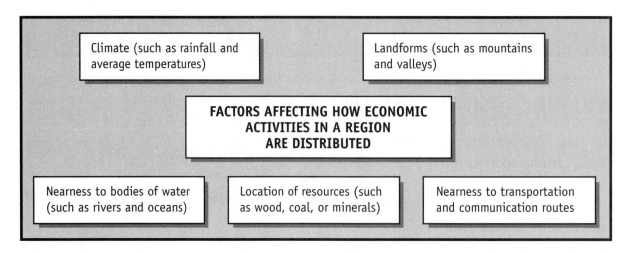

Farming. For example, a sunny climate with plenty of fertile soil and fresh water makes an area good for farming. Farming is more difficult without these conditions. People therefore tend to farm in fertile valleys and coastal areas with long growing seasons. Grasslands are good for grazing. Mountains and deserts are usually more thinly populated. This was true of ancient Egypt, Mesopotamia, India and China. In these cradles of civilization, agriculture first arose in river valleys with warm and sunny climates, fertile soil, and water for irrigation.

Trading Activities. Trading activities also affect where people lived. The map below shows major trading routes and urban areas in Europe in the 1400s. Notice the number of important cities near the coasts. In most cases, these cities were connected to the sea by major rivers. Sea-worthy vessels could sail up to the port, which was protected from the open sea. These ports also collected goods from inland areas. These goods were sent downstream by river. Because of their importance as trading centers, the populations of these towns grew. These towns then became major centers of other economic activities, such as shipbuilding, fishing, buying and selling grain, and making cloth.

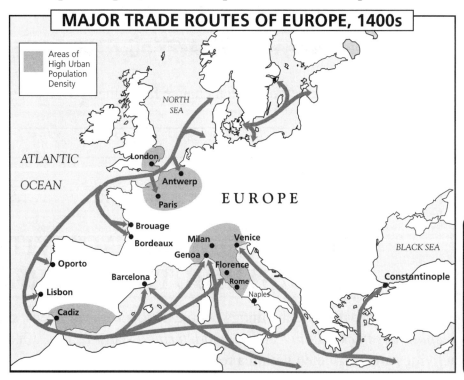

As the map shows, southern Spain, northern Italy, southeastern England and northwestern France — all bordering on or near the ocean — had become leading population centers by 1400.

APPLYING WHAT YOU HAVE LEARNED

▼ What are some of the factors that explain where people choose to settle?

_____

_____

_____

_____

New Forms of Transportation. Later, when European countries industrialized in the late 1700s and early 1800s, the distribution of economic activities changed. People began working in factories. The construction of canals and the invention of the steamship and railroad introduced new forms of transportation. Railroads made it easier to connect mines, factories, and cities by land. People built factories close to key resources or near large cities. For example, iron was produced close to sources of iron ore or coal, and this iron was then shipped by rail to other locations. New cities emerged at places where railroad routes criss-crossed.

THE CHANGING DISTRIBUTION OF ECONOMIC ACTIVITIES

When natural resources run out, new technologies are invented, trade routes shift, or the climate changes, then the location of economic activities within a region may also change.

For example, in Africa today the Sahara Desert is expanding southwards more than 100 miles a year into the grassy **Sahel** region — the lands between the Sahara Desert to the north and tropical rainforests to the south. This change is making farming and the grazing of livestock in the Sahel more difficult. This decrease in fertile land has led to starvation and the migrations of farming communities to the more humid areas of West Africa.

The Sahel region of Africa was once fertile land.

WHAT YOU SHOULD KNOW

☐ You should know that a region is an area with common features. A physical region is an area with common physical characteristics, such as climate and landforms.

☐ You should know that a human region is an area with characteristics shared by people living there. These characteristics may include language, religion and history.

☐ You should know that the physical and human characteristics of a region can change over time. Regions themselves may expand, contract or even disappear.

☐ You should know that economic activities (*such as farming, mining, fishing and manufacturing*) are distributed within a region based on its landforms, the location of resources, transportation and communication routes, and other factors.

☐ You should know that changes in technology, transportation, communications or resources can lead to changes in the distribution of these activities.

CHAPTER STUDY CARDS

Regions

Region. An area with common characteristics, which differ from those of surrounding areas. There are both physical and human regions:

★ **Physical Regions.** An area that shares common physical characteristics — such as climate, plant and animal life, and land forms. Examples: the Amazon Rainforest and the Sahara Desert.

★ **Human Regions.** An area defined by the common characteristics of the people living there. A **country** is a human region.

Cultural Regions

Cultural Regions. Regions based on common cultural characteristics, such as religious beliefs, customs, and art forms. They are a type of **human region**.

★ **Middle East.** This area is both a physical and cultural region.

★ **Latin America.** Mexico, Central America, the West Indies, and South America, where most people speak Spanish or Portuguese, and follow the Catholic religion.

How Regions Change Over Time

Physical and human regions can change:

★ **Changes to Physical Regions.** Changes to a physical region often take millions of years to occur. Example: the disappearance of the land bridge linking Alaska to Siberia.

★ **Changes to Human Regions.** Changes to human features may occur more quickly because of the effects of shifting trade, war, disease, or contact with other cultures.

The Distribution of Economic Activities Within a Region

Several factors influence how economic activities are distributed:

★ **Climate**

★ **Landforms,** such as mountains and valleys.

★ **Nearness to Bodies of Water.**

★ **Location of Resources**, such as wood, coal and minerals.

★ **Nearness to Transportation and Communication Routes.**

TESTING YOUR UNDERSTANDING

1. Which characteristics might help to define a physical region?

    A. the number of people living there
    B. the types of plants found there
    C. the religious practices of people in the region
    D. the common history of the people there

> **HINT**
>
> First **examine** the question. It tests your understanding of the differences between a physical and a human region. You should **recall** that a physical region is based on the physical characteristics of a place, such as its landforms, climate and plant life. Human regions are based on the common characteristics of the people living in an area. **Applying** this knowledge to the answer choices, you should realize that Choices A, C, and D refer to human characteristics used to define human regions. Therefore, the best answer is **Choice B**. A physical region may be defined by its shared forms of plant life.

Now try answering some additional questions on your own.

Look at the map to the right.

2. Based on the map, what goods were most likely traded in Timbuktu?

    GEOG B: 6.3

    A. salt and gold
    B. diamonds and silk
    C. tea and pepper
    D. wood and sand

WEST AFRICAN TRADE ROUTES, 800-1500

3. Based on the map, what conclusion can **best** be drawn about West Africa?

    A. No trade routes crossed the Sahara Desert.
    B. Rivers played no role as main trade routes for the region.
    C. Wheat was once farmed throughout the Sahara Desert.
    D. The region's economy was influenced by its trade in salt and gold.

    GEOG B: 6.3

Look at the maps below.

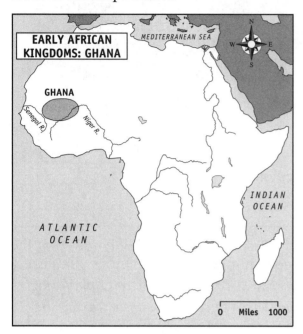

Ghana (750-1200)

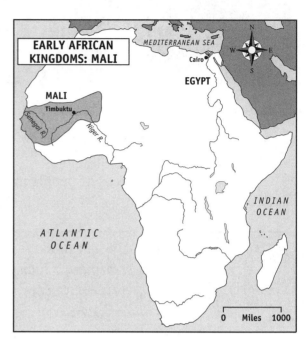

Mali (1240-1400)

4.   Over time, the characteristics of regions may change.

Which statement best describes changes to human regions in West Africa?

A. The later Kingdom of Mali covered more territory than Ghana.

B. The later Kingdom of Mali was smaller because of climate changes.

C. The later Kingdom of Mali developed new farming methods to survive.

D. The later Kingdom of Mali had a less powerful military force than Ghana.

> GEOG
> B: 7.3

5.   Which area can best be identified as a single cultural region, based on the languages, religious beliefs, and customs shared by its people?

A. Asia

B. Africa

C. Latin America

D. North America

> GEOG
> B: 6.4

6.   Many factors play a role in determining how economic activities in a region are distributed.

> GEOG
> B: 6.3

In your **Answer Document**, identify two factors that determine how economic activities in a region are distributed. (2 points)

_____

_____

CHAPTER 9

MOVEMENT

In this chapter, you will learn how people, products and ideas move from place to place. You will also learn what factors influence the migration of peoples, the movement of goods and the diffusion of ideas.

MAJOR IDEAS

PEOPLE IN SOCIETIES, BENCHMARK C
GEOGRAPHY, BENCHMARK D

A. Different **push-and-pull factors** cause people to migrate. "Push" factors include the desire to escape oppression, poverty, political conflict or environmental disaster. "Pull" factors include the search for greater freedom or economic opportunity, or the desire to reinforce cultural ties.

B. The **uneven distribution** of natural resources encourages world trade.

C. Contacts between cultures can lead to changes in belief systems, art, science, technology, languages, and systems of government.

D. Various factors can promote or delay the movement of people, ideas, and goods. These factors include physical features (*such as landforms and bodies of water*), culture, war, trade, and technological innovations.

WHY PEOPLE MIGRATE

Migration is the movement of people from one area to another. There are many reasons that cause people to migrate. Geographers divide these reasons into "push" and "pull" factors:

PUSH FACTORS	PULL FACTORS
◆ Oppression ◆ Poverty ◆ Political Conflicts ◆ Environmental Factors	◆ Freedom ◆ Economic Opportunity ◆ Cultural Ties

People often migrate because of both "push" and "pull" factors. Let's take a closer look at the factors that cause people to migrate.

OPPRESSION / FREEDOM

Throughout history, many countries have persecuted or mistreated some of their citizens for their religious beliefs, political beliefs, or ethnic identity. Societies have even enslaved some of their citizens to provide a work force. People sometimes migrate to escape these conditions. They are "pulled" to a new place where they believe they can live in greater freedom. Here are two examples of people who migrated to escape oppression and find freedom.

CASE STUDY: JEWISH MIGRATIONS

Under the Roman Empire, Jewish people were driven from Israel when they rebelled against Roman rule. In the Middle Ages, Jews often faced prejudice and discrimination from their Christian neighbors. In 1290, England moved to expel its Jewish community. France followed in 1394. In 1492, Ferdinand and Isabella of Spain ordered all Jews to convert to Christianity or leave Spain. From these countries,

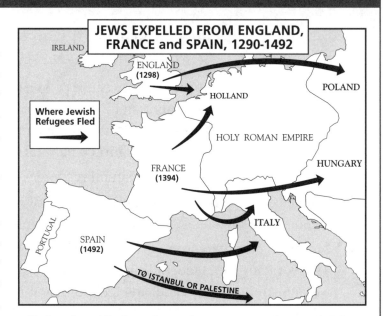

Jews migrated to Holland, Hungary, Poland and Italy, where they were welcomed. Many Jews also fled to the Ottoman Empire, where they settled in Istanbul or Palestine.

CASE STUDY: THE PILGRIMS

In the 1600s, disagreements over religious practices led one Protestant sect to migrate from England. The Pilgrims faced religious persecution from the King and the Church of England. They were often punished, jailed and fined for their beliefs. They fled England for the Netherlands, but soon decided to relocate in the Americas. In 1620, they established a colony at Plymouth, Massachusetts.

APPLYING WHAT YOU HAVE LEARNED

▼ Explain how the Jewish and Pilgrim migrations illustrate the roles played by both "push" and "pull" factors.

_____

_____

_____

_____

POVERTY / ECONOMIC OPPORTUNITY

When a society suffers from extreme poverty, this "pushes" many to attempt to escape. The motivation to migrate is all the greater if people have heard or read that conditions elsewhere are better. For example, during the Black Death in Europe, serfs left their lords' manors and migrated into nearby towns, where they sought new economic opportunities.

CASE STUDY: THE SPANISH IN THE NEW WORLD

After the Spanish conquest of the Americas, many Spaniards went to "New Spain" in search of greater economic opportunities. By the early part of the sixteenth century, thriving Spanish colonies were to be found throughout the New World. Spaniards seeking to enrich themselves established mines and plantations on the islands of the West Indies and in Mexico, Central America and Peru. Their use of weapons and horses allowed forced labor to be imposed on the Native American population.

The native population was forced to dig mines for gold and silver or to plant and harvest crops for sale in Europe. In addition, enslaved Africans were brought across the Atlantic to the Americas to serve as a workforce. Wealthy Spanish colonists organized and ran the enterprise for their own profit. They became the new elite of this society, enjoying luxury and wealth.

Spaniards meeting with Native American Indians.

POLITICAL CONFLICTS AND WARS

Political conflicts and war often lead people to migrate. People flee their homes when armed conflict breaks out. Such fighting might occur because of an invasion by neighbors or because of a civil war caused by conflict between rival groups.

CASE STUDY: ESCAPE FROM THE HUNS

The Huns were a semi-nomadic people in Central Asia who lived off the meat from their herds and from food obtained by hunting and gathering. These Huns were also fierce warriors who excelled at horsemanship and at inflicting terror on those they attacked. As they moved westward, the Huns attacked and destroyed the settlements of the Goths — Germanic tribes living on the edge of the Roman Empire. In 370 A.D., to escape the Huns, 200,000 Goth men, women and children fled into the Roman Empire. Some may have been drawn to Rome because of cultural ties that had developed over time. People are attracted to areas where they have relatives or some knowledge of the culture. But this migration placed pressure, in turn, on the Roman Empire, contributing to its later collapse.

Hun warriors were feared by Goths.

APPLYING WHAT YOU HAVE LEARNED

▼ Most scholars believe the ancient Hebrews lived in slavery in Egypt as described in the Bible. To escape slavery, the Hebrews fled Egypt about 1400–1200 B.C. and moved to Canaan (*present-day Israel*) their ancient homeland. Which "push" and "pull" factors explain why the Hebrews migrated? Explain your answer.

_____

_____

_____

_____

ENVIRONMENTAL FACTORS

Changes in the environment, such as cooling or rising temperatures, or a series of droughts, may lead people to migrate. Sudden environmental catastrophes, such as floods, fires, and earthquakes, also may force people to migrate.

CASE STUDY: DESTRUCTION OF POMPEII

Pompeii was a city in the Roman Empire. The area had a substantial population, which had grown wealthy on the region's fertile soil. On August 24, 79 A.D., Mount Vesuvius, a nearby volcano, erupted. Smoke, ash and burning pebbles flew from the top of the volcano and rained down on the city of Pompeii. Fumes caused delirium in some victims, then suffocated them. A few people were able to escape this environmental disaster. Most Pompeiians were overcome by gas or buried in the falling ash. Volcanic deposits soon covered Pompeii in a layer more than 30 feet thick.

Mt. Vesuvius erupting.

THE MOVEMENT OF GOODS

Movement includes the movement of goods as well as the migration of peoples. Because of differences in location, climate and natural resources, not all areas have the same raw materials or can produce the same things. To obtain goods they cannot make themselves, different areas trade with each other. **Trade** is the exchange of goods.

For example, the crowded cities of the Roman Empire often could not grow enough food to feed all of the people who were living there. Parts of North Africa, including Egypt, were able to grow more grain than they needed. They shipped their excess grain across the Mediterranean Sea to sell in Italy. Another example of differences in resources occurred in Africa. In the rainforests of West Africa, there are deposits of gold but very little salt. Merchants from North Africa carried blocks of salt out of the Sahara Desert to trade others for gold.

You will learn more about how the unequal distribution of natural resources leads to specialization and trade in Unit 4, the Economics and Government unit, later in this book.

APPLYING WHAT YOU HAVE LEARNED

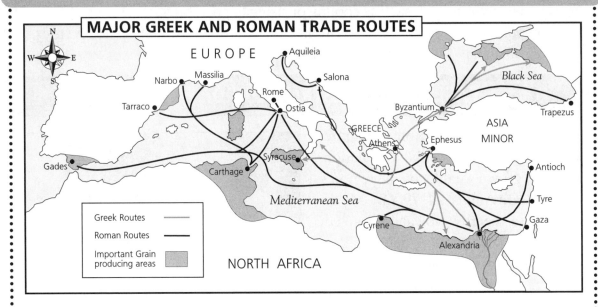

▼ Which cities in the Mediterranean did Rome trade with? _____

_____

_____

_____

_____

▼ What might explain why both the Greeks and Romans traded with grain-producing areas in the Mediterranean region?

_____

_____

_____

_____

CONTACTS BETWEEN CULTURES

Diffusion refers to how something diffuses or spreads. A drop of ink, for example, will spread through a glass of water until the ink and water blend into a single mixture. When different cultures come into contact, new ideas and products are often introduced from one culture to the other. The idea or product then spreads. This process is known as **cultural diffusion**. Such contacts between different cultures often lead to changes in belief systems, art, science, technology, language, and forms of government.

THE SPREAD OF NEW PRODUCTS

Sometimes contact between two different cultures leads to an exchange of products. Travelers and merchants bring the new products back to their homelands. Use of these new products quickly spreads.

CASE STUDY: CHINESE INVENTIONS FOSTER EUROPEAN EXPLORATION

During the Middle Ages in Europe, China developed gunpowder, the compass, and printing. European merchants like **Marco Polo** brought news of these inventions back to Europe. Borrowing from the Chinese, Europeans used gunpowder to construct cannons and adapted the compass to improve their seafaring skills. These Chinese inventions allowed the rulers of Spain and Portugal to launch voyages of exploration across the Atlantic Ocean.

Marco Polo was 17 when he left Venice with his father and uncle for China. This illustration shows their arrival in China.

CASE STUDY: THE COLUMBIAN EXCHANGE

European and Native American cultures encountered each other for the first time in 1492. This encounter led to the *Columbian Exchange* — the introduction of new products to both cultures. Europeans brought horses, goats, chickens, wheat, and goods like cannons, crossbows and steel to the Americas. At the same time, Native Americans had developed many foods unknown to Europeans, including tomatoes, chocolate, potatoes and corn, as well as tobacco. These were now introduced into Europe.

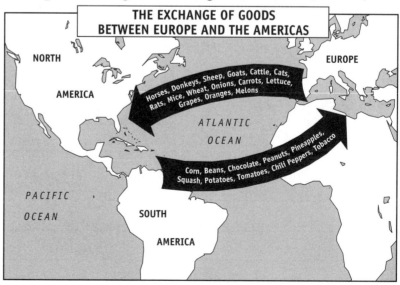

THE EXCHANGE OF GOODS BETWEEN EUROPE AND THE AMERICAS

NORTH AMERICA

EUROPE

Horses, Donkeys, Sheep, Goats, Cattle, Cats, Rats, Mice, Wheat, Onions, Carrots, Lettuce, Grapes, Oranges, Melons

ATLANTIC OCEAN

Corn, Beans, Chocolate, Peanuts, Pineapples, Squash, Potatoes, Tomatoes, Chili Peppers, Tobacco

PACIFIC OCEAN

SOUTH AMERICA

APPLYING WHAT YOU HAVE LEARNED

▼ How might history have been different if the cultures of Europe and the Americas had never come into contact? Explain your answer.

_____

_____

_____

THE SPREAD OF NEW IDEAS

Contacts between different cultures can lead to an important exchange of ideas.

CASE STUDY: THE SPREAD OF CHINESE CULTURE

Japan's location close to China brought many aspects of Chinese culture to Japan. The rulers of Japan claimed to be emperors, like the rulers of China. Chinese writing, music, art, pottery, weaving, building and cooking influenced Japanese styles and tastes. The ideas of Buddhism and Confucianism came from China and interacted with Japanese traditions to create new values and beliefs. Confucianism taught loyalty to the ruler, while Buddhism taught the Japanese to reject selfish desires.

China greatly influenced Japan's writing and other aspects of Japanese culture.

APPLYING WHAT YOU HAVE LEARNED

▼ Japan's location close to China had a great influence on its culture. Can you think of another example in which the culture of a country greatly influenced the culture of one of its neighbors? Explain.

_____

_____

_____

CASE STUDY: AZTECS, MAYA, AND INCAS

When one society is more powerful or technologically advanced, it sometimes attempts to impose its culture on weaker societies. This was the case in the early sixteenth century after Spain conquered the Aztec and Inca Empires in Middle and South America. Native American forms of government collapsed and were replaced by rule from Spain. The defeated Native Americans were forced to accept the Catholic religion. The use of the Spanish language gradually replaced the use of Aztec and Inca languages in Mexico and Peru.

APPLYING WHAT YOU HAVE LEARNED

▼ Is it fair for a culture that is more technologically advanced to impose its culture on a people that is not as advanced? Explain your answer.

_____

_____

FACTORS AFFECTING THE SPEED OF MOVEMENT

Various geographic and other factors may encourage, slow down, or even prevent the movement of people, products, and ideas from place to place.

PHYSICAL FEATURES

Physical geography often helps shape the movement of people, goods, and ideas. Mountains, deserts, rainforests and oceans can reduce or even prevent movement. For example, for thousands of years, the peoples of the Americas and Europe did not know of one another because they were separated by the Atlantic Ocean. Contacts between North Africa and sub-Saharan Africa were minimal because these regions were separated by the Sahara Desert.

People, goods, and ideas most often move through valleys, coastal plains, rivers and seas. For example, the Indian subcontinent is cut off from the rest of Asia by the Himalayan and Hindu Kush Mountains. For centuries, these protected the Indus Valley from invaders. However, both Alexander the Great and later Muslim invaders entered the Indian subcontinent through the Khyber Pass in the Northwest. From here, new ideas, goods, and people gradually spread to the rest of India.

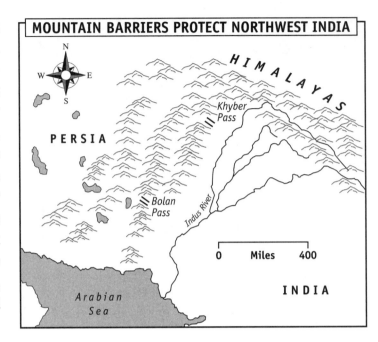

CULTURE

Differences in culture may make it difficult for new ideas, goods or people to enter a place or to find acceptance. For example, the emperors of China once looked on all non-Chinese cultures as inferior. They limited all Chinese contact with foreigners. As the West industrialized, China itself fell behind because of its lack of contacts with the outside world.

WAR

War may cause people to migrate. It can also lead to the development and spread of new ideas. For example, during the Crusades, Europeans traveled to the Holy Land to free it from Muslim control. In the process, Europeans were exposed to Muslim beliefs and

Crusaders about to enter the Holy Land

lifestyles. This interaction of Europeans and Muslims helped to stimulate a demand for Muslim and Asian goods in Europe.

TRADE

Trade also encourages the spread of people, ideas, and goods. The desire for East Asian spices and luxury goods led Christopher Columbus to search for an all-water passage to Asia by sailing westward. His explorations led to the encounter between Europe and the Americas, and to a new exchange of goods and ideas. This encounter further led to European colonization of the Americas.

TECHNOLOGICAL INNOVATIONS

Technological innovations often encourage the spread of ideas, people, and goods. If one society makes an important technological innovation, others often borrow the idea. For example, the ancient Hittites were the first to develop a process that allowed them to produce iron tools, weapons, and ornamental objects. Their iron tools and weapons were harder and had sharper edges than those made from bronze or copper. They were able to conquer Egypt, but Egypt and neighboring societies soon copied the Hittites and made their own iron goods. Some technological innovations directly encourage movement. The compass and other new navigation tools made the European explorations of the 1500s possible. In 1450, **Johann Gutenberg** invented movable type. This allowed books and pamphlets to be printed cheaply. News and ideas spread more quickly. Gutenberg's printing press helped launch the Protestant Reformation by spreading Martin Luther's criticisms of the Catholic Church.

The Hittites used iron to develop a three-man chariot, a technological innovation in warfare.

APPLYING WHAT YOU HAVE LEARNED

▼ Select one of the factors affecting the movement of people, goods, and ideas, and explain how it either encourages or prevents such movement.

_____

_____

_____

APPLYING WHAT YOU HAVE LEARNED

▼ Give one example of contact between different cultures. Explain how this led to the diffusion of belief systems, art, technology, language or government forms.

_____

_____

WHAT YOU SHOULD KNOW

☐ You should know that different push-and-pull factors cause people to migrate. "Push" factors include the desire to escape oppression, poverty, political conflict or environmental disaster. "Pull" factors include the search for greater freedom or economic opportunity, or the desire to reinforce cultural ties.

☐ You should know that the uneven distribution of natural resources encourages world trade.

☐ You should know that contacts between cultures can lead to changes in belief systems, art, science, technology, languages and systems of government.

☐ You should know that various factors (*physical features, culture, war, trade, and technological innovations*) can promote or delay the movement of people, ideas, and goods.

CHAPTER STUDY CARDS

Factors that Lead to Migration

★ **Push Factors:** The desire to escape oppression, poverty, political conflicts, and environmental disasters.

★ **Pull Factors:** The search for greater freedom or for economic opportunity, and the desire to reinforce cultural ties.

Factors Affecting the Spread of Movement

★ Physical features   ★ War
★ Culture   ★ Trade
★ Technological innovations

Effects of Contacts Between Cultures

When different cultures come into contact, new ideas and products are often spread from one culture to the other.

★ **Spread of New Products.** For example, the spread of goods from the Middle East to Europe during the Crusades

★ **Spread of New Ideas.** For example, Japan's nearness to China introduced many aspects of Chinese culture to Japan.

★ **Societal Changes.** Contacts between cultures can lead to changes in belief systems, art, science, technology, languages, and systems of government.

CHECKING YOUR UNDERSTANDING

Examine the map below.

1. What process is illustrated by the map?

   A. the spread of democracy

   B. the movement of goods

   C. changes in belief systems

   D. religious unity

   PEOPLE
   C: 7.3

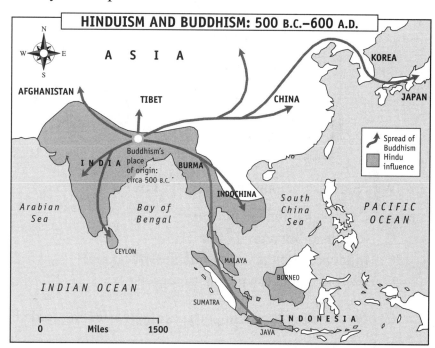

HINT

*First, **examine** the question. It tests your ability to interpret the map. The map shows the spread of Hinduism and Buddhism from the Indian subcontinent to the rest of Asia. You should **recall** that the spread of belief systems, such as religions, is one form of cultural diffusion. If you **apply** this knowledge to the choices, you will find that the best answer is **Choice C**.*

Now try answering some additional questions on your own.

2. Hindu scholars contributed to mathematics by developing the decimal system and the concept of zero. Arab mathematicians transmitted these ideas to Western Europe. What conclusion can best be reached from these facts?

   A. Hindu and Arabs developed the first civilizations.

   B. The study of mathematics first began in Asia.

   C. Through contacts between cultures, new ideas are sometimes spread.

   D. Europeans had no ideas to share with Hindus and Arabs.

   PEOPLE
   C: 7.3

3. The Greeks often had dealings with other Eastern civilizations.

Which feature promoted contact between the Greeks and the ancient civilizations of the Middle East?

A. a common language
B. a series of wars
C. trade across the sea
D. new methods of communication

GEOG
D: 7.5

Look at the graphic organizer below.

4. Which phrase belongs in the center box?

A. Factors that reduce poverty
B. Results of increased trade
C. Influences on that economic growth
D. Factors that cause people to migrate

GEOG
D: 6.8

5. Geography can play an important role in affecting trade between regions.

In your **Answer Document**, identify and explain one geographic cause for trade between different regions. (2 points)

GEOG
D: 6.9

_____

_____

6. The explorations of Christopher Columbus and other Europeans had a lasting impact on Native American cultures.

In your **Answer Document**, identify and describe two ways that European contact with the Americas affected Native American cultures. (4 points)

PEOPLE
C: 7.3

_____

_____

_____

_____

_____

CHAPTER 10

PEOPLE AND THE ENVIRONMENT

The last of the five themes of geography concerns the relationship between people and their environment. In this chapter, you will learn how the physical environment influences where people live and how they live. You will also learn how people modify their environment.

MAJOR IDEAS

GEOGRAPHY, BENCHMARK C

A. **Environmental factors**, such as bodies of water, landforms, climate, vegetation, weathering and seismic activity, influence where people settle and how they live.

B. People **modify** (*change*) their environment by building dams, creating farms, building towns and cities, and producing and using energy.

C. Human modification of the environment can have both **positive** and **negative consequences**.

D. Some general effects of human settlement on the environment include **urbanization**, **desertification**, and **deforestation**.

HOW PEOPLE ARE AFFECTED BY THE ENVIRONMENT

There are many ways in which people are affected by their physical environment.

BODIES OF WATER

Water is essential to human life. The earliest civilizations arose in river valleys. Even today, most cities are located near a major body of water. Bodies of water, such as rivers, lakes and seas, can serve to unite a people. Ancient Egyptians, for example, developed their civilization along the Nile River.

The Nile was used to irrigate lands along the river.

LANDFORMS

People are affected by **landforms**, such as mountains, hills, plains, and deserts. People generally settle in flat, fertile valleys and plains, where they can build homes and grow crops more easily. Fewer people live in mountains, swamps or desert areas. Lifestyles are also affected by landforms. For example, the Incas developed root crops, like the potato, and terrace farming, so that they could grow food in the Andes Mountains.

CLIMATE

Climate often has a profound effect on where and how people live. The Vikings of Norway wore heavy clothing made of wool, animal hides, and fur. This protected them from the cold. In contrast, people who live in warm areas, like Egypt, wear light clothes to keep themselves cool.

VEGETATION

Vegetation (*plant life*) is influenced by climate, landforms, soil, and nearness to bodies of water. The type of vegetation in an area greatly affects human lifestyles. People often make use of local plants as sources of food, clothing, and building materials. For example, the steppes of Central Asia are dry grassy hills and plains. On these lands, animal domestication and herding became the dominant way of life. For this reason, the peoples of Central Asia have generally been herders who were skilled at horsemanship.

As this illustration from 300 B.C. shows, Central Asians were experts in horsemanship.

WEATHERING

Weathering is the wearing down of Earth's surface by the wind, ice, and water. When weathering and erosion wear down the top soil of a region, people and animals can no longer live there and are forced to move.

SEISMIC ACTIVITY

Seismic activity refers to earthquakes and volcanoes. Because of seismic activity in the Pacific region, people in Japan have usually built their homes out of lightweight materials. These materials are less harmful if a building collapses during an earthquake.

APPLYING WHAT YOU HAVE LEARNED

▼ What are some of the ways that the environment can affect where people settle?

_____

_____

▼ Give one example of how your activities are influenced by your environment.

_____

_____

HOW PEOPLE MODIFY THEIR ENVIRONMENT

Just as people are affected by their environment, people can also affect their environment. Here are some of the ways that humans have modified their environment, and the positive and negative consequences that have resulted from these changes:

AGRICULTURE

Agriculture (*farming*) is the growing of food. Civilization first arose after the **Neolithic Revolution**, when people discovered they could plant seeds to grow crops they could eat. Gradually, civilizations turned forests, grasslands, and marshes into farmland.

A Neolithic Revolution grindstone, used to crush grain.

In **slash-and-burn** agriculture, early peoples burnt down forests and grew crops in the ashes. Later farmers learned to leave the land without crops for one season to replenish its nutrients, to rotate crops, or to add fertilizer.

Positive and Negative Effects. Cutting down forests and planting fields have greatly increased our food supply. This has permitted rapid population growth. However, it has also led to pollution of Earth's land, air and water. In some places agriculture has also contributed to deforestation and desertification. You will learn more about these later in this chapter.

URBAN GROWTH

Urbanization is the movement of people into cities. The first cities arose in the Middle East. By 7,000 B.C., Jericho had 3,000 residents. Sumer, the world's oldest known civilization, began on the plains of Mesopotamia in 3,500 B.C. Later ancient cities like Rome had as many as a million people. In the Middle Ages, urban centers were generally smaller. Agricultural improvements in the 1700s, increased overseas trade, and the rise of manufacturing during the Industrial Revolution led to the rapid growth of cities. Today, most people in industrialized countries live in cities. Urbanization changes the environment by concentrating thousands, even millions of people in small, treeless areas. For example, Cleveland was once a forest area. Today, it is home to skyscrapers and concrete streets.

The remains of ancient Sumerian streets and markets.

Positive and Negative Effects. Urbanization has many effects. Many people flourish in urban environments. They interact with other people sharing their common interests and ideas. However, urban centers pollute the environment and use up large amounts of natural resources. The crowding and congestion of modern cities can make life for some people uncomfortable, unhealthful and even dangerous. There is a tendency for these negative effects to increase as urban centers grow in size.

THE BUILDING OF DAMS

People sometimes build dams to drain swamps, to prevent floods, to generate energy, and to store water for drinking and irrigation.

Positive and Negative Effects. Construction of a dam can save thousands of lives by preventing floods and making water available when it is needed. However, artificial dams flood some areas and take away water from other areas.

ENERGY

Various societies have used different forms of energy. Early societies used animal power and slaves. Modern society depends on burning fossil fuels like coal and oil.

Positive and Negative Effects. The use of oil and gas for energy has made our modern society possible. However, it has also created tremendous amounts of pollution, leading to **global warming**. Meanwhile, existing oil reserves are gradually running out. Our world is increasingly dependent on a few countries — mainly in the Middle East — to meet its energy needs. People will need to use new sources of energy, such as solar and wind energy, to keep the world's modern economies running smoothly.

APPLYING WHAT YOU HAVE LEARNED

Complete the chart below to show the positive and negative effects of change:

Human Changes to the Environment	Positive Effects	Negative Effects
Agriculture		
Urban Growth		
Building Dams		
Energy		

THE GEOGRAPHIC IMPACT OF MIGRATION

Human migration can have important effects on the physical and human characteristics of a place. Three important effects of human migration and settlement have been *urbanization*, *deforestation*, and *desertification*.

URBANIZATION

You already know that urbanization is the migration of people from rural areas into cities. Although humans have inhabited Earth for hundreds of thousands of years, cities have only existed for less than 10,000 years. The rise of cities has transformed landscapes, used up resources, and caused pollution. But cities are also now the main centers of human activity. They make life, as we know it, possible.

DEFORESTATION

Human settlement in an area often leads to deforestation. Deforestation has been practiced by humans for thousands of years. One of the earliest evidences of deforestation appears in the Neolithic period. During this period, extensive deforestation occurred, to permit farming. Much of Europe was once covered by forests that were cut down for farmland. Since forests provide oxygen to the atmosphere and

Early humans often cleared land by setting fire to a forest.

protect soil from erosion, there is serious concern about cutting down the world's remaining forests, especially in tropical areas like the Amazon.

DESERTIFICATION

In some cases, more people have settled in an area than its water supplies and other resources can support. In these situations, human settlement has helped turn an area into a desert. Human activities such as cutting down forests, using lake and groundwater supplies for irrigation, and overgrazing with animal herds dries out the topsoil and removes plants holding the soil together. Without enough water or plant life, land in warm areas can easily turns into desert.

WHAT YOU SHOULD KNOW

☐ You should know that environmental factors (*such as bodies of water, landforms, climate, vegetation, weathering and seismic activity*) influence where people settle and how they live.

☐ You should know that people modify their environment by building dams, creating farms, building towns and cities, and producing and using energy.

☐ You should know that human modification of the environment can have both positive and negative consequences.

☐ You should know that some general effects of human settlement include urbanization, deforestation, and desertification.

CHAPTER STUDY CARDS

How People Are Affected by the Environment	How People Modify Their Environment

How People Are Affected by the Environment

★ **Bodies of Water.** Earliest civilizations arose in river valleys near water.

★ **Landforms.** People generally settle in flat, fertile valleys and plains, where they can build homes and plant crops more easily.

★ **Climate.** This has had a large impact on how people live, dress, and eat.

★ **Vegetation.** The vegetation that can grow in an area greatly affects human lifestyles.

★ **Weathering.** Erosion of the topsoil can make farming in an area very difficult.

★ **Seismic Activity.** The presence of earthquakes and volcanoes often determines how homes will be built.

How People Modify Their Environment

Just as people are affected by the environment, people can modify their environment in a number of ways. Each of these can have both negative and positive consequences.

★ **Agriculture**
★ **Urban growth**
★ **Building of dams**
★ **Energy**

Effects of Human Migration/Settlement

★ **Urbanization**
★ **Deforestation**
★ **Desertification**

CHECKING YOUR UNDERSTANDING

1. The Neolithic Revolution introduced agriculture to the world. How did the development of agriculture make later urban growth possible?

   A. Farmers could visit cities for entertainment.
   B. Farmers grew enough food to support urban populations.
   C. Farmers increased air pollution by cutting down trees.
   D. Farmers attracted large numbers of workers to their farms.

   GEOG C: 6.5

*First **examine** the question. It tests your understanding of an effect of the Neolithic Revolution. You should **recall** that the Neolithic Revolution made it possible for a society to grow its own food. In some areas, a surplus of food made it possible for people who were not farmers to live in cities. **Applying** this information to the question, the answer is **Choice B**.*

Now try answering some additional questions on your own.

2. People sometimes modify their environment to meet their needs.

    GEOG
    C: 6.5

    What is a positive consequence of building a dam?

    A. interrupting the life cycles of fish
    B   artificial flooding of areas above the dam
    C. loss of deposits of rich soil from occasional flooding
    D. preventing floods from sudden rains

3. The climate of a region influences the kind of vegetation that grows there.

    GEOG
    C: 6.5

    What potential effect could global warming have on the types of vegetation growing in northern climates?

    A. Farmers will see the variety of crops they can grow in northern climates decrease.
    B. Plants traditionally grown in cooler climates will die out and be replaced by plants better adapted to warmer temperatures.
    C. The variety of vegetation in northern climates will have minimal change.
    D. Northern forests will thrive from warmer temperatures and longer summers.

4. The environment often influences where people live. Which type of environment typically has the highest population density?

    GEOG
    C: 6.5

    A. hilly mountains and plateaus   C. wet bogs and swamp areas
    B. flat, fertile plains and river valleys D. dry and barren desert regions

5. What is an important consequence of the uneven distribution of natural resources?

    GEOG
    D: 6.9

    A. global warming   C. world trade
    B. increased climate change D. reduced cultural ties

6. Which factor is **most likely** to promote the diffusion of new products and ideas?

    GEOG
    D: 7.5

    A. disruption in political ties C. climate change
    B. extensive trade links   D. mountain barriers

7. Millions of people live in regions that are likely to face periodic earthquakes, volcanoes, or tsunamis — huge tidal waves.

    GEOG
    C: 6.5

    In your **Answer Document**, identify two ways that human settlements and activities have been influenced by the potential for seismic activity in a region. (2 points).

    _____

    _____

UNIT 2: GEOGRAPHY CONCEPT MAP

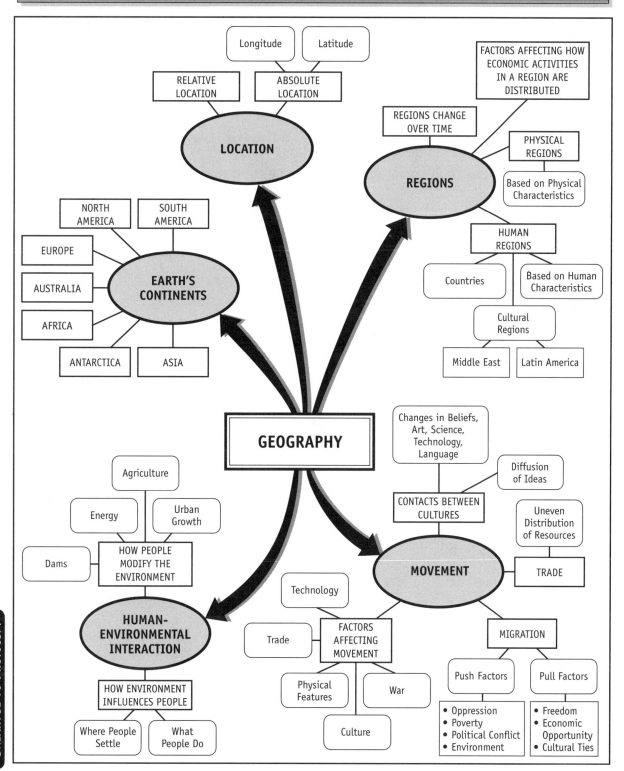

LOCATION
- Longitude
- Latitude
- RELATIVE LOCATION
- ABSOLUTE LOCATION

REGIONS
- REGIONS CHANGE OVER TIME
- FACTORS AFFECTING HOW ECONOMIC ACTIVITIES IN A REGION ARE DISTRIBUTED
- PHYSICAL REGIONS
  - Based on Physical Characteristics
- HUMAN REGIONS
  - Countries
  - Based on Human Characteristics
  - Cultural Regions
    - Middle East
    - Latin America

EARTH'S CONTINENTS
- NORTH AMERICA
- SOUTH AMERICA
- EUROPE
- AUSTRALIA
- AFRICA
- ANTARCTICA
- ASIA

GEOGRAPHY

MOVEMENT
- CONTACTS BETWEEN CULTURES
  - Changes in Beliefs, Art, Science, Technology, Language
  - Diffusion of Ideas
- TRADE
  - Uneven Distribution of Resources
- FACTORS AFFECTING MOVEMENT
  - Technology
  - Trade
  - Physical Features
  - Culture
  - War
- MIGRATION
  - Push Factors
    - Oppression
    - Poverty
    - Political Conflict
    - Environment
  - Pull Factors
    - Freedom
    - Economic Opportunity
    - Cultural Ties

HUMAN-ENVIRONMENTAL INTERACTION
- HOW PEOPLE MODIFY THE ENVIRONMENT
  - Agriculture
  - Energy
  - Urban Growth
  - Dams
- HOW ENVIRONMENT INFLUENCES PEOPLE
  - Where People Settle
  - What People Do

TESTING YOUR UNDERSTANDING

1. Africa contains the Sahara Desert and several mountain ranges. These physical barriers have kept different groups apart from one another.

   What does this show about the role of physical barriers?

   A. They often act to encourage trade.
   B. They speed up the spread of cultural ideas.
   C. They encourage technological innovation.
   D. They can lead to the creation of separate cultural regions.

   `GEOG D: 7.5`

2. Which physical features are located on the European continent?

   A. Sahara Desert and the Nile River
   B. Gobi Desert and the Himalayan Mountains
   C. Andes Mountains and the Amazon River
   D. Pyrennes Mountains and the Seine River

   `GEOG A: 6.1`

3. Deserts are found on many of the world's continents. On which continent is the Gobi Desert located?

   A. Africa   C. Asia
   B. South America   D. Australia

   `GEOG A: 6.1`

4. Which is the best example of a cultural region?

   A. Australia
   B. Middle East
   C. South America
   D. Himalayan Mountains

   `GEOG B: 6.4`

5. A large portion of the African continent is covered by grasslands known as the savanna. Over the centuries, more and more of the savanna has been claimed by the expanding Sahara Desert through the process of desertification.

   Which factor has **most** contributed to desertification in Africa?

   A. overgrazing of animal herds
   B. human disease and famine
   C. planting of trees to fight erosion
   D. seismic activity along the African Rift Valley

   `GEOG C:6.6`

Look at the map below.

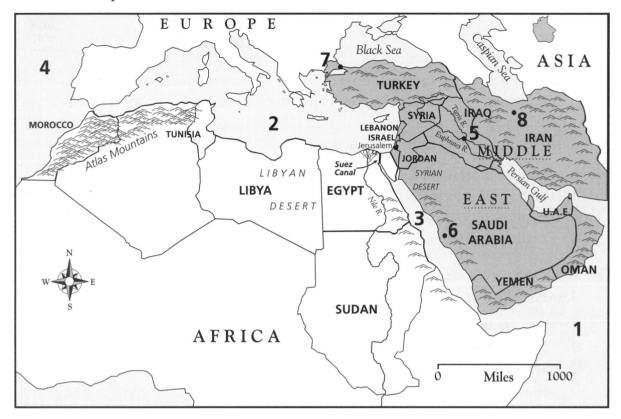

6. Which number on the map indicates the location of the Mediterranean Sea?

A. (1)   C. (3)
B. (2)   D. (4)

GEOG
A: 6.1

7. Which number on the map shows where the city of Baghdad is located?

A. (5)
B. (6)
C. (7)
D. (8)

GEOG
A: 6.1

8. The people of the early Inca civilization lived in the Andes Mountains. There they developed root crops, like the potato, which could be grown in mountain climates.

What does this indicate about human settlement?

A. Landforms can influence human activities in an area.
B. People tend to settle along river systems or coastal areas.
C. Climate has little impact on how people live.
D. People are greatly affected by seismic activity.

GEOG
C: 6.5

9. Which is an example of a physical region?

   A. Ohio
   B. Sahara Desert
   C. Latin America
   D. European Union

   GEOG
   B: 7.4

10. The Sahel is a region in Africa directly south of the Sahara Desert. People in this region traditionally live by herding animals which can eat dry grasses. Climate change is gradually turning the Sahel into desert. How is this change most likely to affect the pattern of economic activities in the region?

    A. People will be unable to herd animals and will migrate.
    B. People will farm crops instead of herding animals.
    C. People will develop heavy industry in place of agriculture.
    D. People will work at tourism and other service industries.

    SKILLS
    B: 7.4

11. Many scholars believe that in ancient times, the Hebrews left Egypt to escape from slavery. Which cause of migration does this example illustrate?

    A. flight from oppression
    B. seeking refuge from political conflict
    C. flight from environmental disaster
    D. attraction to an area based on economic opportunity

    GEOG
    D: 6.8

Look at the graphic organizer below.

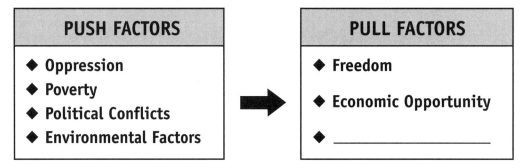

12. Which phrase belongs on the blank line of the graphic organizer?

    A. Monarchial Government
    B. Cultural Ties
    C. Seismic Activities
    D. Drought

    GEOG
    B: 7.4

13. In your **Answer Document**, identify and describe two effects of human migration on the physical and human characteristics of places. (4 points)

    GEOG
    C: 6.6

    _____

    _____

    _____

14. The practices for preparing and taking care of farmland vary from region to region. Which group would typically practice slash-and-burn techniques?

   A. people who live along rivers that deposit rich soil during floods
   B. subsistence farmers who plant an area until the soil loses its fertility
   C. farmers who rely on chemical fertilization and pesticides
   D. nomads who use pastures for their livestock

15. The Romans created an elaborate system of aqueducts, plumbing, and sewers to supply water to remove waste from their homes. This allowed more people to move into urban centers, like the city of Rome. What was a negative consequence associated with this advance?

   A. Roman culture and lifestyles spread to Northern Europe.
   B. The quality of life improved for wealthy Roman citizens.
   C. Romans depended on slaves to build and maintain these systems.
   D. More water was available for Roman farmers for irrigation.

16. On which continent is the Amazon Rainforest located?

   A. Africa   C. Europe
   B. Asia   D. South America

17. Which continent can the country of Indonesia be considered part of?

   A. Africa   C. Europe
   B. Asia   D. South America

18. People modify their environment in a variety of ways to meet their needs. In your **Answer Document**, identify two ways that humans can change their environment. Then choose one of the ways you identified and describe one positive and one negative consequence of that action. (4 points)

19. Migration is the process of moving from one region or country to another. In your **Answer Document**, identify and describe two reasons for human migration. (4 points)

Look at the map to the right.

20. Which latitude and longitude coordinates are closest to Brunei?

A. 17°N, 100°E
B. 22°N, 80°E
C. 5°N, 115°E
D. 10°N, 120°E

GEOG
A: 6.2

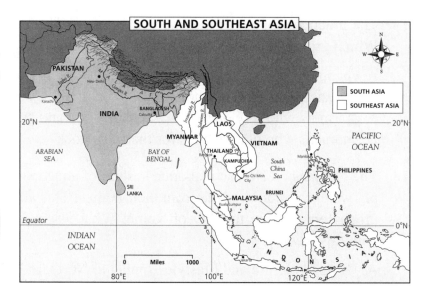

21. Geographers agree that physical and human regions can change. In your **Answer Document**, give two reasons why a physical region or human region might change over time. (2 points).

GEOG
B: 7.3

_____

_____

22. Africa is the second largest continent in area, with an area three times the size of the United States. In your **Answer Document**, identify and describe two important physical features on the continent of Africa. (4 points).

GEOG
A: 6.1

_____

_____

_____

_____

23. Economic activities are things people do to meet their needs — such as farming, fishing, keeping livestock, mining, and manufacturing. Many factors affect how these economic activities are distributed within a region.

In your **Answer Document**, identify two factors that affect how economic activities are distributed in a region. Then explain how each of these factors has an effect on economic activity. (4 points).

GEOG
B: 6.3

_____

_____

_____

_____

UNIT 3

PEOPLE AND SOCIETIES IN HISTORY

In this unit, you will learn about **history** — the study of the past. You learn about the history of the world from the origins of humankind to the European colonization of the Americas.

◆ **Chapter 11. The Birth of Civilization.** In this chapter, you will learn about the origins of humankind and the Neolithic Revolution. You will then learn about the rise of the world's first civilizations and their achievements.

◆ **Chapter 12. The Achievements of the Classical Civilizations.** In this chapter, you will learn about the political and social characteristics of the classical civilizations of Greece, Rome, India and China. You will also learn about their enduring impact on later civilizations.

◆ **Chapter 13. The Feudal Societies of Europe and Asia.** In this chapter, you will learn about the system of feudalism that existed in Europe and Japan. You will then learn about the spread of Islam, the Crusades, and the Mongol conquests.

◆ **Chapter 14. The Renaissance and Reformation.** In this chapter, you will learn how Europeans experienced a rebirth of learning during the Renaissance. You will also learn how the Reformation shattered the unity of the Catholic Church.

◆ **Chapter 15. The Civilizations of Africa and the Americas.** In this chapter, you will learn about the peoples of West Africa and North and South America.

◆ **Chapter 16. Europeans Explore and Expand Overseas.** In this chapter, you will learn how European exploration led to contact with America, and the effect of this connection on Europe, the Americas, and Africa.

KEY TERMS YOU WILL LEARN ABOUT IN THIS UNIT

- Neolithic Revolution
- Civilization
- River Valley
- Multiple-tier Timeline
- Judaism
- Hinduism
- Buddhism
- Christianity
- Islam
- Monotheism
- Slavery
- Gender Roles
- Silk Road
- Feudalism
- Crusades
- Mongols
- Renaissance
- Reformation
- Columbian Exchange
- Reformation
- West African Kingdoms
- Gold-Salt Trade
- Transatlantic Slave Trade
- Mercantilism

LOOKING AT PAST SOCIETIES

You already know that historians analyze information from primary and secondary sources to draw conclusions about the past. Historians must also possess a strong sense of time and a basic understanding of how societies generally work. It is these last two characteristics that we will examine here.

DEVELOPING A SENSE OF TIME

World history covers a vast span of time — from the beginning of humankind to the present. To better understand this vast sweep, historians divide history into **periods** — shorter time spans unified by some common characteristics. There is no exact agreement among historians as to when each historical period began or ended. Historical periods often begin and end in different places at different times. For example, the Middle Ages is a historical period closely tied to Europe, while the Ming Dynasty refers to a period in the history of China. This unit divides history into five major time periods:

ERAS OF WORLD HISTORY

◆ The Birth of Civilization, 3500 B.C. to 500 B.C.

◆ The Classical Civilizations, 500 B.C. to 500 A.D.

◆ The Middle Ages, 500 A.D. to 1350 A.D.

◆ The Renaissance and Reformation, 1350 to 1550

◆ The Age of European Exploration and Expansion, 1400 to 1770

UNDERSTANDING SOCIAL STRUCTURE

In order to study past societies, historians and other social scientists have developed several general concepts to help explain how societies work. These concepts also make it easier to compare the cultural practices and products of different societies.

BASIC NEEDS

Every human society has essentially the same basic needs. Each society must provide food and shelter to its members; protect itself against outside groups; maintain cooperation among its members; and raise and educate its young people.

CUSTOMS

Each society develops its own patterns of behavior to meet these needs. These patterns are known as **customs**. They are passed from one generation to the next. Customs are ways that members of a society do things. These include what they eat, how they dress, how they build their homes, and the holidays they celebrate.

ROLES

Roles are based on rules for the proper behavior of individuals in particular positions and situations. A mother, for instance, is expected to behave in a certain way toward her children. Once a role in society is learned, people know how they are supposed to act. **Gender roles** are roles assigned separately to women and men.

In traditional Japan, women and men had different gender roles.

INSTITUTIONS

Organizations, known as **institutions**, are developed by each society to make social roles clear and to take care of social needs. Such institutions include:

FAMILIES	SCHOOLS	GOVERNMENTS
Families arrange for reproduction, the care of family members, and the upbringing of the young.	Schools teach the young the values of society and prepare them for the responsibilities of adulthood.	Governments protect us from outsiders, promote social cooperation, and regulate individual behavior.

SOCIAL STRUCTURE

In every known society, some members enjoy greater wealth and wider opportunities than others. People who share similar wealth, power, and prestige are said to belong to the same **social class**. The following social classes exist in many societies:

◆ **Upper Class.** This group often inherits wealth and owns a large share of the property in that society. They lead a luxurious lifestyle and often occupy leadership roles in the society.

◆ **Middle Class.** This is an intermediate group of educated and mostly successful people — managers, professionals, shopkeepers, and business owners.

◆ **Working Class.** This group is composed of manual workers who work in factories, mining or transportation, or who work as independent craftsmen.

◆ **Peasants.** These are farm workers or owners of small farms mainly engaged in **subsistence agriculture** (*growing food for themselves*). They have little education and limited experience of the world outside their own villages.

◆ **Lower Class.** These people are uneducated and unskilled. They take the least desirable and worst-paying jobs. Often, members of lower classes face prejudice and other social handicaps.

In the caste system, "untouchables" once did the lowest tasks in society.

Social mobility refers to the ability to move from one social class to another. In some societies, social mobility is not possible. One is assigned a social position based on one's parents. Traditional Hindu society, for example, was divided into castes. There was no movement from one caste to another. One's caste determined what work one could do and who one's friends were. In other societies, it is easier to move from one class to another.

BELIEF SYSTEMS

All societies have some set of beliefs. For example, members of a society may believe that God has appointed their rulers. Many such beliefs are often closely tied to religion. Most **religions** have three common elements:

A **set of beliefs** about the nature of the universe and the existence of God or gods.	A **set of practices** relating to worship and proper conduct in life.	An **organization**, such as a church, which oversees the conduct of religious practices.

For example, Jews, Christians and Muslims all believe in one God and believe that this God created Earth. When studying a religion, you should therefore ask:

◆ **What are its Beliefs?** Does it believe in a God or gods? Do followers believe in life after death? Does the religion have prophets or holy persons?

◆ **What are its Customs and Practices?** Does it have rules for leading a moral life? Are there foods or actions that are forbidden among its followers?

◆ **Does it have a Religious Organization?** Does it have a group of religious leaders? Does it have houses of worship?

THE BIRTH OF CIVILIZATION

In this chapter, you will learn about the origins of humankind, the development of agriculture, and the rise of the first civilizations.

MAJOR IDEAS

HISTORY, BENCHMARK B

A. The earliest humans survived by **hunting** and **gathering** their food. They used **tools** made of wood, bone, and stone. They also learned to make **fire**.

B. About 10,000 years ago, people in the Middle East developed the first agriculture and domesticated animals during the **Neolithic Revolution**.

C. The first **civilizations** arose in fertile **river valleys**. The Sumerians in **Mesopotamia** invented the wheel, sailboat and cuneiform writing. The **Egyptians** developed an advanced civilization along the banks of the **Nile River**.

D. Other early civilizations developed along the **Indus River** on the Indian subcontinent and along the **Huang Ho** (*Yellow River*) in China.

THE FIRST HUMANS

Our knowledge of the earliest human beings comes from the discovery of fossils. Many scientists believe the first human beings appeared in East Africa sometime between 200,000 and 400,000 years ago.

THE FIRST HUMANS

Early humans had several advantages over other animals. Humans had superior intelligence, hands to make tools, and an ability to communicate through speech. As a result, humans were able to pass on their way of doing things to their young. In this way, human cultures developed. **Culture** refers to a people's way of a life. It includes such things as their language, the clothes they wear, how they organize their family, and how they obtain food.

The most important activity of early humans was food gathering. The first humans were **hunters** and **gatherers**. They depended on hunting, fishing, and gathering wild plants for food. They used **tools** made of stone, bone, and wood to carry out these tasks. Early humans learned how to make fire to keep warm, to cook food, and to frighten off animals.

Humans also learned to cooperate to hunt large animals like mammoths — an extinct animal that was related to elephants. Various groups of humans gradually migrated from Africa to Asia, Europe, the Americas and Australia.

THE NEOLITHIC REVOLUTION

About 10,000 years ago, people in some areas began to change from hunters and gatherers to producers of food. Social scientists believe this change first occurred in the Middle East, where wild wheat and barley were plentiful. People noticed they could spread seeds out on the soil and after some time they would grow into crops. People also learned how to **domesticate** animals such as goats, sheep, and cattle. This meant they could keep and breed

these animals rather than hunt them. These advances are now referred to as the **Neolithic Revolution**.

With the introduction of agriculture, people no longer had to wander in search of food. They could build permanent homes and villages and establish a fixed way of life. The Neolithic Revolution also allowed people to grow more food

Early tools used during the Neolithic Revolution.

than they had been able to gather or hunt. As a result, populations grew. However, by settling in one place people also became more exposed to attack by other groups. New social classes developed: warriors defended the village and priests conducted religious ceremonies. The first governments developed as one or more leaders made key decisions for the entire community.

EARLY RIVER VALLEY CIVILIZATIONS

As agricultural societies developed and grew, their way of life changed. Around 3500 B.C., the first **civilizations** arose. A **civilization** is a form of human culture in which some people live in cities, they have complex social institutions, they use some form of writing, and they are skilled at using science and technology.

The first civilizations developed in four separate **river valleys**. Each of these river valleys offered a mild climate and a water highway to other places. Most importantly, each of these valleys formed a flood plain, where an overflowing river deposited fertile soil. This led to abundant harvests.

MESOPOTAMIA (3500 B.C. – 1700 B.C.)

Sometime between 5,000 and 6,000 years ago, the first river valley civilization developed in **Mesopotamia**, the region located between the **Tigris** and **Euphrates Rivers** (*in present-day Iraq*). Mesopotamia is Greek for the "land between two rivers."

Agriculture. Although Mesopotamia was hot and dry, people learned how to irrigate the land by diverting water from the Tigris and Euphrates Rivers. Irrigation allowed farming settlements to flourish and food supplies to increase. Since fewer people could produce more food, other people began to specialize in activities other than farming — some became potters, weavers or metal workers. Others became warriors and priests.

Government and Religion. The people of Mesopotamia built several cities. At first, each city-state, such as **Sumer, Ur,** and **Babylon,** had its own ruler and local gods. Later, these city-states were united under a single ruler. The Mesopotamians were also **polytheistic,** believing in many gods.

Building. The Mesopotamians were the world's first city-builders. They lacked stone bricks or timber to build their cities. Instead, they made buildings from mud bricks and crushed reeds. They built walled cities, temples with arches, and stepped-pyramids known as **ziggurats**. Each ziggurat was made of a series of square levels, with each level slightly smaller than the one below it.

A Mesopotamian ziggurat.

Cultural and Scientific Contributions. Some of the most important inventions in history took place in these ancient times. The **Sumerians,** the people of Sumer, invented the wheel and the sailboat. They also developed tools and weapons of copper and bronze — made by melting tin and copper together.

The Sumerians invented the world's earliest known writing system, **cuneiform**, a form of symbol writing on clay tablets. The Sumerians also devised a calendar, dividing the year into 12 months. The Babylonian number system was based on 60, providing the basis for our seconds and minutes today.

Legal System. The Babylonians developed the earliest known written law code — the **Code of Hammurabi**. It covered almost every occurrence in daily life. Its aim was to ensure justice, protect the weak, and fight evil. The Code treated nobles and commoners differently. Some of the Code's provisions punished criminals quite harshly, demanding "an eye for an eye, and a tooth for a tooth."

A cuneiform writing tablet.

APPLYING WHAT YOU HAVE LEARNED

▼ Which contribution do you think was most important — cuneiform writing, the wheel, the sailboat, or the Code of Hammurabi? Explain your answer.

_____

_____

_____

_____

EGYPT (3200 B.C. – 500 B.C.)

Egypt is located in North Africa. The world's longest river, the **Nile**, runs through it. Each year, the Nile floods the lands along its banks, depositing fertile soil. With this rich soil and an ample supply of fresh water, Egyptian farmers were able to grow large amounts of food. Farmers along the Nile supported a large number of craftsmen, warriors, priests, and nobles. Ease of communication along the river encouraged the development of a highly centralized government.

Government and Society. The most powerful person in ancient Egypt was the **pharaoh** (*king*). The pharaoh governed Egypt as an absolute ruler. The pharaoh owned all the land, commanded the army, made laws, controlled irrigation and grain supplies, and defended Egypt from foreigners. Egyptians considered the pharaoh to be a god.

Next in the social order came the priests and nobles. Below them came the warriors, scribes, merchants and craftsmen. At the lowest level of society were the peasants and slaves. They spent their time farming, herding cattle, and working on building projects for the pharaohs.

Religion. The ancient Egyptians believed a person's body should be preserved after death, in preparation for the afterlife. When pharaohs died, their bodies were embalmed and buried in a special room under a large triangular stone tomb known as a **pyramid**. Here, they were surrounded with gold, jewels, and other precious objects for use in the afterlife. Egyptians imagined the afterlife as similar to life before death.

Pharaoh Sesostois III, (c. 1860 B.C.)

EGYPTIAN ACCOMPLISHMENTS

Medicine. Egyptians developed knowledge of the human body through embalming (preserving). They performed surgical operations, such as setting fractures.

Hieroglyphics. Ancient Egyptians developed one of the earliest forms of writing, based on picture symbols. Hieroglyphics appeared on temples, pyramids and on scrolls of reed paper, known as **papyrus**.

Building and Art. Egyptian architects and engineers built magnificent pyramids, palaces, and temples of stone. They decorated their buildings with paintings and sculptures.

Hieroglyphic writing from a tomb.

Geometry and Astronomy. Egyptians developed geometry to build their projects. By observing the stars, they developed a calendar based on 365 days.

APPLYING WHAT YOU HAVE LEARNED

▼ Identify one way in which Egyptian and Mesopotamian societies were similar.

_____

▼ Identify one way in which Egyptian and Mesopotamian societies differed.

_____

INDIA

More than 5,000 years ago, the **Indus River Valley** became another of the earliest centers of human civilization. As in Egypt and Mesopotamia, a river deposited rich soil over the neighboring plain during its annual flood.

Agriculture and Building. Farmers grew barley, wheat, dates and melons. Food surpluses allowed people to build large cities like Harrappa and Mohenjo-Daro. Each of these cities had more than 30,000 people. Remarkably, almost all the houses were connected to public sewers and a water supply. These people, known as **Harrappans**, were also the first people known to make cotton cloth.

Trade and Collapse. Trade was an important part of the Harrappan economy. Many small clay seals, probably used for trading purposes, have been discovered by archaeologists. They have also found kilns for making pottery and evidence of the use of metals. The Harappans developed their own form of writing, although scholars are still unable to decipher it. No one knows exactly why this civilization collapsed, but its end occurred suddenly.

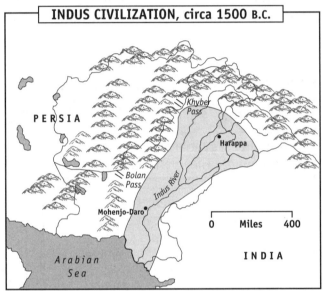

INDUS CIVILIZATION, circa 1500 B.C.

APPLYING WHAT YOU HAVE LEARNED

▼ What were some of the achievements of the civilization that developed in the Indus River Valley? _____

_____

_____

CHINA

About 500 years after the settlement of the Indus River Valley, China's first civilization emerged in the fertile plains along the Huang Ho (*Yellow river*).

Agriculture. As along the Nile and Indus Rivers, the fertility of the soil along the Huang Ho was increased by the river's occasional overflowing of its banks. Around 4,500 B.C., people began growing millet (*a type of grain*). Later, they learned to farm soybeans and to raise chickens, dogs, and pigs.

Government. Around 1700 B.C., a ruling family, or **dynasty**, known as the **Shang** took power. They built the first Chinese cities and established their capital at Anyang, near the Huang Ho. The Shang ruled with the help of powerful nobles. Shang kings were leaders of the military, They were also looked upon as the high priests of society. Shang kings were viewed as the most qualified to offer sacrifices to their royal ancestors.

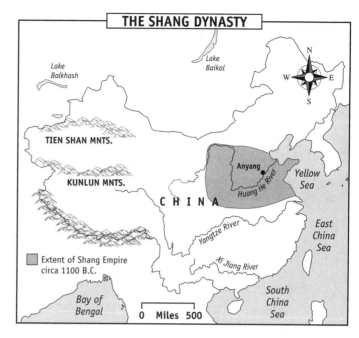

Cultural Contributions. The Chinese under the Shang were skilled at many crafts. Their special skill in bronze work can be seen in many objects dating from this period. They also were the first to make **silk** from a silkworm's cocoon. Finally, they developed a system of writing with pictographs, known as **characters**. Each character represented one word.

APPLYING WHAT YOU HAVE LEARNED

Complete the chart below by filling in the missing information.

Civilization	Location	Agriculture	Government	Contributions
Mesopotamia				
Egypt				
Indus River Valley				
Huang Ho				

APPLYING WHAT YOU HAVE LEARNED

▼ In Chapter 7, you learned to write a research report. Select one of the early river valley civilizations you learned about in this chapter and write a short report about its legacy to the world today. Use the Internet and at least one trade book for your research. Also include a bibliography with your report.

WHAT YOU SHOULD KNOW

☐ You should know that the earliest humans survived by hunting and gathering their food. They used tools of wood, bone, and stone, and learned to make fire.

☐ You should know that about 10,000 years ago, people in the Middle East first developed agriculture and learned to domesticate animals. This transformation is known as the Neolithic Revolution.

☐ You should know that the first civilizations arose in fertile river valleys. The Sumerians in Mesopotamia invented the wheel, sailboat and cuneiform writing. The Egyptians developed an advanced civilization along the banks of the Nile. Ruled by pharaohs, the Egyptians built pyramids and made contributions to medicine, geometry, astronomy, and art.

☐ You should know that other early civilizations developed along the Indus River on the Indian subcontinent and along the Huang Ho (*Yellow River*) in China.

CHAPTER STUDY CARDS

Neolithic Revolution

★ **Agriculture.** People saw that they could grow food by planting seeds in the ground.

★ **Food Surpluses.** People began to change from hunters and gatherers to producers of food.

★ **Domestication of Animals.** People learned to domesticate animals such as goats, sheep, and cattle.

★ **Villages.** People no longer had to wander in search of food and could now establish villages with permanent homes.

★ **Social Classes.** Populations grew, and new social classes developed.

Early River Valley Civilizations

The first civilizations developed along rivers with fertile soil from floods.

★ **Mesopotamia.** The region between the Tigris and Euphrates Rivers; invented the sailboat, wheel, calendar, and bronze.

★ **Egypt.** Developed along the Nile River in North Africa; Egyptian society was ruled by a powerful pharaoh.

★ **India.** The Indus River deposited rich soil over the neighboring plain.

★ **China.** China's first civilization emerged in the fertile plains along the Huang Ho.

CHECKING YOUR UNDERSTANDING

Look at the map below.

1. A group of archeologists discovered a preserved mummy, hieroglyphics written on stone walls, and an embalmed pharoah.

   In which location was this site most likely found?

   A. Site A
   B. Site B
   C. Site C
   D. Site D

   HIST
   B: 7.2

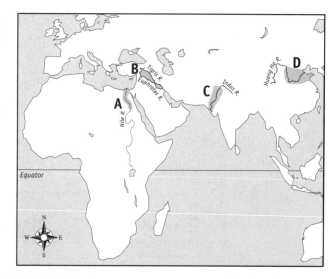

> **HINT**
>
> *First, **examine** the question. It tests your ability to interpret a map that shows the location of four ancient river valley civilizations. You should **recall** that hieroglyphics, well-preserved mummies, and pharaohs were part of Egyptian civilization found along the banks of the Nile River. Choices B, C, and D are all sites located near other river systems. If you **apply** this knowledge to the choices, the best answer would be **Choice A**.*

Now try answering some additional questions on your own.

2. What did each of the ancient civilizations indicated by the letters on the map have in common?

   HIST
   B: 6.4

   A. They were ruled by a pharaoh.
   B. They first began along river valleys.
   C. They farmed wheat and barley.
   D. They buried their rulers in large pyramids.

3. During which period did the domestication of animals and the farming of crops first occur?

   HIST
   B: 6.3

   A. Ice Age   C. Age of Classical Civilizations
   B. Neolithic Revolution   D. Renaissance

4. How did the introduction of agriculture affect early peoples?

    A. Societies became nomadic.
    B. Food production declined.
    C. Civilizations developed.
    D. Populations declined rapidly.

    HIST
    B: 6.3

5. What is one similarity between the ancient civilizations of Egypt and China?

    A. They both had a democratic government.
    B. They both believed in one God.
    C. They both had written forms of communication.
    D. They both carried on trade with the Americas.

    HIST
    B: 6.4

6. Throughout history, certain characteristics have helped to define a civilization. Identify two of these characteristics (2 points)

    HIST
    B: 6.3

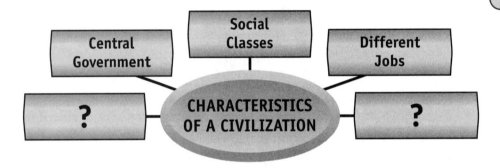

7. In your **Answer Document** identify and describe two advantages that the ancient Phoenicians had that allowed them to expand trade and increase their economic power. (4 points)

    HIST
    B: 6.3

    _____

    _____

    _____

    _____

    _____

    _____

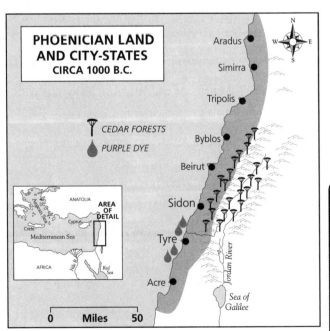

THE ACHIEVEMENTS OF THE CLASSICAL CIVILIZATIONS

In this chapter, you will learn about the impact of classical civilizations after 500 B.C. You will also learn about major world religions and how to interpret a multiple-tier timeline.

MAJOR IDEAS

HISTORY, BENCHMARK B
PEOPLE IN SOCIETY, BENCHMARKS A AND C

A. Greek culture was characterized by a questioning spirit and major achievements in art, literature, history, philosophy and mathematics. Greeks also developed the first **democracy**.

B. Rome was the heir to Greek civilization. Romans developed a **republican** form of government, based on the rule of law. As Rome expanded, it changed to an empire. Romans excelled at engineering, established the rule of law, adopted Christianity, and spread the Latin language.

C. In India, Aryans established the **caste system** and the **Hindu** religion. **Buddhism** also originated in India.

D. China was ruled by a series of dynasties. **Shih Huang-ti** unified China and built the **Great Wall**. **Confucianism** became China's dominant belief system.

E. Major world religions developed in this period: **Hinduism**, **Buddhism**, **Judaism**, **Christianity** and **Islam**.

CLASSICAL CIVILIZATIONS OF THE WEST: GREECE AND ROME

Civilization gradually spread from Mesopotamia and Egypt to other places on the Mediterranean, including Phoenicia, Israel, Persia, Greece, Italy and Carthage.

GREECE

Ancient Greece consisted of a large mountainous peninsula, the islands of the Aegean Sea, and the coast of present-day Turkey. Greeks were unified by their language and religion. They were **polytheists** — believing in many gods and goddesses — including Zeus, Athena, and Apollo, who were supposed to live on Mount Olympus.

Because of its hilly terrain, parts of Greece, like Athens, came to depend on trade. Greeks produced wine, olive oil, and pottery, which they traded with other peoples of the Mediterranean. Through these contacts, the Greeks became exposed to key achievements of other ancient civilizations, such as the **alphabet** invented by the Phoenicians.

The Rise of City-States. Mountains caused centers of population to be cut off from one another. As a result, separate **city-states** developed. Two of the most important were Sparta and Athens:

◆ **Totalitarian Sparta.** Spartans were a war-like people. They forced those they defeated to work as slaves on their farms. Life was organized around military needs. Strict obedience and self-discipline were emphasized.

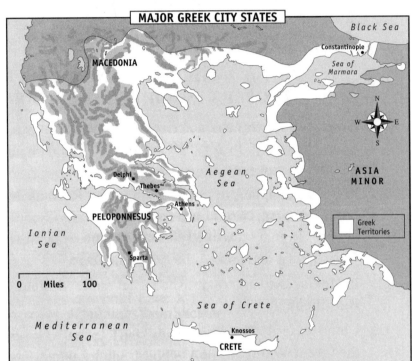

◆ **Democratic Athens.** Athens developed the world's first **democracy**. Every Athenian citizen could partici-

pate in government by voting directly on issues facing the city-state. However, only a minority of Athenians were citizens. Women, foreigners, and slaves could not take part in government. Although the Athenians believed in democracy, like other city-states they relied on slaves, often captured in war, to perform much of the work.

The Golden Age of Greek Culture. In the 5th century B.C., the Greek city-states went to war against Persia, which had set out to conquer them. After defeating the Persians, Greece enjoyed a "**Golden Age**" — a period when people enjoy prosperity and make significant achievements in the arts and other fields.

Art, literature, and philosophy flourished in Athens during these years. Athenians believed human reason was powerful enough to understand the world and to solve its problems. A series of philosophers — **Socrates**, **Plato**, and **Aristotle** — asked hard questions and applied their reasoning powers to answer them. What is the best way to act? What is goodness? How does nature work? Greek sculptors and architects tried to create statues and buildings with perfect proportions. The first historians tried to tell the story of the past.

Pericles, a Greek statesman, championed democracy. He used revenues collected from other city-states to rebuild Athens and constructed the **Parthenon** and other magnificent temples. However, a rivalry soon developed between Athens and Sparta, which led to thirty years of warfare. Sparta finally emerged as the victor.

Alexander the Great

Alexander the Great. In 338 B.C., the king of Macedonia, an area north of Greece, brought all the Greek city-states under his control. His son, **Alexander the Great**, went on to conquer most of the Mediterranean world, including Egypt and Persia. His conquests reached as far as the Indus River Valley. Alexander the Great forged a new culture, **Hellenism**, which was largely Greek, but which also included elements from the different cultures that he had conquered. Although Alexander's empire collapsed after his early death, his conquests helped to spread Greek culture and learning throughout the ancient world.

Democracy. Athens developed the first known democratic government — a system in which citizens take part in governing.

Science and Mathematics. Key advances were made by Pythagoras, Euclid, and Archimedes — mathematicians who are still studied today.

Literature and History. The Greeks developed the first known dramas and historical writings.

ANCIENT GREEK ACHIEVEMENTS

Art and Architecture. The Greek ideal of beauty was based on harmony and proportion. In architecture, the Greeks built temples with beautiful columns, such as the Parthenon in Athens. Sculptures depicted human beauty.

Philosophy. Greeks believed in the dignity of the individual. Through the use of reason, they believed humans could understand how the world worked. The greatest Greek philosophers were Socrates, Plato, and Aristotle.

APPLYING WHAT YOU HAVE LEARNED

▼ How was Athenian democracy different from American democracy today?

_____

_____

ROME

One of the most influential civilizations in history was Rome. Rome is located on a fertile plain in the middle of Italy near the west coast. To the north, the Alps Mountains protected Rome from most invaders. The sea provided further protection, while serving as a route for trade and expansion. The Romans were heirs to Greek culture. They believed in the same gods and goddesses, although they gave them Roman names. They also knew of Greek achievements in science, art, history and literature.

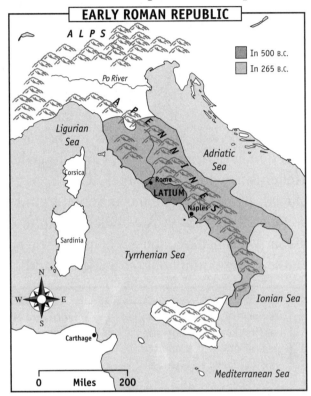

The Roman Republic. Early Rome contained two main social classes: **patricians** (*wealthy landowning families*) and **plebeians** (*small farmers, craftsmen, and merchants*). In early times, the Romans overthrew their king and made Rome into a **republic** — a system of government by representation. Republican Rome was governed by a patrician assembly known as the **Senate**, and by elected officials, known as **Consuls**.

The Twelve Tables. The Roman Republic issued the **Twelve Tables** to protect the plebeians. These written laws were placed in a public meeting place for all to see. The Twelve Tables covered civil, criminal, and religious law, and provided a foundation for later Roman law codes. Under Roman law, all "citizens" were equal under the law and innocent until proven guilty. At the same time, Rome also permitted the existence of slavery.

Rome Expands into an Empire. After uniting Italy, Rome defeated Carthage, its main rival in the Mediterranean. By 146 B.C., Rome dominated the Mediterranean world. The expansion of Rome changed its basic character. The Roman army became a professional force instead of a citizens' army. **Julius Caesar**, a general, threatened to seize absolute power, but was assassinated in 44 B.C.

Roman General Julius Caesar, leading an invasion of Britain.

The Pax Romana. Caesar's nephew, **Augustus**, became the first Roman Emperor. Augustus began a long period of peace, known as the **Pax Romana**, which extended throughout Western Europe and the Mediterranean world. Rome brought all political power under its control, but used the rule of law to govern its vast empire. They built aqueducts, stadiums, and other buildings as centers of Roman culture. The Romans promoted trade and offered Roman citizenship to loyal subjects throughout the empire.

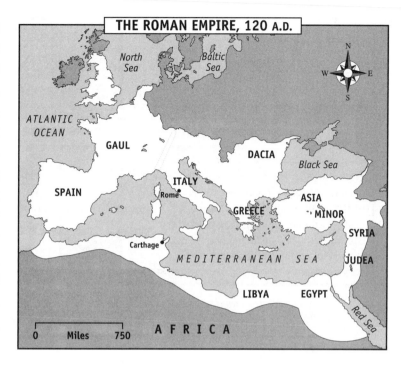

The Rise of Christianity. The Romans permitted the existence of other religions in their empire. However, they expected conquered peoples to worship their emperor as divine (*godlike*). Despite facing persecution, Jews and Christians refused. The Romans destroyed the Jewish temple in Jerusalem and drove the Jews out of Israel. Many Jews fled to Europe, Persia, and North Africa. Despite attempts by the Romans to eliminate Christianity, the religion slowly began to spread. In the 4th century, Emperor **Constantine** became a Christian. Not long afterwards, Christianity became the official religion of the Roman Empire.

Jews and Christians were often persecuted.

Fall of the Roman Empire. In the third century A.D., the Roman empire was attacked by fierce tribes from Europe and Central Asia. The Roman Emperor attempted to reverse the decline by dividing the empire into two parts in 284 A.D. Rome was weakened by a series of corrupt emperors, by a lack of loyalty from its paid troops, and by economic difficulties. The Western Empire finally collapsed in 476 A.D. The Eastern Empire would last another 1,000 years. Despite their decline, the Romans made many important and lasting contributions to world civilization.

Law. Roman concepts of justice, equality before the law, and natural law based on reason shaped later legal systems.

Language. Latin was the language of Rome. Several European languages evolved from it, including Spanish, French, Portuguese, Italian, and Romanian.

ACHIEVEMENTS OF THE ROMAN EMPIRE

Engineering. The Romans built thousands of miles of roads to connect distant parts of the empire with Rome. They built bridges and aqueducts to supply water to their cities. They developed concrete and the use of arches and domes.

Christianity. The adoption of the Christian religion by the Roman Empire was a major turning point in the spread of Christianity.

APPLYING WHAT YOU HAVE LEARNED

▼ What debt did the Romans owe to the ancient Greeks? _____

_____

▼ Imagine you are writing a speech about the legacy of the Roman Empire. What would you identify as its most important contributions?

_____

_____

_____

CLASSICAL CIVILIZATIONS OF THE EAST: INDIA AND CHINA

INDIA

Around 1500 B.C., the **Aryans**, tribes from Central Asia, invaded the fertile river plains of India. They brought their own religion, known as **Hinduism**. Hindus believe in many gods. They also believe in **reincarnation** — that after death, a person's soul is reborn in another living thing.

The Aryan conquest led to the creation of the **caste system**, dividing Indians into rigid social classes. A person could not move from one caste to another. One could only perform certain jobs based on one's caste. **Untouchables** were considered below all other groups and performed the lowliest tasks.

About 500 B.C., another new religion emerged in India. It was known as **Buddhism**. Buddhists believe that excessive desires cause all human suffering, and that to find inner peace one must renounce them. This can only be achieved by giving up all wealth, by meditating, and by respecting all living things.

After Buddha's death, **King Asoka** in Northern India converted from Hinduism to Buddhism. This tolerant ruler sent Buddhist missionaries throughout his empire to spread Buddhism. Buddhism later spread to other countries. Meanwhile, the **Gupta Empire** arose in India. Its Hindu leaders built universities and supported the arts. Their mathematicians developed the ideas of zero, infinity, and a decimal system. Artists painted colorful murals, while writers composed beautiful plays and poems.

Siddhartha Gautuma, or "Buddha," the founder of Buddhism

CHINA

During the period from 1027 B.C., to 220 A.D., China was governed by several ruling families or **dynasties**. The first of these was the **Zhou** (1027–221 B.C.). Zhou rulers claimed to govern with the **Mandate of Heaven**. They claimed Heaven would support good rulers and overthrow bad ones. Future rulers used this "Mandate" to justify their authority.

Confucius. Considered one of the greatest Chinese philosophers, Confucius (551–479 B.C.) lived during the late Zhou dynasty, a time of civil war in China. His philosophy, known as **Confucianism**, was based on respecting traditional ways of performing expected social roles and duties. Confucius placed great emphasis on the family. He also believed that rulers should govern for the benefit of their subjects, while subjects should obey their ruler. Following these rules would maintain social peace and harmony.

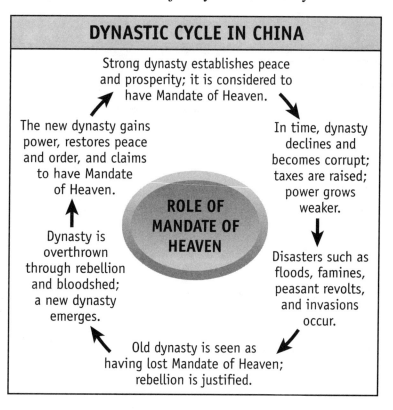

DYNASTIC CYCLE IN CHINA

Strong dynasty establishes peace and prosperity; it is considered to have Mandate of Heaven.

The new dynasty gains power, restores peace and order, and claims to have Mandate of Heaven.

In time, dynasty declines and becomes corrupt; taxes are raised; power grows weaker.

ROLE OF MANDATE OF HEAVEN

Dynasty is overthrown through rebellion and bloodshed; a new dynasty emerges.

Disasters such as floods, famines, peasant revolts, and invasions occur.

Old dynasty is seen as having lost Mandate of Heaven; rebellion is justified.

Ch'in Dynasty. After the Zhou were overthrown, **Shih Huang-ti** united China and became its "First Emperor" (221–206 B.C.). He established a strong central government and introduced a single form of writing and uniform measurements throughout China. Shih connected existing walls to create the **Great Wall of China**, protecting China from invaders to the northwest He treated all Chinese social classes as virtual slaves to his own will. His rule was so harsh that his dynasty ended on his death.

The Great Wall of China.

Han Dynasty. The next dynasty, the **Han** (206 B.C.–220 A.D.), established examinations to select candidates for government service. Examinations were based on knowledge of the writings of Confucius and other Chinese scholars. Examinations were open to all and were viewed as a way for talented commoners to improve their social position. During the Han Dynasty, merchants established overland trade routes to other centers of civilization. The **Silk Road** connected China to the Middle East and Rome. Over these routes, China exported silk, iron and bronze, and porcelain in exchange for gold, linen cloth, glass, ivory, and horses. Contacts with India led to the introduction of Buddhism into China.

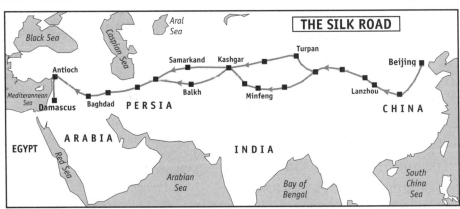

APPLYING WHAT YOU HAVE LEARNED

▼ Imagine your class is debating whether Shi-Huang-ti was a good or bad ruler of China. What would be your position? How would you support your position?

_____

_____

THE ENDURING LEGACY OF CLASSICAL CIVILIZATIONS

Area of Impact	GREECE	ROME	INDIA	CHINA
Concepts of Government and Citizenship	Ancient Athens developed the world's first democracy, but women, slaves, foreigners were not considered citizens.	Romans developed written laws and the first representative republic based on elected officials. Rome later became an empire.	Tolerant rulers, like King Asoka, accepted several religions.	Established Mandate of Heaven. Shih-Huang Ti was first emperor. Under Han, candidates for government service had to take a test.
Scientific and Cultural Advances	Achieved advances in geometry, philosophy, drama, and architecture.	Established concepts of law, engineering (arches) and Latin languages.	Set up universities, arts (literature and poetry), mathematics: the decimal system, and the use of zero.	Found how to make silk. They introduced the making of porcelain.
Spread of Religions	Ancient Greeks worshipped many gods and goddesses.	Traditional Roman gods and goddesses were based on Greeks. Later Rome adopted the Christian religion.	Hinduism (reincarnation) and Buddhism (follow Buddha's example by giving up all selfish desires).	Followed the philosophy of Confucius, which emphasized respect, tradition and family.
Slavery and Systems of Labor	Ancient Greeks used those captured in war as slaves.	Early Rome consisted of free farmers, but the later empire came to rely on slave labor.	Lower castes provided labor. Untouchables performed the most distasteful tasks.	Chinese Emperor used slave labor to build the Great Wall of China and other large projects.

APPLYING WHAT YOU HAVE LEARNED

▼ Describe the political and social characteristics of one of the above ancient civilizations and show how its influence is still felt in the world today.

_____

_____

MAJOR WORLD RELIGIONS

In this section, you will learn about one of the most important legacies of the ancient world: the emergence of major world religions.

HINDUISM

Hinduism has no single holy book, but Hindu writings like the **Upanishads** and the **Bhagavad-Gita** provide guidance and inspiration. Hinduism is the most popular religion of modern India, with more than 700 million Hindus in the world today.

Gods. Hindus believe that there are many gods and goddesses. Each of these gods, however, is a manifestation (*form*) of one Supreme Being.

Reincarnation. Hindus believe that at death, a person's soul is reborn as another living thing. This creates an endless cycle of rebirth for each soul.

MAJOR BELIEFS OF HINDUISM

Karma. *Karma* refers to a person's behavior in life, which Hindus believe determines that person's form in the next life. People who live a good life will be reborn in a higher caste. Those who do not are reborn in a lower caste.

Sacred Objects. Hindus believe the Ganges River is sacred and has the power to wash away sin and evil. The cow is also considered sacred, and religious Hindus do not eat beef.

BUDDHISM

Buddhism began in India around 500 B.C. Prince **Siddhartha Gautama** lived a life of luxury. One day, he looked beyond his palace walls and was shocked by the human suffering he saw. This prompted him to leave his family and to set out in search of truth. After years of searching, he came to believe suffering was caused by selfish human desires. To end suffering, a person must come to accept the world as it is and block out all selfish desires. Missionaries carried his ideas throughout India and then to China, Korea and Japan.

Basic Philosophy. Buddhism is based on a philosophy of self-denial and meditation. Buddhists also believe in reincarnation.

Gods and Holy Books. Buddhists do not believe in a single Supreme Being (*God*). They also do not have a primary holy book. Their basic beliefs are found in books called **Sutras**.

MAJOR BELIEFS OF BUDDHISM

Four Noble Truths. These truths explain life's meaning. They explain that pain and suffering is caused by human desires, such as for material wealth or selfish pleasures. Only by giving up these desires can a person find peace and harmony.

Eightfold Path. To give up human desires, Buddhists believe one should follow this path: give up wealth, act in a worthy manner, speak truthfully, live righteously, respect all living things, and meditate.

Nirvana. By following the Eightfold Path, an individual can escape the soul's endless reincarnations and achieve **nirvana** — a state of eternal bliss.

JUDAISM

The Hebrew (*or Jewish*) civilization developed as long as 4,000 years ago in the area along the Mediterranean occupied by present-day Israel, Lebanon, and Jordan. **Judaism**, the religion of the ancient Hebrews, was the first religion to believe in one God. According to Jewish tradition, the ancient Hebrews migrated from Israel to Egypt to escape food shortages from drought. They remained in Egypt for hundreds of years, where they became enslaved. **Moses** later led the Hebrews out of slavery in Egypt. According to the Bible, Moses presented his people with the **Ten Commandments**, rules for moral conduct, which he said came directly from God. The Hebrews returned to Israel and defeated its occupants.

KEY FEATURES OF JUDAISM

Monotheism. Other ancient peoples were **animists** (*believing each object had its own spirit*), or **polytheists** (*believing in many gods*). In contrast, the Hebrews were **monotheists** (*believing in only one God*).

Ten Commandments. Judaism associated goodness with morality. The Commandments are a code for living a moral life. They consist of ten simple laws which forbade stealing, murder, adultery, and other forms of immoral behavior.

Old Testament. The history of the ancient Hebrews and their relationship with God is told in the first books of the **Bible**, known as the **Old Testament**. Jews refer to the first five books of the Old Testament as the **Torah**.

CHRISTIANITY

Christianity began about 2,000 years ago in the Middle East. It is based on the beliefs of **Jesus Christ**. Jesus was a Jew born in Bethlehem. He preached forgiveness, mercy, and sympathy for the poor and helpless. However, the Romans regarded him as a troublemaker. The Romans crucified Jesus for claiming he was the Messiah or savior. After the death of Jesus, a band of his followers, known as the **Apostles**, helped to spread the new Christian religion. Many were attracted to their belief in an afterlife in which the poor and humble would be rewarded. Eventually, Christianity became the dominant religion of the Roman Empire.

MAJOR BELIEFS OF CHRISTIANITY

Role of Jesus. Christians believe Jesus was the son of God, and sacrificed himself to save humankind from punishment for their sins. Christians also believe that after his death, Jesus was resurrected and rose to Heaven.

Christian Conduct. Christians believe they will be saved and will go to Heaven after death if they have faith in Christ as their savior and treat others with love and respect. Christians believe in the Golden Rule — "do unto others as you would have them do onto you."

The Christian Bible. The sacred book of Christianity consists of the **Old Testament** (*the Jewish Bible*) and the **New Testament**, which describes the life of Christ and the works of the Apostles.

ISLAM

Islam was founded by an Arab merchant named **Mohammed**. He had a vision that commanded him to convert the tribes on the Arabian Peninsula to belief in a single God, known in Arabic as "**Allah**" — the same God worshipped by Jews and Christians. Mohammed lived in Mecca, an oasis town situated on caravan routes of the Arabian Peninsula. Soon local merchants became jealous of his growing influence. Fearing for his life, Mohammed fled from Mecca to the city of Medina in 622. In Medina, Mohammed emerged as a popular religious leader. He soon gathered an army to retake Mecca in a **jihad** or "holy war." In 632, two years after recapturing Mecca, Mohammed died. His followers believe Mohammed was God's last prophet on Earth. His teachings are contained in the **Koran** (*Qu'ran*), Islam's holiest book. The **Five Pillars of Faith** are the basic religious duties that all followers of Islam must fulfill.

FIVE PILLARS OF FAITH

Confession of Faith
Muslims must affirm: "There is no God but Allah and Mohammed is his prophet."

Prayer
Muslims must pray five times a day, while facing the city of Mecca.

Charity
Muslims must give money to the poor and pay taxes to the mosque.

Fasting
During the month of Ramadan, Muslims cannot eat or drink during daylight hours.

Pilgrimage
If physically able, a Muslim must make a pilgrimage (*religious trip*) to Mecca.

APPLYING WHAT YOU HAVE LEARNED

▼ The rise of major world religions has brought much kindness to the world, but has also led to wars and bloodshed. Do you think the world has benefited or been harmed by the emergence of religions? Explain your answer.

_____

_____

_____

_____

WHAT YOU SHOULD KNOW

☐ You should know that Greek culture was characterized by a questioning spirit and major achievements in art, literature, history, philosophy and mathematics. Greeks also developed the first democracy.

☐ You should know that Rome was the heir to Greek civilization. Romans developed a republican form of government, based on the rule of law. As it expanded, Rome changed to an empire. Romans excelled at engineering. Through their empire they spread of the rule of law, Christianity, and the Latin language.

☐ You should know that in India, Aryans established the caste system and the Hindu religion. In addition, Buddhism originated in India, and soon spread throughout Asia.

☐ You should know that China was ruled by a series of dynasties. In addition, Confucianism became the dominant belief system of China during the Han Dynasty. Shih Huang-ti, the "First Emperor," unified China and built the Great Wall.

☐ You should know that major world religions include Hinduism, Buddhism, Judaism, Christianity and Islam.

CHAPTER STUDY CARDS

Greek Civilization

★ **City-States.** Mountains cut off centers of population from each other. This led to the development of separate city-states.

★ **Sparta.** A Greek city-state that was totalitarian in nature. Life was organized around military needs.

★ **Athens.** Developed the world's first democracy, but women, foreigners and slaves could not take part in government.

★ **Golden Age of Greek Culture.** During this period art, literature, and philosophy flourished in Athens. Philosophers such as **Socrates**, **Plato**, and **Aristotle** questioned nature and life. Artists and writers strived for ideal beauty.

Roman Civilization

Rome was located on a fertile plain in the middle of Italy near the west coast.

★ **Roman Republic.** Rome was once a **republic** — a system of government by representation. Roman society contained two main social classes: patricians and plebians.

★ **Twelve Tables.** This was a Roman code of laws that provided that citizens were equal under the law and were innocent until proven guilty.

★ **Roman Empire.** After uniting the city-states of Italy, Rome defeated Carthage, its main rival in North Africa.

★ **Pax Romana.** A long period of peace lasting 400 years that emerged under Augustus.

Indian Civilizations	Chinese Civilization
★ **Aryans.** Tribes from Central Asia that invaded the fertile river plains of India. ★ **Hinduism.** Aryans introduced Hinduism to India. Hindus believe in many gods and in reincarnation. They created a caste system, dividing Indians into rigid classes. ★ **Gupta Empire.** Its Hindu leaders supported the arts and built universities. They developed the idea of zero in mathematics, infinity and the decimal system. ★ **Buddhism.** Buddha discovers that the cause of human suffering was selfish human desires. Buddhism spreads from India to China and Southeast Asia.	China's early history was marked by several ruling families known as **dynasties**. ★ **Zhou Dynasty.** Claimed to govern with the **Mandate of Heaven** — the support of heaven to justify their authority. ★ **Confucius.** Chinese philosopher who introduced respect for traditional ways and performing social roles and duties. Rulers should govern for the benefit of their subjects. Subjects should obey rulers. ★ **Shih Huang-ti.** The ruler who united China and became its "First Emperor." Also built the Great Wall of China.

CHECKING YOUR UNDERSTANDING

Look at the map below.

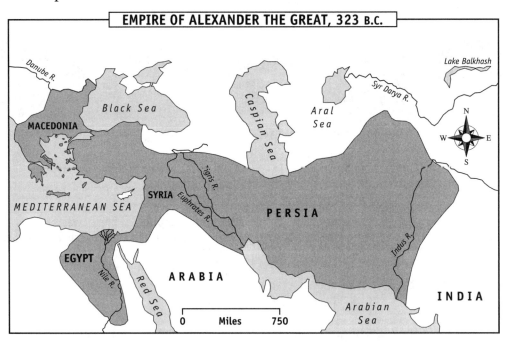

EMPIRE OF ALEXANDER THE GREAT, 323 B.C.

1. What was a lasting effect of Alexander's conquests?

   A. Greeks learned to build stone pyramids for their kings.
   B. Sparta and Athens regained their independence.
   C. The subjects of his empire adopted the Christian religion.
   D. Greek culture spread from Egypt to the Indus River.

HIST
B: 7.2

Examine *the question. It asks you to interpret the map and think about a cause-and-effect relationship. What was a lasting effect of Alexander's conquests. You should* ***recall*** *that Alexander conquered a vast empire from Egypt to the Indus River. Greek culture was introduced to all of these regions. Choices A, B, and C are all statements that are untrue. If you* ***apply*** *this knowledge to the choices, the best answer would be* ***Choice D***.

Now try answering some additional questions on your own.

2. Which society was the first to practice direct democracy?

    A. ancient Athens   C. Gupta Empire
    B. dynastic China   D. ancient Rome

> HIST
> B: 7.2

3. In what way were the Code of Hammurabi and the Twelve Tables similar?

    A. They promoted a belief in one God.
    B. They established written legal standards.
    C. They provided records of economic activity.
    D. They supported democratic government.

> HIST
> B: 7.2

4. Which statement most likely represents the view of a citizen of ancient Athens visiting Sparta?

    A. "The government and society in Sparta are too strict. The people have little if any voice in government."
    B. "I feel as though I have never left home. I find everything here is the same as it is in Athens."
    C. "This society allows greater freedom of expression than I have ever experienced back home in Athens."
    D. "I have never heard of a society like this, where people believe in only one God."

> HIST
> B: 7.2

5. A book contained the following passage: "The journey to Mecca began at Beirut Airport, but it was not until that afternoon that I put on the *Ihram* [robe] and drove on the road from Jiddah to Mecca. The road was crowded with cars, buses and trucks packed with pilgrims chanting the Hajj refrain."

    Which religion was the author describing in this passage?

    A. Christianity
    B. Islam
    C. Hinduism
    D. Judaism

> PEOPLE
> A: 6.2

6. Roman women could own property and could make wills leaving their property to whomever they chose.

What conclusion could be drawn from this statement?

A. Roman women had the right to vote.
B. Roman women enjoyed some legal rights.
C. Roman women were equal to men.
D. Roman women could hold political offices.

PEOPLE
A: 6.1

7. What factor helped prevent the ancient Greek city-states from uniting to form a single country?

A. lack of a common language
B. size of its desert regions
C. mountainous topography
D. cold, hostile climate

GEOG
C: 6.5

8. How did the caste system influence traditional rural Indian society?

A. by creating fixed social classes
B. by promoting political instability
C. by reducing the powers of landowners
D. by contributing to greater social mobility

PEOPLE
A: 6.1

9. Religion has played a major role in influencing ancient and present-day life.

In your **Answer Document**, identify one major religion and list two of its beliefs or principles. (2 points)

PEOPLE
A: 6.2

_____

_____

10. The world today owes much to the African, Greek, Roman, Chinese, Arab and European civilizations.

In your **Answer Document**, identify and describe two cultural or scientific legacies of ancient Africa, Greece, Rome, China, India or Arab civilizations. (4 points)

PEOPLE
C: 6.4

_____

_____

_____

_____

CHAPTER 13

THE FEUDAL SOCIETIES OF EUROPE AND ASIA

In this chapter, you will learn about conditions in Europe and Asia under feudalism. Historians often refer to this period as the Middle Ages (or *Medieval times*).

MAJOR IDEAS

HISTORY, BENCHMARKS A AND C
CITIZENSHIP RIGHTS AND RESPONSIBILITIES, BENCHMARK B

A. After the fall of the Roman Empire, Europe fell into a period of chaos.

B. To protect themselves, Europeans developed the system of **feudalism**. Feudalism was a political, economic and social system. Under feudalism, the king gave land to his **nobles** in return for their service. Nobles provided the king with knights. **Serfs** worked the land for their noble lords.

C. **Islam** quickly spread throughout the Middle East, North Africa and Spain. Scholarship and culture flourished in the Islamic world.

D. Christians and Muslims fought for control of the Holy Land during the **Crusades**. The Crusaders introduced Europeans to new goods and ideas.

E. The **Mongols** from Central Asia conquered both China and Russia.

F. A feudal system developed in Japan under the **Shoguns**.

G. A **multiple-tier timeline** shows events in several areas or topics at once.

THE BARBARIAN INVASIONS

Even when the Roman Empire was at its height, Germanic tribes like the Goths, Vandals, and Franks lived beyond Rome's frontiers. The Romans considered these peoples "barbarians." Eventually, these tribes defeated the Romans, causing the empire's collapse. Barbarian tribes then established new kingdoms in many parts of Western Europe. They mixed their own customs and beliefs with what they learned from the Romans, and gradually adopted Christianity.

Visigoths fought Roman warriors.

The constant migrations and warfare of this period disrupted trade and made travel unsafe. Bridges and roads fell into disrepair. Cities, towns and villages were abandoned. Raiders, like the **Vikings** attacked towns. Shortages of food and other goods grew. People **bartered** for goods without using money. People gave up their interest in learning. Churches and monasteries became the only places with people who could read and write.

BARBARIAN KINGDOMS IN EUROPE, 500 A.D.

CHARLEMAGNE AND THE FRANKS

Charlemagne became king of the Franks in 768. He expanded the Frankish practice of giving land to his nobles in exchange for their promises of loyalty and service. His nobles served him with knights on horseback. At the same time, the nobles gave land to those below them in exchange for similar promises of loyalty and service. Peasants provided service to their lords for security. Charlemagne expanded the Frankish kingdom to include present-day France, Germany, Holland, Belgium, and Northern Italy. In 800, he was crowned **Holy Roman Emperor** by the Pope (*head of the Church*). Although his empire did not last, Charlemagne established the social, cultural, and political foundations that influenced much of Western Europe for the next several centuries.

Charlemagne

SKILL BUILDER: MULTIPLE-TIER TIMELINES

A timeline shows a group of events placed on a line in **chronological order** — the order in which these events happened. The earliest event appears on the left with the most recent event on the right. The purpose of a timeline is to show relationships between events.

UNDERSTANDING B.C. and A.D.

In most of the world today, dates are based on when it is believed Jesus Christ was born. These dates are divided into two groups: **B.C.** and **A.D.** Sometimes **B.C.** is shown as **B.C.E.** — **B**efore the **C**ommon **E**ra. As time passes:

- **B.C. dates** go from higher numbers (500 B.C.) to lower numbers (200 B.C.)
- **A.D. dates** go from lower (100) to higher numbers (2008).

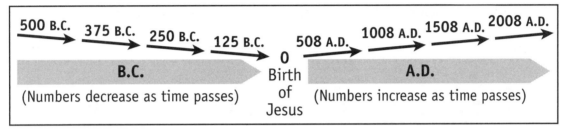

INTERPRETING MULTIPLE-TIER TIMELINES

The type of timeline we just reviewed is sometimes called a **single-tier timeline**. It contains a single line with dates and events in chronological order. However, historians sometimes want to review events in two places or based on two themes at once. In that case, a **multiple-tier timeline** is useful. It shows more than one line of events occurring within the same time period.

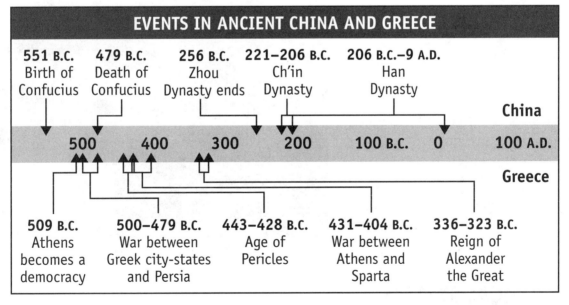

Notice that the title of this multiple-tier timeline is "Events in Ancient China and Greece." The timeline helps you to compare when different events occurred in these two separate regions of the ancient world.

APPLYING WHAT YOU HAVE LEARNED

1. Which happened first, the death of Confucius or the birth of democracy in Athens?

   _____

2. Which lasted longer, the Ch'in dynasty or the reign of Alexander the Great?

   _____

3. What was happening in Greece in the same year that Confucius died in China?

   _____

FEUDAL SOCIETY IN EUROPE

To protect themselves from violence and to provide for basic economic needs, people throughout Western Europe adopted the system used by the Franks. This new arrangement became known as **feudalism**. The **feud** was the land given to the lord for his service. Feudalism in Europe was characterized by a number of key social, economic, and political relationships.

A SOCIAL SYSTEM

A major characteristic of feudal society was the development of a strict class structure based on the control of land and military power. Local nobles (*lords*) were given land by their rulers in exchange for military service. The lords had small armies made up of **knights** (*armed warriors on horseback*). **Serfs** (*peasants*) worked the land. People were born as serfs, knights, or lords and could not change their social position.

Each feudal knight was a skilled warrior.

A POLITICAL SYSTEM

Under the feudal system, the leading nobles controlled political life. The king relied on them for his armies, and they often fought among themselves or challenged the king's authority. Civil wars were frequent, and powerful nobles often grabbed the throne for themselves.

AN ECONOMIC SYSTEM

During the Middle Ages, most people lived on manors. A **manor** consisted of the lord's house and the peasants who lived on the surrounding lands. Each manor produced its own food, clothing, and shelter. Serfs gave their lord part of their harvest and performed other services in return for the use of land. The lord protected serfs from attacks by outsiders and let them use his mill and oven. Each lord had almost complete power over serfs on his manor. He could pass laws, impose taxes, and act as a judge. **Serfs** were bound to the land and had no voice in most matters. They had virtually no rights.

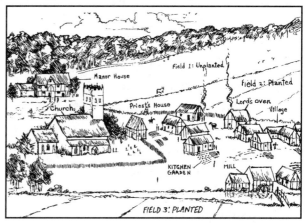

APPLYING WHAT YOU HAVE LEARNED

▼ Describe the conditions that led to the rise of feudalism in Europe.

_____

▼ Feudalism has been called a "political, economic and social system." Explain why this is a good description.

_____

_____

ROLE OF THE ROMAN CATHOLIC CHURCH

During the Middle Ages, the Roman Catholic Church was the single most powerful organization in Western Europe. There were many reasons for this.

REASONS FOR THE CHURCH'S POWER

| The Role of Faith. People were very religious. They believed the Church represented God and held the power to send a person to Heaven or Hell. Most felt united by their common faith. | Power and Wealth. Many nobles left land to the Church when they died, hoping to gain entry into Heaven. The Church became Europe's largest landowner. Church wealth also increased through **tithes** (*church taxes*). | Center of Learning. The Church was the main center of learning. Church officials were usually the only people who could read and write. Rulers often relied on Church officials, since they were the most educated people. |

THE BYZANTINE EMPIRE

Although the western half of the Roman Empire collapsed in the 5th century, the eastern half of the empire, known as the **Byzantine Empire**, survived for a thousand years beyond the fall of Rome. At the crossroads of Europe and Asia, the Byzantine Empire was a natural center for trade. Silk and spices from the east, furs from Russia, and grains, olives and wines from the empire itself brought great wealth. The emperor held absolute power and governed with the help of a vast centralized bureaucracy. The Byzantines developed their own form of Christianity. They were greatly influenced by Greek culture, and spoke mainly Greek. **Emperor Justinian** created a comprehensive code of Roman law.

THE ISLAMIC RELIGION SPREADS

Meanwhile, Islam had united the various Arab tribes with a common religion and language (*Arabic*). Arabs then set out on a "holy war" against non-believers. The Arabs were desert fighters who fought with enthusiasm to gain entry into Heaven. Over the next century, Muslim Arabs created a vast empire — an area as large as the Roman Empire at its height. They conquered the Middle East, North Africa, and Spain.

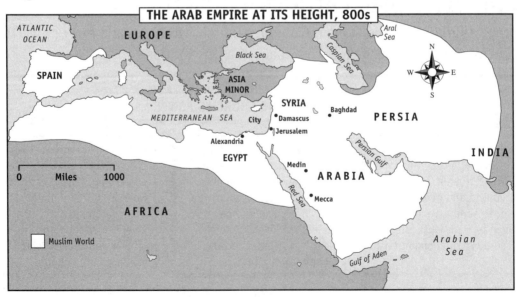

THE GOLDEN AGE OF ISLAMIC CULTURE

Muslim Arabs were influenced by the great civilizations of the ancient Middle East, as well as by the achievements of Greece and Rome. Arab rulers were known as **caliphs**. The capital of the caliphate moved first to **Damascus** in Syria and then to **Baghdad** in Iraq. During these centuries, while learning was in decline in Western Europe, a **Golden Age** of culture flourished in the Islamic world.

Mathematics. Arab scholars borrowed the concept of zero from India and developed Arabic numerals, which were eventually adopted by other cultures. These developments led to great advances in algebra and geometry.

Arts and Crafts. Mohammed forbade making images of God or people. Islamic art is largely made up of geometric designs, flowers, and stars. Their textiles, leather works, and rugs are highly prized.

ARAB CULTURAL ACHIEVEMENTS

Medicine. Arab doctors discovered that blood moves to and from the heart. They learned to diagnose many diseases, including measles and smallpox.

Architecture. Muslim rulers built beautiful palaces and mosques, richly decorated with mosaics, calligraphy, and geometrical designs.

APPLYING WHAT YOU HAVE LEARNED

▼ Some historians have claimed that it would be impossible to overstate the importance of the Catholic Church during the Middle Ages. Would you agree?

_____

_____

_____

_____

▼ What were some of the contributions of the Islamic civilization to the world?

_____

_____

_____

_____

▼ Make your own concept map illustrating the political, economic, and social characteristics of European feudalism.

CONFLICT AND CONQUEST

An important series of military conflicts shook Europe, Asia, and North Africa at the height of the Middle Ages.

THE CRUSADES

For hundreds of years, Christians had traveled to Jerusalem to worship where Jesus was born. However, when a particular group of Muslims gained control of Jerusalem, they drove Christians out of the Holy Land. The Pope called on all Christians to fight a holy Crusade to retake the Holy Land.

The **Crusades** were a series of military conflicts that were religious in nature. The word "Crusade" comes from the Latin word for cross. The Crusaders wore red crosses on their tunics. Seven Crusades were fought over the next two centuries between Christian Europeans and Muslims in the Middle East. The Crusades brought rulers and nobles from different parts of Europe together in a common cause. Although the Crusaders never achieved more than temporary control of Jerusalem, the Crusades had many important effects:

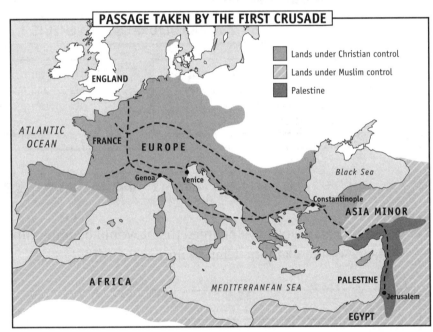

PASSAGE TAKEN BY THE FIRST CRUSADE

Lands under Christian control
Lands under Muslim control
Palestine

ENGLAND
ATLANTIC OCEAN
FRANCE
EUROPE
Genoa
Venice
Black Sea
Constantinople
ASIA MINOR
AFRICA
MEDITERRANEAN SEA
PALESTINE
Jerusalem
EGYPT

THE EFFECTS OF THE CRUSADES

New Ideas and Products.
Europeans had greater exposure to new ideas, such as the use of zero in mathematics, and to foreign products, such as silk, rice, spices, coffee, perfumes, cotton cloth, raisins, and glass mirrors.

Increased Trade.
The European demand for foreign products, like spices, sugar, lemons and rugs, eventually led to increased trade with other parts of the world.

Growth of Intolerance.
The Crusades led to the Christian persecution of Jews and Muslims, as well as to the Muslim persecution of Christians.

APPLYING WHAT YOU HAVE LEARNED

▼ Many Muslims saw the Crusades as an invasion inspired by European greed and prejudice. Most European Christians felt they were recapturing the Holy Land. Both groups thought they were performing a holy mission. Why did these groups view the same events so differently?

_____

_____

_____

_____

THE MAGNA CARTA, 1215

Conflicting interests between the king, the Catholic Church and the nobles led to the surprising emergence of individual rights in medieval England. To regain lost lands in France, **King John** increased taxes and demanded forced loans from his nobles. He also had a dispute with the Catholic Church. Civil war broke out when the **barons** (_leading nobles_), with the help of the English Church, rebelled. In 1215, King John agreed to their terms and signed the **Magna Carta**. In this charter, he promised that: "No freeman should be taken, imprisoned or be deprived of his property except by lawful judgment of his peers or by the

King John

law of the land." Another provision of the Magna Carta stated that the king could not raise taxes to wage war without the consent of the kingdom. Finally, the Magna Carta established a council of barons to enforce the agreement. The charter limited royal power and established individual rights in England.

THE MONGOL INVASIONS

Stretching across Eurasia is a band of dry, treeless grasslands ringed by mountains known as the steppes. The **steppes** allowed nomadic peoples to herd animals and to perfect their horsemanship and fighting skills. Throughout much of history, nomads like the Mongols have pushed out of this region and conquered their neighbors.

Ghengis Khan (1162–1227) united the Mongols and conquered much of China. His successors conquered Persia, Russia and the rest of China, creating one of the world's largest empires. In the 1200s, **Marco Polo** visited Mongol China. He was amazed at Chinese inventions like gunpowder and the compass. His return to Europe sparked new interest in Asia.

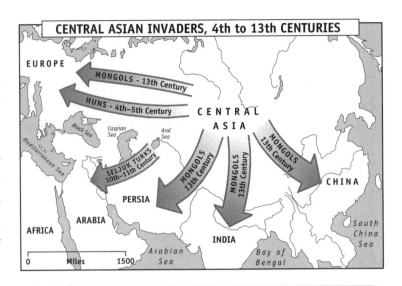

CENTRAL ASIAN INVADERS, 4th to 13th CENTURIES

APPLYING WHAT YOU HAVE LEARNED

▼ In what way did the conflicts between peoples in the Middle Ages promote change? _____

_____

JAPAN'S FEUDAL PERIOD, 1200 TO 1600

One part of Asia that the Mongols were never able to conquer was Japan. However, by the 1100s, the Japanese emperor's power had so weakened that Japan collapsed into civil war. A system of **feudalism**, similar to that which existed in Europe, eventually arose.

THE SHOGUN

In 1192, Japan's most powerful noble had the emperor appoint him as Japan's "Supreme Military Governor" or **Shogun**. For the next 600 years, the Shoguns were the real rulers of Japan, while the emperors acted as mere figureheads. The Shogun stood at the top of the Japanese feudal system. He gave land to the **daimyo** (*noble landowners*). To provide military protection for their lands, the **daimyo** recruited **samurai** warriors. Each samurai swore an oath of loyalty to the emperor and to his local daimyo.

JAPANESE SOCIETY

EMPEROR
Held highest rank in society but had no political power

Daimyo
Large landowners

Shogun
Actual ruler

Samurai Warriors
Loyal to Daimyo and Shogun

Peasants
Four-fifths of the population

Artisans
Craftspeople such as artists and blacksmiths

Merchants
Low status but gradually gained influence

The samurai promised to follow a strict code of honor, known as **Bushido**. Bushido emphasized the loyalty of the samurai to the daimyo. If a samurai warrior dishonored his daimyo, he was expected to take his own life. In return for their loyalty, the daimyo provided the samurai with social status and economic support.

ART FORMS FLOURISH AMID TURMOIL

In 1274, the Mongol ruler of China, **Kublai Khan**, sent a large force to invade Japan. The Mongols were defeated, but the costs of preparing for the invasion weakened the Shogun's power. Japan fell into a period of chaos and civil war. For the next century, the daimyo controlled their own lands with little interference from the central government. Despite this chaos, this was a period of intense cultural activity. The art of flower arranging, the tea ceremony, landscape painting, and the art of gardening all developed at this time. Japanese painting in this period stressed contemplation, meditation, and spiritual enlightenment. Each art form represented an attempt to reflect on life and the beauty of nature.

APPLYING WHAT YOU HAVE LEARNED

▼ How was feudalism in Japan similar to feudalism in Europe? _____

_____

▼ On a separate piece of paper, make your own multiple-tier timeline showing events in feudal Europe and events in feudal Japan.

WHAT YOU SHOULD KNOW

☐ You should know that after the fall of the Roman Empire, Europe fell into a period of chaos. To protect themselves, Europeans developed the system of feudalism. Feudalism was a political, economic and social system.

☐ You should know that Islam quickly spread throughout the Middle East, North Africa and Spain. Christians and Muslims fought for control of the Holy Land during the Crusades. The Crusaders introduced Europeans to many new goods and ideas.

☐ You should know that in England, King John granted his subjects special rights in Magna Carta.

☐ You should know that Mongols from Central Asia conquered China and Russia.

☐ You should know that a multiple-tier timeline can show events in several areas.

☐ You should know that Japan developed a feudal system like that of Europe.

CHAPTER STUDY CARDS

Feudalism

Feudalism arose in Europe from the chaos after the fall of Rome. It provided security and protection in a period of great turmoil.

★ **Social System.** Society was divided between the king, nobles, knights, and serfs.

★ **Political System.** The king ruled with the advice of his leading nobles. The nobles served the king with their knights — armed warriors on horses.

★ **Economic System.** Serfs worked on the land of their lord. Most people lived on the manor, which was self-sufficient.

Conflict and Conquest

★ **Spread of Islam.** Islam spread from Arabia throughout the Middle East and then to North Africa and Spain.

★ **Crusades.** Christian Europeans challenged Muslims for control of the Holy Land during the Crusades.

★ **Mongols.** Mongols, a group of nomadic horsemen from Central Asia, attacked China and the West.

★ **Japanese Feudalism.** In the 1200s, a system of feudalism similar to European feudalism developed in Japan. The Shogun gave land to his daimyo, who pledged their loyalty.

CHECKING YOUR UNDERSTANDING

1. Which was a characteristic of feudalism in both Europe and Japan during the Middle Ages?

   A. Merchants enjoyed more power than other classes.
   B. Political power was held by a strong central government.
   C. Rulers collected taxes to support large standing armies.
   D. Rulers allowed the use of their lands in exchange for military service.

   HIST C: 7.3

*First, **examine** the question. It tests your ability to compare feudalism from Europe and Japan. You should **recall** that under feudalism in both regions, the ruler gave lands to his followers in exchange for military service. The other choices are wrong. Merchants did not have more power than nobles. Rulers relied on their nobles to provide knights, rather than paying to support large standing armies. **Apply** what you know to select the best answer, which is **Choice D**.*

Now try answering some additional questions on your own.

2. What was one important legacy of the Golden Age of Muslim culture?

    A. attempts to colonize North America

    B. frequent conflicts between Christians and Jews

    C. advances in mathematics, science, and medicine

    D. policies to reduce trade between the Middle East and China

PEOPLE
C: 7.4

Use the map below to answer question 3.

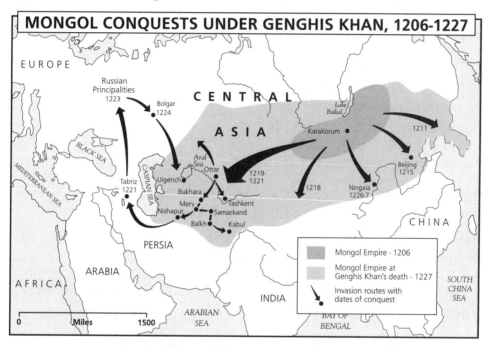

3. Which statement about the Mongols is **best** supported by the map?

    A. The Yuan dynasty kept China cut off from outside influence.

    B. Most Chinese people lived in river valleys.

    C. Genghis Khan extended Mongol influence throughout Asia.

    D. The city of Samarkand was part of the Yuan Empire.

HIST
C: 7.4

4. Which phase **best** characterizes the early Middle Ages in Western Europe?

    A. the manor system and feudal ties

    B. absolute monarchies and strong central governments

    C. decreased emphasis on religion in daily life

    D. extensive trade with Asia and the Middle East

HIST
C: 7.3

5. Which characteristic is most closely associated with feudalism in Japan?

    A. nobles protected serfs from attack

    B. samurai were loyal to the daimyo

    C. people lived on manors

    D. serfs worked the land

HIST
C: 7.3

UNLAWFUL TO PHOTOCOPY

6. "Western Europe went into a long, deep sleep. Learning was found only in the religious orders. Roads and bridges fell into disrepair. Fear and chaos reigned." What period in history does this quotation describe?

    A. rise of Christianity
    B. after the collapse of the Roman Empire
    C. the start of the Crusades
    D. the rise of Islam

    HIST
    C: 7.3

7. Which characteristic describes most feudal societies?

    A. an exchange of land for services
    B. widespread economic opportunity
    C. a representative government
    D. the protection of individual rights

    HIST
    C: 7.3

8. What was a lasting effect of the Crusades?

    A. They strengthened the power of the serfs in Europe.
    B. They increased trade between Europe and Asia.
    C. They brought European influence to Africa.
    D. They promoted the idea of religious freedom.

    HIST
    C: 7.4

9. Which statement **best** describes the role of the Catholic Church in Western Europe during the Middle Ages?

    A. The Church encouraged individuals to question authority.
    B. Church leaders were involved solely in spiritual activities.
    C. The Church gained influence as the world became more secular.
    D. The Church provided a sense of stability, unity, and order.

    HIST
    C: 7.3

10. In what way were European medieval knights and Japanese samurai warriors similar?

    A. They pledged oaths of loyalty to their leader.
    B. They pledged devotion to their nation-state.
    C. They pledged service to their church.
    D. They pledged support to their shogun.

    HIST
    C: 7.3

11. Feudalism in Western Europe can be characterized by a number of social, economic, and political relationships.

    In your **Answer Document**, describe two relationships that characterized feudal society in Western Europe. (2 points)

    HIST
    C: 7.3

_____

_____

THE RENAISSANCE AND REFORMATION

In this chapter, you will learn about the changes that occurred in Europe from the 1300s to 1500s, ushering in the modern world.

MAJOR IDEAS

HISTORY, BENCHMARK C

A. The rise of towns and trade, increases in royal power, the devastation of the Black Death, and the introduction of gunpowder led to a decline of feudalism.

B. The **Renaissance** marked a "rebirth" of culture. Renaissance humanists looked to the classical civilizations of Greece and Rome for inspiration. Painting and sculpture became more realistic, and literature and architecture borrowed from classical styles.

C. **Johann Gutenberg's** invention of movable type made it easier and cheaper to copy leaflets and books, leading to the spread of new ideas.

D. Martin Luther launched the **Protestant Reformation** when he criticized the Church's sale of indulgences. The Reformation shattered the unity of the Catholic Church.

THE DECLINE OF FEUDALISM

Feudalism was the dominant system in Europe for hundreds of years. However, beginning in the 1200s, feudalism in Western Europe began to decline.

Growth of Trade. The Crusades and travel in the later Middle Ages increased trade and commerce, both within Western Europe and with the East.	**Growth of Towns.** Increased trade led to the growth of towns. Some peasants moved to towns where they were able to obtain their freedom.	**Growth of Middle Class.** Merchants in towns increased in power as they grew more wealthy.

REASONS FOR THE DECLINE OF FEUDALISM

Rise of Powerful Kings. Kings increased their power at the expense of nobles. They demanded payments in money instead of knightly service.	**Gunpowder.** The use of gunpowder, introduced from China, made knights on horseback less important. Kings with standing armies gained new power over nobles.

THE PLAGUE

Another major factor leading to the end of feudalism was the widespread devastation caused by the plague. In the mid-1300s, rats with fleas carrying a disease known as the **Black Death** (*bubonic plague*) entered Europe from Asia, carried on trading ships. Between 1347 and 1351, nearly 25 million people — about one-third of Europe's population — died in this epidemic. The Black Death created a labor shortage in Europe. Large numbers of peasants escaped from serfdom when landowners and towns offered them freedom in exchange for work. Along with the other factors identified earlier, the devastation of the plague helped lead to the end of serfdom and the old feudal order in Western Europe.

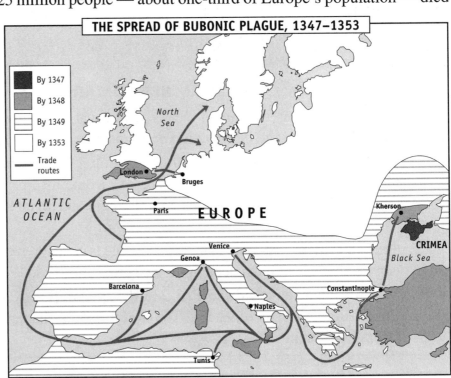

THE SPREAD OF BUBONIC PLAGUE, 1347–1353

- By 1347
- By 1348
- By 1349
- By 1353
- Trade routes

North Sea

ATLANTIC OCEAN

London
Bruges
Paris
EUROPE
Kherson
CRIMEA
Black Sea
Venice
Genoa
Barcelona
Naples
Constantinople
Tunis

APPLYING WHAT YOU HAVE LEARNED

▼ What are some of the factors that contributed to the end of feudalism?

_____

_____

▼ Imagine you are living in London in 1348. Write a letter to your relatives living in the countryside describing the impact of the Black Death on your city.

THE RENAISSANCE

A new interest in learning about the classical civilizations of ancient Greece and Rome developed in the city-states of Italy in the 1300s and 1400s. This period of great intellectual and artistic creativity later became known as the **Renaissance** or "rebirth." Writers and artists believed they were experiencing a revival of classical culture.

THE RENAISSANCE BEGINS IN ITALY

The Renaissance began in the Italian states because of their strategic location. Situated on the Mediterranean along major sea routes to Asia, the Italian city-states, like Florence and Venice, had grown rich from East-West trade and banking. Italy was also the home to many classical ruins from ancient Rome. Wealthy Italian merchants and nobles acted as patrons supporting artists, writers and scholars. Different Italian city-states competed to create the most impressive public buildings and works of art.

ITALIAN CITY-STATES DURING THE RENAISSANCE

MAJOR CHARACTERISTICS OF THE RENAISSANCE

During the Renaissance, traditional beliefs came under challenge. People began to show a greater interest in the material world and less concern in the life hereafter. There was a growth in **secularism** — looking at the world from a non-religious standpoint. Scholars used observation and experience to explain the world, rather than simply looking to Church teachings. Renaissance thinkers had confidence in the powers of human reason to explain the world. **Humanists** placed greater emphasis on the uniqueness and worth of each person. The Church had taught that man was sinful, but humanists now celebrated the wonders of human life.

ACHIEVEMENTS OF THE RENAISSANCE

Renaissance artists, architects and writers created a legacy of lasting achievements that still influence us today,

ART

Before the Renaissance, art in Italy was greatly influenced by Byzantine styles. Religious paintings were highly decorative, often with gold and jewels, but appeared flat and not very lifelike. Figures often floated in space without shadows. The size of a figure was based on its importance, not where it was placed in the picture.

Painting from the Middle Ages

In the 1300, the painter Giotto astonished Italians by painting in an entirely new style, using scenes with figures in lifelike space. Giotto's figures stood firmly on the ground, became smaller as they receded in space, were given depth by realistic shading, and showed emotions with their faces and gestures. Over the next century, each generation of Italian artists made improvements to make their paintings more realistic. Renaissance artists worked out the basic laws

The announcement of the angel to Saint Anne, by Giotto.

of **perspective** to create the illusion of space — how objects appear to decrease in size as they move away from us. Artists also studied human anatomy to depict human figures. **Leonardo da Vinci** discovered how to use shadowing and blurred outlines, especially on the eyes and mouth, to make his subjects appear incredibly alive.

ARCHITECTURE

Renaissance architects studied the ruins of buildings from ancient Rome to develop a new Renaissance style. They abandoned the pointed arches and elaborate details of the Middle Ages for a simpler, more classical style. They used the columns and circular arches of classical architecture as decorative touches. In Florence, citizens had built a large cathedral but did not know how to complete its giant roof. They held a competition among architects. **Filippo Brunelleschi**, who had studied Roman buildings, was chosen as the winner. His dome created an immense interior space — at the time, the largest church in the world.

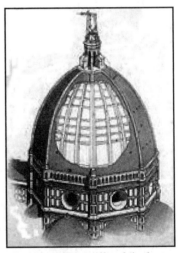

Section of Brunelleschi's dome

LITERATURE

Renaissance humanists studied classical Roman and Greek literature, poetry and philosophy. On the eve of the Renaissance, **Dante** helped create the Italian language in his *Divine Comedy*. Another writer of this period was **Boccaccio**, who wrote the *Decameron*, a book about seven ladies and three gentlemen who leave Florence for a villa in the country to escape the plague. Over ten days they tell each other 100 different stories. Later writers, including **Geoffrey Chaucer** and **William Shakespeare**, borrowed heavily from these stories.

Other Renaissance writers described the dignity of man, the pleasures of the senses, and how a nobleman should behave at his prince's court. The artist **Benvenuto Cellini** wrote a book about his own life. **Niccolo Machiavelli** wrote works of history as well as a guidebook for Renaissance princes. Machiavelli's ideas on ruling a country have had a profound impact on many political leaders. As the Renaissance spread to other countries, writers such as **Francois Rabelais** in France and **Miguel Cervantes** in Spain completed works in their own native languages.

ACHIEVEMENTS OF THE RENAISSANCE

ART:
Leonardo Da Vinci represented the ideal "**Renaissance man.**" He was a painter, sculptor, designer, and inventor. His paintings include *Mona Lisa* and *The Last Supper*.

Michelangelo. His paintings on the ceiling of the Sistine Chapel in Rome are considered among the greatest works of art of all time. His major sculptures, made in an astonishingly life-like style, include *David*, *Moses*, and the *Pieta*.

LITERATURE:
Niccolo Machiavelli wrote *The Prince*, advising rulers to do anything necessary to maintain and increase their power, including the use of deceit and force. He believed "the end justifies the means."

William Shakespeare wrote plays whose popularity have endured for centuries. His dramas *Hamlet*, *Macbeth*, and *Romeo and Juliet* explore the full range of human activities and emotions.

SCIENCE AND TECHNOLOGY:
Nicholas Copernicus stated that the earth and other planets revolved around the sun. This idea contradicted Church teachings, which said the Earth was the center of the universe.

Galileo Galilei and **Francis Bacon** rejected reliance on authorities and developed the **scientific method**, which emphasized direct observation, measurement, and experimentation.

Michelangelo's Pieta

William Shakespeare

Nicholas Copernicus

APPLYING WHAT YOU HAVE LEARNED

▼ Which Renaissance artist, writer, or scientist do you think made the most enduring contribution to modern-day society? Explain your answer.

_____

_____

_____

▼ Form small groups with your classmates. Have each group make an oral presentation to the class about one Renaissance artist, architect or writer.

GUTENBERG'S REVOLUTION IN PRINTING

For thousands of years, Europeans had copied all of their scrolls and books by hand. Such manuscripts were often highly illustrated, valuable and rare. Block printing was invented in China and introduced to Europe in the 1300s. The printer cut out every word he needed to print on the face of a wooden block. This left the letters raised. The block was inked, paper was laid on it and pressed down. With blocks, the printer could make copies of a book, but the blocks took a long time to cut, and each block could print only one page. **Johann Gutenberg** developed a printing press with movable type in Germany around 1450. Gutenberg created individual letters of metal, which were held together in a frame. The type for each page could then be broken down and reused. It was much easier to reset type than to carve an entirely new wood block. The invention of movable type, along with the use of a special press and oil-based inks, allowed the mass production of printed books for the first time.

Johann Gutenberg

APPLYING WHAT YOU HAVE LEARNED

▼ How was Gutenberg's work important for spreading new ideas? Explain your answer. _____

_____

_____

THE PROTESTANT REFORMATION

The spirit of inquiry of the Renaissance led to a questioning of the authority of the Catholic Church. Many reformers were already questioning church abuses. For example, many bishops and priests sought luxury and riches instead of a spiritual life. They collected revenues from places they never visited, and even committed individual immoral acts.

THE IMPACT OF LUTHER AND HIS IDEAS

In 1517, **Martin Luther** posted **Ninety-five Theses** (*arguments*) on a church door in Germany. Luther called for reforms within the Catholic Church. He especially challenged the Pope's right to sell **indulgences** — pardons for committing a sin, allowing the purchaser to enter Heaven. Luther believed that neither priests nor the Pope had special powers to provide salvation to individuals. Luther taught that only through personal faith in God could a person be saved and go to Heaven. The Pope **excommunicated** (*expelled from the Catholic Church*) Luther for holding these beliefs. Luther found protection from several German princes. He eventually responded to the Pope's condemnation by establishing his own new church.

Martin Luther in 1529.

Gutenburg's invention of movable type helped Luther and his followers spread their ideas. These reformers printed thousands of pamphlets in native languages, such as German and French, to win popular support. Luther also translated the Bible into German, since he believed that people should be able to interpret its text for themselves. This helped promote the development of a standard version of the German language. Lutherans rejected the Catholic Church's authority.

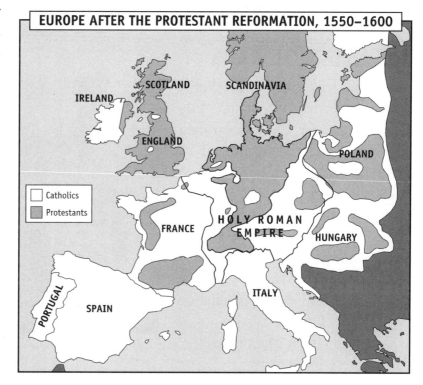

EUROPE AFTER THE PROTESTANT REFORMATION, 1550–1600

IRELAND
SCOTLAND
SCANDINAVIA
ENGLAND
POLAND
FRANCE
HOLY ROMAN EMPIRE
HUNGARY
PORTUGAL
SPAIN
ITALY

☐ Catholics
▨ Protestants

Other Reformers. Warfare between Catholics and Lutherans began almost immediately. Soon other reformers, like **John Calvin** in Switzerland, started churches of their own. These reformers were called **Protestants** because they protested against the Catholic Church.

EFFECTS OF THE REFORMATION

End of Religious Unity.
The religious unity of Western Europe, which had lasted for a thousand years, was shattered forever. Europe's religious differences led to a century of warfare between Protestants and Catholics.

Growth of Royal Power.
Without a powerful central Church, the power of European kings began to grow. In England, **King Henry VIII** broke with the Pope and became the head of the Church of England in 1534.

Persecution. Rulers tried to ensure that their subjects were all of one faith. This often led to the persecution of religious minorities.

THE CATHOLIC CHURCH FIGHTS BACK

The Protestant Reformation greatly weakened the power of the Catholic Church. As Protestantism swept across Europe, the Catholic Church reacted by making limited reforms and curbing earlier abuses. This movement is known as the **Catholic Counter-Reformation**. At the **Council of Trent**, the Church redefined Catholic beliefs and ended the sale of indulgences. The Church also banned Protestant books and established the **Inquisition**, a court whose purpose was to punish **heretics** — those who denied Church teachings.

A CENTURY OF WARS

Under the leadership of the Pope, and with the support of the Holy Roman Emperor, Catholics fought to prevent the further spread of Protestantism. They even won back some areas to Catholicism. Germany and the Netherlands became involved in a series of bloody wars, ending in the **Thirty Years War** (1618–1648). As a result, one-third of the German population was killed. Europeans also faced widespread famine and disease.

Sometimes protesters against the Church were burned at the stake.

APPLYING WHAT YOU HAVE LEARNED

Describe the impact of the following developments on Europe:

Development	Description	Impact
End of Feudalism		
Renaissance		
Invention of the Printing Press		
Protestant Reformation		

WHAT YOU SHOULD KNOW

☐ You should know that the rise of trade and towns, growth of royal power, devastation of the Black Death, and introduction of gunpowder all contributed to the decline of serfdom and feudalism in Western Europe.

☐ You should know that the Renaissance marked a "rebirth" of culture. Renaissance humanists looked to the classical civilizations of Greece and Rome for inspiration. Painting and sculpture became more realistic, and architecture and literature looked to classical styles.

☐ You should know that Johann Gutenberg's invention of movable type made it easier and cheaper to print leaflets and books, and to spread new ideas.

☐ You should know that Martin Luther launched the Protestant Reformation when he criticized the sale of indulgences. His actions shattered the unity of the Catholic Church in Europe.

CHAPTER STUDY CARDS

Decline of Feudalism

Feudalism declined for a number of reasons:

★ **Growth of Towns.** Towns began to grow when trade increased. As trade grew, the use of money replaced the barter system.

★ **Changes in Warfare.** The use of gunpowder (invented in China) made knights on horse-back and castles less important as a way of fighting.

★ **Black Death.** The Black Death, begun in the 1340s, killed one-third of Europe's population.

★ **Cost of labor.** Many peasants escaped serfdom and fled to towns where they were offered freedom in exchange for work.

Renaissance

The Renaissance sparked a "rebirth" of classical culture in Italy from 1350 to 1500s.

★ **Humanism.** Renaissance thinkers celebrated human achievements and focused on the uniqueness and worth of each individual.

★ **Secularism.** Thinkers used observation and reason to explain the world, rather than following church teachings.

★ **Achievements.** Vernacular literature, realistic sculpture, perspective in painting, and invention of the printing press.

★ **People.** Leonardo da Vinci, Michelangelo, Boccacio, Galileo, Niccolo Machiavelli.

The Protestant Reformation

Martin Luther objected to the Catholic Church's sale of indulgences. In his **Ninety-five Theses** (1517), Luther challenged the Pope's authority. Luther broke from the church.

Effects of the Protestant Reformation:

★ Ended religious unity in Europe.

★ Others, like **John Calvin**, started Protestant churches of their own. **Henry VIII** of England broke with the Catholic Church.

★ Led to a century of religious wars between Catholics and Protestants.

★ Helped kings to strengthen their power.

Catholic Counter-Reformation

The Catholic Church fought back against the rise of Protestantism.

★ **Council of Trent.** Ended the sale of indulgences and began a ban on certain books.

★ **Inquisition.** Tried and executed those suspected of heresy — non-Catholic beliefs.

★ **Religious Wars.** Catholic rulers cooperated with the Pope in fighting Protestantism. Catholics and Protestants fought against each other.

CHECKING YOUR UNDERSTANDING

1. What **best** explains why Italian city-states dominated trade routes on the eve of the Renaissance?

   A. They were strategically located for trade from Asia.
   B. They were situated north of the Alps.
   C. They were located on the Baltic and North Seas.
   D. They were unified under Mongol rule.

   HIST
   D: 7.5

*First, **examine** the question. It tests your understanding of the causes of the Renaissance. You should **recall** that the Italian city-states benefited from their strategic location for East-West trade. If you **apply** this knowledge to the choices, you will find that Choices B and C fail to correctly describe the location of Italy. Choice D is also wrong because Italy was never ruled by the Mongols. Thus, the best answer is **Choice A**.*

Now try answering some additional questions on your own.

2. Which statement **best** describes a change that occurred during the Renaissance?

    A. Feudalism became the dominant political system.
    B. The use of reason and logic was discouraged.
    C. Technology and science became less important.
    D. A new questioning spirit and attitude emerged.

    > HIST
    > D: 7.5

3. What explains why the Renaissance began in Italy?

    A. Italian city-states had grown wealthy from trade between Europe and Asia.
    B. Farmers produced great agricultural surpluses on flood plains.
    C. Italian merchants supported the Neolithic Revolution.
    D. Protestant scholars migrated to Italy to escape persecution.

    > HIST
    > D: 7.5

4. Which development was an effect of the Protestant Reformation?

    A. the posting of the Ninety-five Theses
    B. the decline in the power of the Catholic Church
    C. the sale of indulgences
    D. the end of religious warfare

    > HIST
    > D: 7.5

5. Why was the Catholic Church under criticism from reformers on the eve of the Protestant Reformation?

    A. It had sponsored expeditions to the Middle East.
    B. It was too concerned with worldly power and riches.
    C. It had refused to sell indulgences to peasants.
    D. It had allowed the Bible to be printed and distributed.

    > HIST
    > D: 7.5

6. What was a major characteristic of the Renaissance?

    A. The unity of the Catholic Church was shattered.
    B. The manor became the center of economic activity.
    C. The major language of common people became Latin.
    D. The classical cultures of Greece and Rome were studied and imitated.

    > HIST
    > D: 7.5

| Gutenberg invents the printing press. | Martin Luther stresses the central role of faith for salvation. | The Council of Trent meets. |

7. Which development in European history do these events most concern?

A. the Renaissance

B. the Reformation

C. the Neolithic Revolution

D. the Age of Feudalism

HIST
D: 7.5

8. Which invention helped to spread the ideas of the Protestant Reformation?

A. movable-type printing press

B. magnetic compass

C. steam engine

D. triangular sail

HIST
D: 7.5

9. Compare the two pictures below. In your **Answer Document**, describe two ways in which Renaissance architecture differed from the architecture of the Middle Ages. (2 points)

HIST
D: 7.5

Notre Dame Cathedral, Paris, France

St. Maria Degli Angeli Cathedral, Florence, Italy

_____

_____

_____

10. The Renaissance brought many important and long-lasting changes to life in Europe.

HIST
D: 7.5

In your **Answer Document**, identify two changes that occurred during the Renaissance. Then explain how each change you identified affected life in Europe. (4 points)

_____

_____

_____

_____

CHAPTER 15

THE CIVILIZATIONS OF AFRICA AND THE AMERICAS

In this chapter, you will learn about civilizations that existed outside of Europe and Asia.

MAJOR IDEAS

HISTORY, BENCHMARK D

A. A series of kingdoms developed in West Africa, largely based on the gold-salt trade. These kingdoms were **Ghana**, **Mali**, and **Songhay**.

B. Through trade, both the **Islamic religion** and the **Arabic language** influenced these West African kingdoms. **Timbuktu** became an important center of Islamic learning under **Mansa Musa**.

C. The **Maya**, **Inca**, **Aztec**, and **Mississippian civilizations** flourished in the Americas before the arrival of Christopher Columbus.

D. Maya, Inca, and Aztec peoples lived in centralized empires with all-powerful rulers. The Maya and Aztecs practiced human sacrifice as part of their religion. These civilizations developed many unique foods, including corn, potatoes, tomatoes, and chocolate.

THE WEST AFRICAN KINGDOMS

Much of North Africa is occupied by the **Sahara Desert**. Just below this desert is a wide band of grassland known as the **savanna**. The savanna stretches across the entire width of Africa, from the Atlantic to the Indian Ocean. It is excellent for grazing herds. South of the savanna lie the tropical rain forests of equatorial Africa. The people of West Africa developed their own religions and customs. **Griots**, or storytellers, passed on oral traditions.

As in ancient times, camel caravans are still used to cross the Sahara Desert.

THE GOLD AND SALT TRADE

The Sahara acted as a barrier that separated the peoples of sub-Saharan Africa from the Mediterranean world and the rest of Eurasia. Despite this separation, trade across the desert was never cut off completely. Arab merchants, traveling on camels that were able to go several days without water, crossed the Sahara. They were motivated by the gold and other riches they could obtain from trade with West African societies.

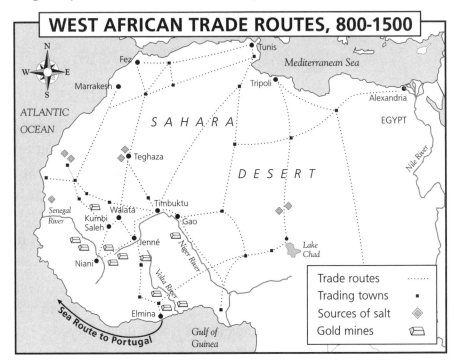

At the same time, West Africans lacked salt, which is vital to human survival. Salt was needed to preserve food and to add flavor. While sub-Saharan Africa lacked salt, it had most of the world's known gold reserves. Muslim merchants, moving in caravans across the desert, picked up large blocks of salt on their journey to exchange for gold. A thriving trade in gold and salt developed. Muslim merchants also purchased enslaved Africans. African kingdoms located along these trade routes grew rich from this trade.

APPLYING WHAT YOU HAVE LEARNED

▼ In West Africa, salt was once known as "white gold." Was this label justified?

_____

_____

_____

THE RISE OF AFRICAN KINGDOMS

Starting around the eighth century, West Africa saw the rise of a series of powerful kingdoms. For the next 800 years, their civilizations dominated West Africa — leading to an increased exchange of ideas, the rise of cities, and greater wealth.

KINGDOM OF GHANA (750–1200)

The Kingdom of Ghana was founded around 750 A.D. Ghana reached the height of its power around 900. The people of Ghana used their ability to make iron swords, spears, and lances to defeat their neighbors and to gain control of West Africa's major trade routes. Caravans brought salt south to Ghana, and returned north with gold from areas southwest of Ghana.

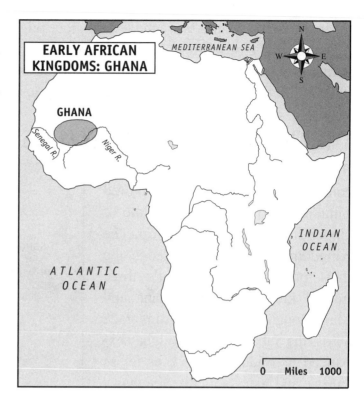

The power of the kings of Ghana rested on their ability to tax trade passing through the region, especially the salt and gold trade. The rulers of Ghana built a capital city, developed a large cavalry force and governed a wide area. Their people followed traditional religions, believing in spirits. As its population grew, Ghana's food supply became insufficient. In 1076, Ghana was invaded by Muslims from North Africa. Ghana never fully recovered from the invasion and eventually dissolved into several smaller states.

KINGDOM OF MALI (1240–1400)

In 1240, the people of Mali conquered Ghana. Their rulers established a new empire and brought both gold and salt mines under their control. Mali's rulers converted to Islam, although most of their people did not adopt the Islamic faith.

Mali's most famous ruler, **Mansa Musa**, expanded his kingdom greatly. He respected traditional West African ways, but also brought Muslim scholars and experts from Egypt. He built new mosques, schools, and law courts.

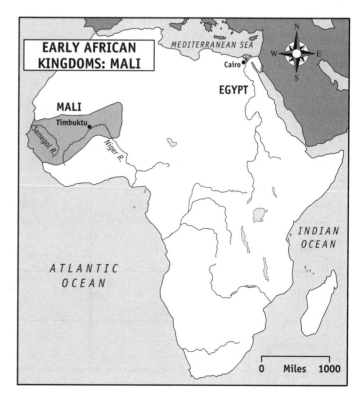

In the 1330s, Mansa Musa made a religious pilgrimage to Mecca. Mansa Musa turned his capital city of **Timbuktu** into a flourishing center of trade and learning. Because of the importance of studying the Koran, more West Africans learned to read and write in Arabic. Later rulers of Mali proved less capable than Mansa Musa, and the empire collapsed in the 1400s.

THE KINGDOM OF SONGHAY (1475–1600)

By 1470, the Songhay people had conquered their neighbors, captured Timbuktu and brought the middle of Upper Niger under their control. The Kingdom of Songhay emerged as the most prosperous of Africa's three trading kingdoms. Like Ghana and Mali, Songhay grew rich from trade across the Sahara Desert. Songhay expanded its trading network as far as Europe and Asia. Not only Songhay's rulers, but also many of the common people adopted Islam. **King Askia Muhammed** divided the country into provinces and ruled according to Muslim law. Despite its wealth and power, the Kingdom of Songhay lasted only about 100 years. In 1591, Songhay

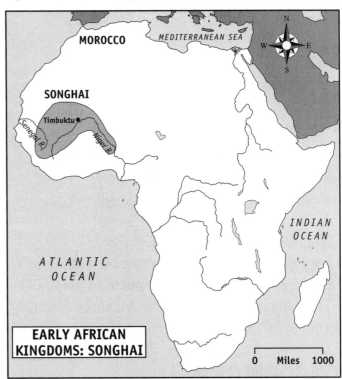

fell to an invading army from Morocco. The fall of Songhay marked the end of the great West African kingdoms. West Africa divided into a number of smaller independent areas.

APPLYING WHAT YOU HAVE LEARNED

Fill in the chart below comparing the three West African kingdoms:

Kingdom	Time Period	Control of Trade	Influence of Islam
Ghana			
Mali			
Songhay			

PRE-COLUMBIAN CIVILIZATIONS IN THE AMERICAS

While complex civilizations were flourishing in Asia, Africa, and Europe, equally striking developments had been occurring in the Americas. In this section, you will learn about the pre-Columbian civilizations that flourished before the peoples of the Americas ever encountered Europeans.

THE FIRST AMERICANS

Scientists believe that during the Ice Age, Asia and Alaska were attached by a land-bridge where the Bering Strait is found today. As long as 25,000 years ago, groups of Asian hunters crossed this landbridge, following the migrations of animal herds. Over time, these people settled throughout North America, Central America, the islands of the Caribbean, and South America. Separated by vast mountains, dense jungles, grass-lands, and deserts, these "Native Americans" soon developed their own languages and cultures.

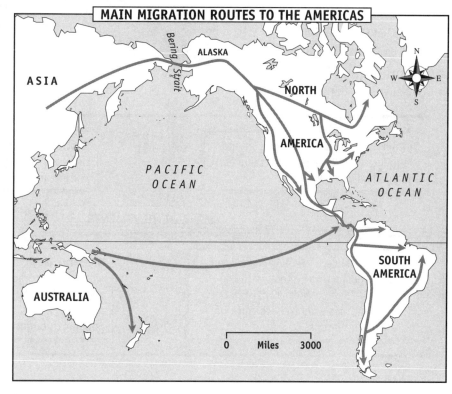

The peoples of the Americas experienced their own Neolithic Revolution in which they learned to grow corn (*maize*) and other crops. Several complex civilizations emerged in **Mesoamerica** (*present-day Mexico and Central America*). Historians refer to these civilizations as **pre-Columbian** because they existed in the Americas before the arrival of the explorer Columbus in 1492.

THE MAYA, 1500 B.C. – 1546 A.D.

More than 3,000 years ago, the Maya developed a complex civilization in the rainforests of present-day Guatemala.

Around 800 A.D., the Maya migrated northward to the Yucatan Peninsula in present-day Mexico, where they built a new series of city-states. No one knows why they moved. One of these later Maya cities is still well-preserved at **Chichen Itza**. Its stone pyramids served as tombs for nobles and religious leaders. Some pyramids reached heights as tall as modern skyscrapers. Although archeologists once thought the Maya were extremely peaceful, they have discovered that they practiced human sacrifices. Constant warfare from the 13th to the 16th centuries led to the final decline of Maya civilization. The Maya started the cultivation of corn, introduced ball games, and made many other contributions that influenced the later peoples of Mesoamerica.

Chichen Itza

Builders. The Maya built huge cities in the jungle with large palaces, temples, and pyramids.

Writing System. The Maya developed their own hieroglyphics — a writing system using picture symbols.

MAYA ACHIEVEMENTS

Math and Science. The Maya developed a complex numbering system, with the use of zero. Their calendar consisted of 365 days and was used to keep track of the changing seasons.

Artistry. Maya artists painted colorful murals to decorate their pyramids, palaces, and temples. They developed a ball game, played in a rectangular court, that became popular throughout the Americas.

THE AZTECS, 1200–1521

The Aztecs (*or Mexica*) were actually an alliance of several Native American groups living in Central Mexico. Around 1300, the Aztecs settled in the Valley of Mexico. They learned to grow corn and acquired other skills from their neighbors. Over the next two centuries, they engaged in frequent warfare to conquer other peoples of the region. Eventually, their empire ruled over 10 million subjects. They built their capital city at Tenochititlan, (*today Mexico City*), on islands in a giant lake. By 1500, its population was 500,000.

The Aztecs were ruled by an all-powerful emperor. They had an elaborate social structure, with nobles, merchants, and farmers. Like other Native American cultures, the Aztecs worshipped many gods. The Aztecs believed the Sun God needed human blood to continue his journeys across the sky. For this reason, the Aztecs practiced human sacrifices on a massive scale. Captured warriors from other tribes were sacrificed, as well as Aztecs who volunteered for this honor. The Aztecs believed these sacrifices were necessary to keep the universe in motion. As many as 20,000 people were sacrificed each year to the Aztec Sun God.

The Aztecs were accomplished warriors.

THE INCA EMPIRE, 1200–1535

The Inca Empire developed along the Pacific coast and in the Andes Mountains of South America. A series of earlier civilizations preceded the Inca. The rugged mountain terrain required that these people cooperate to survive. They bred llamas and alpacas to carry goods and to provide wool and food. To farm in the Andes, people had to carve terraces into the sides of the mountains, like giant staircases. They also grew root crops like potatoes.

Around 1400, the Inca began extending their rule along the Andes Mountains. Eventually they ruled an empire covering much of present-day Peru, Ecuador, Bolivia, and Chile. Like the Aztecs, they were ruled by an all-powerful emperor. They built stone roads, connected by footbridges, stretching over ten thousand miles to unite the distant corners of their empire. The Inca never developed a form of writing, but used **quipu** — bundles of knotted and colored ropes — to count, keep records, track crops, and send messages.

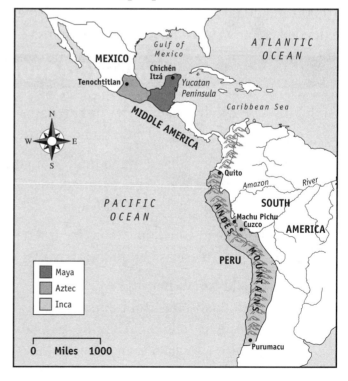

With their superb engineering skills, the Inca constructed vast stone buildings high in the Andes. The ruins of **Machu Picchu**, an ancient fortress city is the best surviving example of Inca building skills. Its stone walls are so expertly cut and fit together, without mortar, that a knife cannot be inserted between them.

MISSISSIPPIAN CIVILIZATIONS, 900–1350 A.D.

A Mississippian settlement

Mississippian culture flourished along the banks of the Mississippi River. Their culture soon spread to many parts of what is today the Central and Eastern United States. Mississippian peoples were influenced by trade with Mesoamerica. They adopted Mesoamerican agriculture and building techniques. Mississippians became known as **mound builders**, because of the enormous flat-topped temple mounds they built in the centers of their large, well-organized cities. They were mainly farmers who grew corn. The beginning of large scale agriculture allowed them to establish large permanent settlements. At a time when many European cities were little more than villages, the Mississippians built a large city near present-day St. Louis. Its surrounding wooden fence was almost two miles long, and enclosed a city of between 10,000 and 20,000 people. Mississippians also established an extensive trade network that extended as far west as the Rocky Mountains.

WHAT YOU SHOULD KNOW

☐ You should know that a series of kingdoms developed in West Africa, largely based on the gold-salt trade. These kingdoms were Ghana, Mali, and Songhay.

☐ You should know that through trade, both the Islamic religion and Arabic language influenced these West African kingdoms. Timbuktu became an important center of Islamic learning under Mansa Musa.

☐ You should know that the Maya, Inca, Aztec, and Mississippian civilizations flourished in the Americas before the arrival of Christopher Columbus.

☐ You should know that the Maya, Inca, and Aztec peoples lived in centralized empires with all-powerful rulers. The Maya and Aztecs practiced human sacrifices as part of their religion. They developed many important food crops, including corn, potatoes, tomatoes, and chocolate.

CHAPTER STUDY CARDS

Gold-Salt Trade

★ The Sahara Desert separated sub-Saharan Africa from the Mediterranean world.

★ Some Arab merchants crossed the Sahara, motivated by the gold-salt trade.

★ West Africans lacked salt, which was needed for survival. Salt was also used to preserve food and to add flavor.

★ While sub-Saharan Africa lacked salt, it had most of the world's known gold reserves.

★ Muslim merchants, in caravans, picked up blocks of salt to exchange for gold.

First Americans

★ Some 25,000 years ago, Asian hunters crossed the land bridge connecting the Bering Strait with North America.

★ These hunters and gatherers followed the animal herds.

★ Over time, these people settled throughout North America, Central America, the islands of the Caribbean, and South America.

Rise of West African Kingdoms

★ **Kingdom of Ghana.** Ghana's rulers built a capital city, developed a large cavalry force, and governed a wide area.

★ **Kingdom of Mali. Mansa Musa**, ruler of Mali, expanded his kingdom greatly. He respected traditional West African ways, but brought Muslim scholars and experts from Egypt. **Timbuktu** became a center of learning.

★ **Kingdom of Songhay.** Songhay emerged as the most prosperous of Africa's three trading kingdoms. Its rulers and people were Muslim.

Pre-Columbian Civilizations

★ **Maya Empire.** More than 3,000 years ago, the Maya developed a complex civilization in the rainforests of present-day Guatemala.

★ **Aztec Empire.** Over two centuries, the Aztecs engaged in frequent wars to conquer other peoples in Central Mexico.

★ **Inca Empire.** The Inca Empire developed along the Pacific coast and in the Andes Mountains of South America; they developed potatoes as food.

★ **Mississippians.** Grew corn and constructed mounds around the Mississippi River.

CHECKING YOUR UNDERSTANDING

1. What best explains the prosperity of the kingdoms of West Africa?

    A. They were located along the Tigris and Euphrates Rivers.

    B. They imported silks and spices from China.

    C. They followed Hindu beliefs.

    D. They benefitted from the trade in gold and salt.

    HIST
    D: 7.6

*First, **examine** the question. It tests your understanding of cause-and-effect relationships. You should **recall** that a series of West African kingdoms prospered from their control of the trade in salt and gold. Now **apply** this information to the four choices. These kingdoms did not develop along the Tigris and Euphrates Rivers, did not import Chinese goods, and were not followers of Hinduism. Choices A, B, and C are therefore wrong. The best answer is **Choice D**.*

Now try answering some additional questions on your own.

2. Which characteristic was shared by the Kingdom of Ghana and the Mongol Empire?

    A. They thrived on taxing the peasants.
    B. They had large, well equipped armies.
    C. They adopted the cultural achievements of the Chinese.
    D. Their rulers made pilgrimages to Mecca.

    > PEOPLE
    > A: 6.1

3. What conclusion can **best** be reached from Mansa Musa's reign in Mali?

    A. Christianity was the dominant religion in Africa at this time.
    B. Trade was not necessary for a civilization to prosper.
    C. Islam had little impact outside the Middle East.
    D. Complex civilizations developed in West Africa, independent of Europe.

    > HIST
    > D: 7.6

4. What did the Aztecs, Inca, and Maya possess that made them civilized?

    A. strong naval forces
    B. a written language and literature
    C. arts, architecture, and cities
    D. a monotheistic religion

    > HIST
    > D: 7.5

5. "In Timbuktu, there are numerous judges, teachers, and priests, all properly appointed by the king. He greatly honors learning. Many handwritten books imported from North Africa are sold. There is more profit made from this commerce than from all other merchandise."

    What does this description of Timbuktu by a 14th century traveler demonstrate?

    A. Timbuktu participated frequently in war.
    B. Timbuktu emphasized literacy and trade.
    C. Timbuktu protected the human rights of all citizens.
    D. Timbuktu chose its political leaders through democratic elections.

    > HIST
    > D: 7.6

6. How did the Inca modify their physical environment?

   A. They built large fishing fleets to feed their populations.

   B. They established extensive trade agreements with Europe.

   C. They raised cattle and horses on the pampas.

   D. They built footbridges that connected their roads across the Andes

HIST
D: 7.5

7. In what way were the Romans, Mongols and Aztecs similar?

   A. They developed writing systems.

   B. They extended control over neighboring peoples.

   C. They adopted democratic governments.

   D They established industrial economies.

PEOPLE
A: 7.1

8. Where did most of the wealth of the West African kingdoms of Ghana and Mali come from?

   A. the purchase of slaves from Europeans

   B. the creation of colonies on the Mediterranean coast

   C. taxes on goods brought by Indian merchants

   D. control of the trans-Saharan trade in gold and salt

HIST
D: 7.6

9. What does the Aztec use of the calendar and the Mayan writing system illustrate about pre-Columbian cultures in the Americas?

   A. These civilizations traded extensively with Africa.

   B. These civilizations had major cultural accomplishments before they ever came into contact with Europe.

   C. These civilizations declined from invasion and disease.

   D. These civilizations converted to Islam.

HIST
D: 7.5

10. What impact did trade across the Sahara have on the kingdoms of West Africa?

   A. It helped spread the Arabic language and the Islamic religion.

   B. It developed new foods like corn, tomatoes and potatoes.

   C. It led to the invention of paper, gunpowder and the compass.

   D. It introduced the system of feudalism.

HIST
D: 7.6

11. The kingdoms that developed in West Africa can be identified by several important characteristics. In your **Answer Document**, identify two of these characteristics and describe their importance to West African civilization. (4 points)

HIST
D: 7.6

_____

_____

_____

LOOKING AT THE THE ROLE OF WOMEN

Gender roles refer to the different positions taken in society by women and men. Throughout history, the role of women has varied greatly from one civilization to another. In most societies, women did not receive equal rights until relatively recent times. The fact that women bore and raised children, while men went to war and represented the family in public life, encouraged this trend.

Mesopotamia. Most girls stayed at home with their mothers, where they learned cooking and housekeeping. Women were responsible for raising the children and crushing the grain. There were enormous variations in the rights enjoyed by women in different social classes. Wealthier women were able to go to the marketplace to buy goods, could complete legal matters in their husband's absence, and could even own property. These women could engage in business for themselves, and obtain divorces. A few women enjoyed even higher status in Mesopotamian society.

Ancient Greece. The male citizens of the city-states of ancient Greece generally regarded women as inferior and excluded them from public life.

◆ **Athens.** In Athens, women were provided with a male guardian — either her husband or closest male relative. Although Athenian women could own clothing, jewelry, and slaves, they could not own land or enter into contracts. Instead, women managed the household, subject to their husband's will.

◆ **Sparta.** By 600 B.C., Sparta had conquered its southern neighbors. The defeated men and women were required to work on Spartan lands as slaves. Fearing a revolt, Sparta became an armed camp. Marriages were arranged by parents. Women had little say in the selection of their husbands. Spartan women, nevertheless, enjoyed greater status than elsewhere in Greece. Many were given an education and physical training. They generally married at the age of 18, later than other Greek women, to insure healthier and stronger babies.

Ancient Rome. Romans placed a high value on marriage, home and the family. This strongly influenced their treatment of women. Under Roman law, women passed from the authority of their fathers to that of their husbands. Women were not allowed to hold office. However, it was acceptable for men to seek their wife's advice — so long as it was given in private. Women could also hold property and make wills. Among the lower classes, many women even worked outside the home. Romans adopted a traditional view of gender roles, in which women were responsible for household chores and men represented the family outside.

Han China. Under Confucianism, the woman was considered at the bottom of the family structure and subject to the will of her husband or other male relative. Women were generally responsible for running the family. They did not receive an education outside the home. Wealthy men could marry more than one wife. The practice of foot-binding (*feet were tightly wrapped in bandages so they could not develop normally*) illustrates the effort made to limit female independence.

The Middle Ages. The role of women was determined by the attitudes of the Catholic Church and the nobility. Both agreed that women should be obedient to men. Woman's inferior status was blamed on Eve's disobedience in the Garden of Eden. Women's lifestyles varied according to their social status. Among peasants, a close partnership often existed between the man and his wife. Both worked side-by-side in the fields. Women ran the home and looked after the livestock. Among the nobility, only a handful of women received an education.

West African Kingdoms. In many traditional African religions, both boys and girls were separated from the community and underwent special ceremonies at puberty; marriages were arranged by families; the groom paid a dowry to his bride's family. Under Islam, women were limited to running the household while their husbands represented the family outside it — summed up by the Ghanaian proverb: "A woman is a flower in a garden; her husband is the fence around it."

Mesoamerica. Gender roles were established at birth. Boys were given a machete by their fathers, and girls received a stone instrument used to grind maize from their mothers, Each gift represented their future roles. Boys were taught crafts, and the girls were taught to cook and other necessities. Women held a variety of roles in the family, from harvesting grains and preparing the food, to caring for the animals. Women could hold jobs outside the home. Some sold goods in the market or were skilled artisans. Others were priestesses who worked in temples.

Aztec women planting crops.

APPLYING WHAT YOU HAVE LEARNED

▼ Divide the class into small groups. Select one of the civilizations described and research other differences between the genders. Or select a famous woman from that culture. Then present an oral report to the class.

EUROPEANS EXPLORE AND EXPAND OVERSEAS

In this chapter, you will learn about Columbus' voyage westward to reach Asia, and how this voyage led to the encounter between Europe and the Americas. The European encounter with the peoples of the Americas brought the major civilizations of the world together for the first time and had a profound impact on all peoples.

MAJOR IDEAS

HISTORY, BENCHMARK D

A. The Renaissance spirit of inquiry and new technologies encouraged Europeans to engage in overseas exploration in the 1400s. Spain and Portugal led European nations in exploring the seas.

B. Columbus' first voyage led to the first encounter between Europe and the Americas in 1492. This encounter resulted in the introduction of new foods, livestock, and diseases to the Americas and Europe, Asia and Africa, known as the **Columbian Exchange**.

C. The Spanish conquest of the Aztecs and Incas led to the European **colonization** of the Americas, the introduction of Christianity, and the deaths of millions of Native Americans from European diseases.

D. Europe became enriched from colonizing the Americas. An influx of foodstuffs and other goods raised living standards.

E. European colonization of the Americas had a great impact as well on the peoples of sub-Saharan Africa and Asia. Africans were enslaved and shipped to the Americas. Asians were affected by increased trade with the West and the establishment of new trading outposts.

THE AGE OF DISCOVERY

The spirit of inquiry of the Renaissance led Europeans to explore the oceans. Europeans adapted technological innovations from other cultures to improve their navigation skills. These innovations included the compass from China, the triangular lateen sail used by the Arabs, and the movable rudder. The conquest of the Byzantine Empire by the Ottoman Turks in 1453 cut Europe off from trade with East Asia. As a result, incentives were created to find new all-water passages to the East.

Desire for Foreign Products. The Crusades, Marco Polo's reports, and other contacts had greatly stimulated European interest in East Asian goods like spices, perfumes, and silks.	**Search for New Trade Routes.** Renaissance Europeans desired to explore the oceans. European rulers correctly believed that control of trade with East Asia would bring them vast wealth.

MOTIVES FOR OVERSEAS EXPLORATION

Technology. Better navigation skills and instruments, like the compass and movable rudder, allowed Europeans to sail farther than ever before.	**Religion.** Christian rulers in Europe wanted to spread their religion through overseas exploration.

APPLYING WHAT YOU HAVE LEARNED

▼ Identify two reasons Europeans became engaged in overseas exploration:

- _____

- _____

SPAIN AND PORTUGAL LEAD THE WAY

Spain and Portugal led the way in looking for an all-water route to East Asia. Both countries were located on the Atlantic Ocean and had the resources needed to finance costly overseas exploration. Spain's rulers hoped to spread Catholicism and to glorify their country through overseas exploration. **Prince Henry** of Portugal (1394–1460), developed a new, lighter sailing ship and sponsored expeditions along the coast of Africa.

◆ **Christopher Columbus** (1451–1506) was convinced he could reach Asia by sailing west. Others believed the world was round but too large to reach Asia this way. In 1492, he landed in the Americas instead of reaching the East Indies. His "discovery" of the Americas provided new sources of wealth that forever altered the world economy.

◆ **Vasco da Gama** (1460–1524), a Portuguese explorer, discovered an all-water route from Europe to India by sailing around the southern tip of Africa in 1497. His discovery made it possible for Europeans to obtain Asian goods without relying on overland routes.

Vasco da Gama

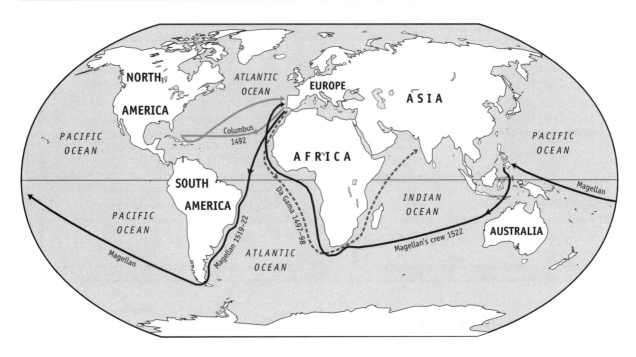

◆ **Ferdinand Magellan** (1480–1521) another Portuguese explorer, led the first expedition of ships to **circumnavigate** (*circle*) the world in 1519. Sailing around South America and across the Pacific, Magellan confirmed that the world was round.

APPLYING WHAT YOU HAVE LEARNED

▼ Why is Columbus more famous today than either Da Gama or Magellan?

_____

_____

▼ Would you favor renaming Columbus, Ohio as Magellanville? Explain.

_____

THE EUROPEAN CONQUEST OF THE AMERICAS

The impact of the arrival of Europeans was especially profound on Native American Indians. Spanish **conquistadors** (*conquerors*) and priests arrived shortly after the first explorers. They conquered native peoples, seized their gold and silver, brought new diseases, and converted some native peoples to Christianity. Small numbers of Spanish soldiers — using horses and firearms, and acting with local allies — quickly overcame large numbers of Native Americans and conquered the two largest American empires of that time: the Aztecs in Mexico and the Incas in Peru.

THE CONQUEST OF MEXICO

In 1519, **Hernando Cortés** sailed to Mexico with a force of soldiers in search of gold and silver. Cortés met the Aztec Emperor **Montezuma**. The Aztecs at first believed that the Spaniards were gods and showered them with gifts. Later, Cortés left the Aztec capital and found allies among the enemies of the Aztecs. With a few hundred Spaniards and several thousand Native American warriors, Cortés successfully defeated the Aztecs in 1521.

Cortés and his army of conquistadors easily defeated the Aztecs.

Cortés' easily triumphed over the Aztecs who fought with clubs, spears, and bows, while the Spaniards had guns, steel swords, dogs, horses and cannons. The Aztecs were also worn down by an outbreak of smallpox, accidentally introduced by the Europeans. The Aztecs had no immunity against smallpox and other diseases brought by the Europeans. Because of these factors, Cortés was quickly able to conquer the powerful Aztec empire.

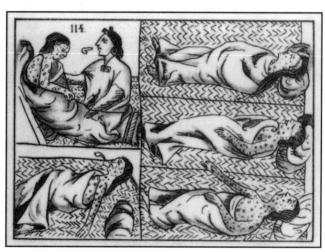
An Aztec artist depicts the suffering from smallpox, a disease introduced by Europeans.

THE CONQUEST OF PERU

In 1530, **Francisco Pizarro** set out to conquer the Inca. High in the Andes Mountains, Pizarro and a handful of soldiers defeated a much larger force of Inca warriors. Pretending friendship, Pizarro invited the Inca emperor to visit him. Pizarro and his army ambushed the imperial party and murdered the emperor. Pizarro was then able to conquer the Inca capital by 1533. Again, Native Americans were no match for the more technologically advanced Europeans.

Francisco Pizarro

APPLYING WHAT YOU HAVE LEARNED

▼ Would you consider Cortés and Pizarro as great men or as the destroyers of civilizations? Explain your reasoning.

_____

_____

_____

_____

EFFECTS OF THE ENCOUNTER

The European encounter with the Americas led to an exchange of ideas, customs, and technologies. As you know, such exchanges are referred to as **cultural diffusion**.

NEW FOODS AND INCREASED TRADE FOR EUROPE

One result of the encounter was that the European diet was greatly improved by the introduction of new foods such as tomatoes, corn, potatoes, and chocolate. At the same time, wheat, sugar, cattle, horses, pigs, and chickens were introduced from Europe into the Americas. This is sometimes known as the **Columbian Exchange**.

Raw materials obtained from the Americas hastened European economic development. Wealth from the "New World" enriched European merchants and their kings — especially in those states bordering the Atlantic: Portugal, Spain, England, France and Holland. Western Europe became the center of a vast global trading network, with trade shifting away from the Mediterranean to the Atlantic.

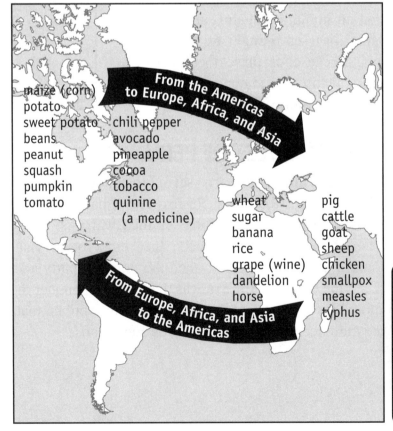

From the Americas to Europe, Africa, and Asia

maize (corn)
potato
sweet potato · chili pepper
beans · avocado
peanut · pineapple
squash · cocoa
pumpkin · tobacco
tomato · quinine
(a medicine)

From Europe, Africa, and Asia to the Americas

wheat · pig
sugar · cattle
banana · goat
rice · sheep
grape (wine) · chicken
dandelion · smallpox
horse · measles
· typhus

THE COLONIAL EXPERIENCE IN LATIN AMERICA

The Spanish conquest of the Americas brought many important changes to American society. Spain sent royal governors to rule its new colonies in the king's name. Gold and silver from the Americas were shipped to Spain, making it the strongest power in Europe in the 16th century. Conquered lands in the Americas were often divided among the soldiers. The conquerors used Native Americans to farm the land and work the mines. This system of forced labor was called the **encomienda system**.

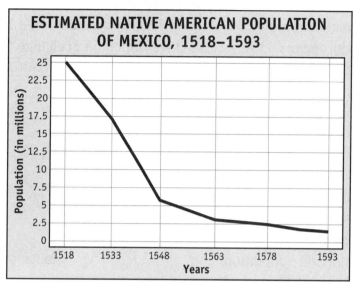

Native American populations declined rapidly because they lacked immunity to diseases brought by the conquerors, like measles and smallpox.

APPLYING WHAT YOU HAVE LEARNED

▼ Form a small group to consider this question: would you describe the encounter between Europe and the Americas as favorable or unfavorable? Consider the perspectives of several different groups in answering this question.

_____

_____

THE TRANS-ATLANTIC SLAVE TRADE

The deaths of many Native Americans from new diseases and harsh working conditions created the demand for a work force for the Spanish colonists, especially in the West Indies.

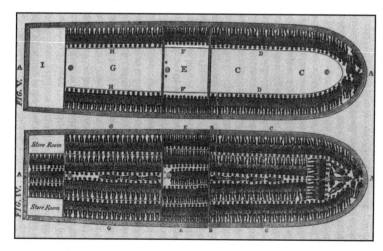

During the Middle Passage, slaves were packed tightly below deck.

A solution was found in the **Trans-Atlantic slave trade**. Slavery had long existed in Africa. Arab traders purchased slaves in West Africa to take north. Slavery was now expanded on a massive scale. People were captured by warring African tribes and traded to European and American slave traders in exchange for guns, rum, and other goods. It is es-

timated that slave traders removed as many as 15 million Africans over the next 300 years. Many of the captives died during the voyage across the Atlantic, known as the **Middle Passage**, because of the horrible conditions on board slave ships. Those who survived found themselves prisoners in a strange land.

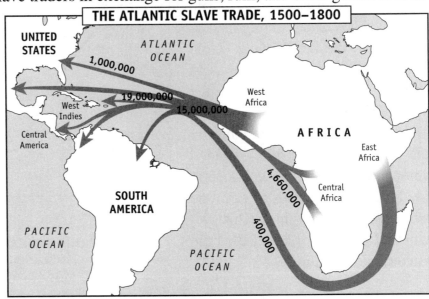

THE LEGACY OF THE TRANSATLANTIC SLAVE TRADE ON AFRICA

Encouraged African Warfare
The slave trade encouraged tribes to go to war with each other to obtain slaves to trade for European guns, rum, and other goods.

Disrupted African Culture
The slave trade destroyed much of Africa's rich heritage and disrupted its development. It create a legacy of violence, bitterness, and social upheaval.

Increased Cultural Diffusion
The exchange of ideas and goods increased. Slave traders brought new weapons and other goods to Africa, while slaves brought their beliefs, legends, and music to the Americas.

APPLYING WHAT YOU HAVE LEARNED

▼ Do you think you could have survived what enslaved Africans typically endured on their passage to the Americas? Explain your answer.

_____

_____

_____

THE COMMERCIAL REVOLUTION

Although most of Europe remained agricultural during this period, the fastest growing part of the European economy was actually in the trade of goods, especially those brought from Asia and the Americas. The **Commercial Revolution** marked an important step in the transition of Europe from the local economies of the Middle Ages to the formation of a truly global economy. The Commercial Revolution had the following aspects:

INCREASED TRADE AND SPECIALIZATION

People began producing more goods for sale rather than for their own use. Trade increased as the Americas exported sugar, rice, tobacco, and other agricultural products grown by enslaved Africans. China provided silks and porcelain, while India exported tea. The East Indies produced spices, and Europe exported woolen cloth and finished goods.

MERCANTILISM

European kings hoped to increase their power through the system of **mercantilism**. Mercantilists taught that real wealth and power were based on amassing gold and silver, which could be used to pay soldiers. For this purpose, France, England and Holland established overseas colonies in imitation of Spain and Portugal. Having colonies is sometimes referred to as **colonialism** or **imperialism**. Each so-called "mother country" exported finished goods to the colonists in exchange for less-costly raw materials. The competition for colonial empires led to a new series of wars between European powers.

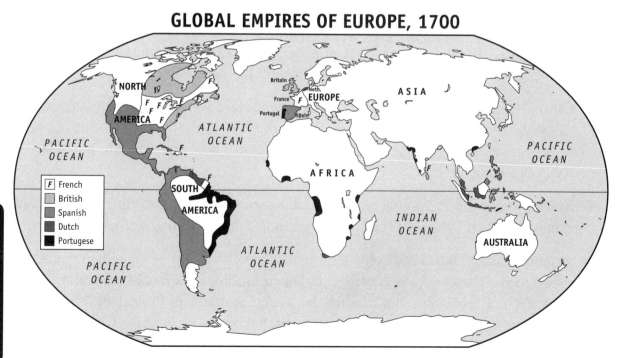

GLOBAL EMPIRES OF EUROPE, 1700

THE EMERGENCE OF CAPITALISM

Merchants and bankers laid the foundations for a new system known as **capitalism**. Under this system, business owners risk their **capital** (*money*) in a business in order to make **profits**. The growth of new businesses led to a demand for huge sums of money. Money was needed to pay for the ships, crews and cargo needed for international trade. Ships also had to be insured because there was a high risk of loss from an accident, stormy weather or war. European rulers also needed money to buy equipment and hire troops to wage war. To raise these large sums, **joint stock companies** were sometimes formed. These ventures were privately-owned companies that sold stock to investors. Investors bought the stock to get a share of the profit. Banks also developed new ways of raising and lending money. Governments borrowed large amounts of money to wage war, creating enormous public debts.

THE IMPACT ON ASIA

These developments affected the peoples of Asia just as they did those living in Europe, the Americas, and Africa.

◆ **Ottoman Empire.** In the Middle East, the Turkish Ottoman Empire increased its trade with Europe. The Ottomans, for example, used tobacco, introduced from the Americas, and guns, first developed in Europe.

◆ **India.** Muslims also extended their influence into Northern India. The **Muslim Mughals** united most of India in the late 1500s. **Shah Jahan** (1628–1658) destroyed Hindu temples and built new palaces and mosques in the Muslim style. His most famous building, the **Taj Mahal**, was constructed as a magnificent tomb for his wife. French, British and Portuguese traders set up trading posts along the coasts of India. The **British East India Company** began acquiring territories in India, and by the late 1700s, this British company controlled most of the Indian subcontinent.

◆ **China.** China stayed isolated from most of these developments The Emperor of China believed that China was superior to the rest of the world and did not need foreign trade. European merchants continued to use gold and silver to buy Chinese silk, porcelain and tea.

◆ **Spice Islands.** Further to the east, the Dutch took control of the "Spice Islands" and established their control of the Dutch East Indies (*today known as Indonesia*).

◆ **Japan.** At first, Japan welcomed European merchants by buying their guns and other goods. However, Portuguese and Dutch missionaries began converting many Japanese to Christianity. But rivalries between Catholic and Protestant missionaries led to conflicts within Japan. The Shogun reacted by totally banning Christianity and by closing off all contact between Japan and the outside world.

APPLYING WHAT YOU HAVE LEARNED

▼ Some economists believe the establishment of the "modern world economy" dates from this period in history. Explain whether you would agree.

_____

THE RISE OF ROYAL POWER IN EUROPE

The spirit of the Renaissance, the effects of the Reformation and the European encounter with the Americas all served to increase the power of European **monarchs** (*hereditary rulers*) and to enrich European society.

EFFECTS OF THE REFORMATION

The religious wars that followed the Reformation provided European rulers with an opportunity to build large standing armies and to increase their wealth through new taxes. The growing middle classes in the towns often allied with the king, who offered greater stability against the nobles. Kings also assumed control of religious affairs within their borders.

DIVINE RIGHT THEORY

Monarchs began to justify their increased power on the basis of **divine right**. According to this theory, the king was God's deputy on Earth, and royal commands expressed God's wishes. The Englishman **Thomas Hobbes** wrote that kings were justified in assuming absolute power because only they could maintain order.

LOUIS XIV, 1638–1715: A CASE STUDY IN ABSOLUTISM

Absolutism refers to a monarch's total control over his subjects. **Louis XIV of France** provided a model for other absolute monarchs. Under his rule, the king's command was law. Critics who challenged the king were punished. To subdue the nobles, Louis built a large palace at Versailles. Leading nobles were expected to spend most of the year at the royal court, under the watchful eye of the king. Louis also interfered in the economic and religious lives of his subjects. He demanded that Protestants convert to Catholicism or leave France. Finally, Louis involved his subjects in a series of wars to expand France's frontiers and to bring glory to his rule.

RUSSIA UNDER THE TSARS

The rulers of Russia adopted the system of royal absolutism on a grand scale. By the end of the 15th century, the local rulers of the region around Moscow had declared their independence from the Mongols and set about conquering neighboring lands. The bulk of Russia's population were **serfs** — peasants required by law to stay on the land and to work for noble landowners. Unlike Western Europe, serfdom continued in Russia and Eastern Europe in this period. Russian nobles exercised almost absolute power over their serfs. In return for their privileges, the nobility pledged absolute loyalty to the Tsar. Two of the most notable Russian rulers during this era were:

Peter the Great

◆ **Peter the Great (1682–1725).** Peter turned Russia from a backward nation into a modern power by introducing Western ideas, culture and technology. He often used brutal methods to force nobles to Westernize. Peter moved the capital of Russia from Moscow to St. Petersburg, a city he built on the Baltic seacoast so that Russia would have a "window on the West." By the end of his reign, Peter had expanded Russian territory, gained ports on the Baltic Sea, and created a mighty Russian army.

◆ **Catherine the Great (1762–1796).** Catherine continued Peter's policies of expansion and Westernization. She promoted limited reforms during her reign by reorganizing the government, codifying the laws, and educating children at state expense. Despite such reforms, she refused to part with any of her absolute power. During her long reign, the conditions of the Russian serfs actually worsened.

Catherine the Great

ENGLAND BECOMES A LIMITED MONARCHY

Unlike France and Russia, England's monarchs were never able to secure absolute rule. In England, strong checks had already been established on the king's power during the Middle Ages. Later events turned England into a limited **constitutional monarchy**, in which subjects enjoyed basic rights and political power was shared between the king and Parliament.

STEPS IN THE DEVELOPMENT OF CONSTITUTIONAL MONARCHY

Magna Carta. In 1215, English nobles forced King John to sign the Magna Carta. This guaranteed that Englishmen could not be fined or imprisoned except according to the laws of the land. Accused persons were considered innocent until proven guilty.

Rise of Parliament. Parliament was established as a legislative body made up of nobles in the House of Lords and elected representatives in the House of Commons. Parliament claimed the right to approve new taxes.

The English Civil War (1642–1649) and the Glorious Revolution (1688). During these two revolutions, Parliament established its supremacy over the king. **King Charles I** was actually beheaded in 1649, and England briefly became a republic. The monarchy was restored, but **James II** was overthrown in 1688. The **Bill of Rights of 1689** confirmed that English monarchs could not collect new taxes or raise an army without Parliament's consent.

THE IDEAS OF JOHN LOCKE

One of the most influential writers to emerge during this period was **John Locke**. Locke believed that governments obtain their power from the people they govern, not from God as divine right theorists supposed.

According to Locke, the main purpose of government was to protect a people's rights to life, liberty, and property. Locke defended people's right to rebel when the government abused its power. A century later, Locke's writings influenced the leaders of the American and French Revolutions.

John Locke

APPLYING WHAT YOU HAVE LEARNED

▼ Describe the role of Magna Carta, the rise of Parliament, the English Civil War, and the Bill of Rights of 1689 in the development of constitutional monarchy.

_____

_____

▼ Form a small group and select a monarch to research for a classroom project. Explain who the ruler was, what he or she did, and why the monarch was important.

WHAT YOU SHOULD KNOW

☐ You should know that the Renaissance spirit of inquiry and new technologies encouraged Europeans to engage in overseas exploration in the 1400s.

☐ You should know that Columbus' first voyage led to the encounter between Europe and the Americas in 1492. This encounter led to the introduction of new foods, livestock, and diseases to the Americas, Europe, and to Asia and Africa.

☐ You should know that the Spanish conquest of the Aztecs and Incas led to European colonization of the Americas, the introduction of Christianity, and the deaths of millions of Native Americans from European diseases.

☐ You should know that Europe became enriched from plundering and colonizing the Americas and from increased trade. An influx of foodstuffs and other goods raised European living standards.

☐ You should know that European colonization of the Americas had a great impact on the peoples of both sub-Saharan Africa and Asia. Africans were enslaved and shipped to the Americas. Asians were affected by increased trade with the West and by the establishment of European trading outposts.

CHAPTER STUDY CARDS

Encounter between Europe and Americas

This encounter had many lasting effects:

★ **Cultural Diffusion.** An exchange of ideas and products between the Americas and the rest of the world. Europeans learned about new foods: corn, potatoes, tomatoes, and, chocolate.

★ **Colonization.** Europeans defeated Native Americans and established vast colonial empires.

★ **Disease.** Native Americans suffered from diseases and conquest. Millions died from exposure to European "diseases."

★ **Slavery.** Led to the Trans-Atlantic slave trade and enslaved millions of Africans.

Commercial Revolution

★ **Mercantilism.** Rulers increased their power by amassing gold through conquest, taxes, and colonies

★ **Colonialism / Imperialism.** The nations of Spain, Portugal, France, Holland, and England developed overseas empires.

★ **Capitalism.** Merchants developed new methods of finance, borrowing and joint-stock companies.

★ **Trans-Atlantic Slave Trade.** Africans captured by other tribes were sold to Europeans on the West African Coast. Millions of Africans were taken in ships under inhumane conditions. Slaves worked under brutal conditions.

CHECKING YOUR UNDERSTANDING

Look at the illustration below.

1. Which system does this illustrate?

   A. isolationism
   B. mercantilism
   C. migration
   D. cultural diffusion

   HINT
   D: 7.7

>
> **HINT**
>
> First, **examine** the question. It tests your ability to interpret an illustration. The illustration shows gold and silver accumulating in a "Mother Country's" treasury. You should **recall** that mercantilists believed that a nation's real wealth and power were based on accumulating gold and silver. If you **apply** this knowledge to the choices, you will find that the best answer is **Choice B**.

Now try answering some additional questions on your own.

2. Which country had the most influence on the colonization of Mexico and Peru in the 1500s?

   A. Spain   C. England
   B. France   D. Netherlands

   HIST
   D: 7.7

3. In the 1520s and 1530s, Hernán Cortés and Francisco Pizarro led expeditions to the "New World." What was a direct result of their efforts?

   A. destruction of the Aztec and Inca Empires
   B. capture of Brazil by Portugal
   C. colonization of Canada by France
   D. exploration of the Philippines and East Indies

   HIST
   D: 7.7

4. What was an important effect of the "Columbian Exchange"?

   A. rapid decline in European population
   B. economic instability in China and Japan
   C. introduction of new foods to both Europe and the Americas
   D. spread of Hinduism into India

   HIST
   D: 7.7

5. During the Commercial Revolution, where did most trading centers develop?

> HIST
> D: 7.7

A. in the mountains
B. along waterways
C. near grasslands
D. on the tundra

6. What conclusion can best be drawn from information on the map?

> HIST
> D: 6.5

A. An extensive road system connected different parts of the Inca Empire.
B. The Moche controlled more territory than the Chimu.
C. Tropical conditions existed throughout the Inca Empire.
D. A common language unified all Andean civilizations.

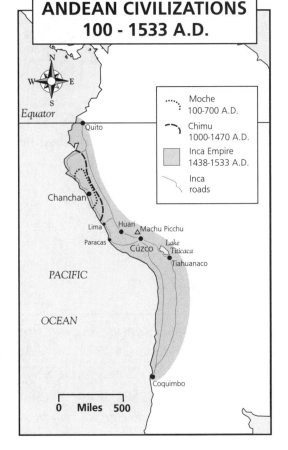

ANDEAN CIVILIZATIONS 100 - 1533 A.D.

Legend:
- Moche 100-700 A.D.
- Chimu 1000-1470 A.D.
- Inca Empire 1438-1533 A.D.
- Inca roads

Quito, Chanchan, Lima, Huari, Machu Picchu, Paracas, Cúzco, Lake Titicaca, Tiahuanaco, Coquimbo

PACIFIC OCEAN

0 Miles 500

7. In 1521, Spanish *conquistadores* conquered the Aztec Empire. What was one reason for their success?

A. Spanish soldiers used their superior military technology against the Aztecs.
B. Aztec religious beliefs promoted nonviolence.
C. Spain joined the Incas in their fight against the Aztecs.
D. The Spanish cavalry outnumbered the Aztec warriors.

> HIST
> D: 7.7

8. Shortly after contact with Europeans in the 1500s, why did the American Indian population suddenly decline?

A. Native peoples could not digest new foods.
B. There was religious persecution resulting from the Spanish Inquisition.
C. Native peoples had no natural immunity to new diseases.
D. Native peoples faced terrible conditions on their sea journey across the Atlantic.

> HIST
> D: 7.7

9. Which was an important result of the colonization of the Americas?

A. Native American societies experienced rapid population growth.
B. European rulers lost power and prestige in the New World.
C. Large numbers of Americans migrated to Europe for a better life.
D. Plantations in the Americas used enslaved Africans to replace native workers.

> HIST
> D: 7.7

Look at the map below.

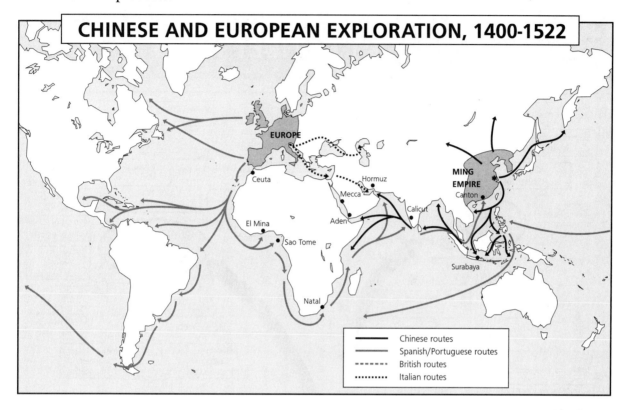

10. What does the map above indicate about exploration?

PEOPLE
D: 7.7

   A. The Portuguese taught the Chinese their sailing knowledge.

   B. Italians explored the east coast of Africa.

   C. The Spanish, Portuguese and Chinese were active explorers.

   D. China practiced isolationism throughout the 15th century.

11. In your **Answer Document**, identify and describe one reason why a small force of Spanish *conquistadores* were able to defeat the Aztecs so quickly. (2 points)

HIST
D: 7.7

_____

_____

12. The encounter between the peoples of Europe and the Americas had both positive and negative effects.

HIST
D: 7.7

In your **Answer Document**, identify and describe one positive and one negative effect of this encounter. (4 points)

_____

_____

_____

UNIT 3: PEOPLE AND SOCIETIES IN HISTORY CONCEPT MAP

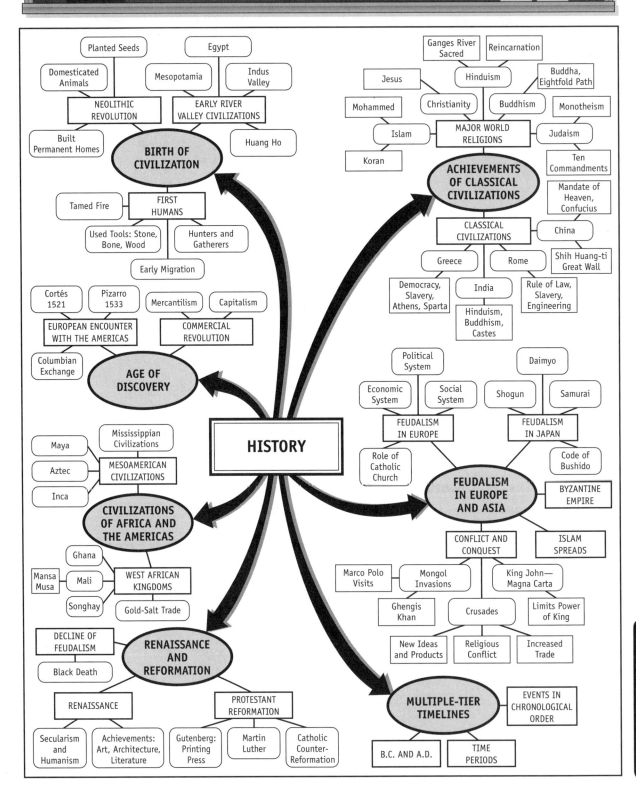

TESTING YOUR UNDERSTANDING

Look at the map below.

1. Egypt was one of the world's earliest civilizations to emerge. Which statement is most accurate based on information in the map?

   A. Most of Egypt's farmland was on the Red Sea.
   B. Egypt's mineral quarries were mainly along the Nile River.
   C. Egypt lacked gold and iron.
   D. Egypt's copper mines were located on the banks of the Nile River.

   **GEOG
   C: 7.4**

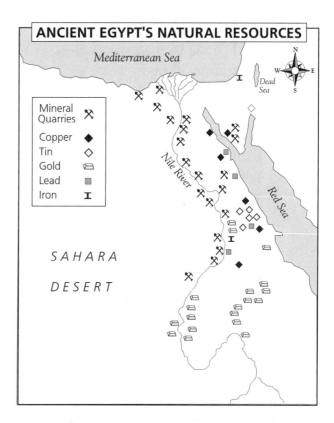

ANCIENT EGYPT'S NATURAL RESOURCES

Mediterranean Sea

Mineral Quarries ⚒
Copper ◆
Tin ◇
Gold ✏
Lead ■
Iron I

Nile River

Red Sea

Dead Sea

S A H A R A

D E S E R T

2. Why were the river valleys of the Tigris-Euphrates, the Huang Ho, and the Indus important centers of early civilization?

   A. They had rich deposits of iron ore and coal.
   B. They were isolated from outside cultural influences.
   C. They contained rich soils from annual floods.
   D. They were easy to defend from invasion.

   **HIST
   B: 6.4**

3. In the 1200s, Marco Polo traveled to Mongol China. What was a significant effect of the travels and writings of Marco Polo?

   A. The introduction of gunpowder to China.
   B. The decline of Mongol rule in China.
   C. The desire for Asian products in Europe.
   D. The introduction of Confucian teachings to Europe.

   **ECO
   B:7.2**

4. Which term identifies the global transfer of foods, plants, and animals that occurred after the first encounter between Europe and the Americas?

A. Scientific Revolution

B. Columbian Exchange

C. New Imperialism

D. Middle Passage

HIST
D: 7.7

5. Which statement is best supported by the graph on the right?

SKILLS
B: 6.4

A. Little trade in enslaved Africans occurred before the 1500s.

B. Slavery was most widely practiced in Sweden, Denmark, and Holland.

C. Conditions of slavery in Brazil were less harsh than in Spanish America.

D. Most enslaved Africans were sent to Brazil, the Caribbean or Spanish America.

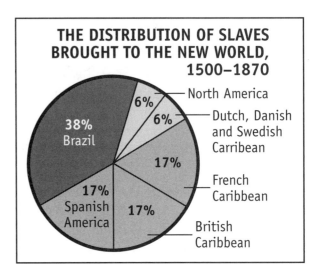

THE DISTRIBUTION OF SLAVES BROUGHT TO THE NEW WORLD, 1500–1870

- North America — 6%
- Dutch, Danish and Swedish Carribean — 6%
- French Caribbean — 17%
- British Caribbean — 17%
- 17% Spanish America
- 17%
- 38% Brazil

Look at the following two pictures.

Remains of Aztec Civilization

Remains of Inca Civilization

6. What do these pictures indicate about ancient Mesoamerican civilizations?

A. They were based on European technology.

B. They used advanced technology to build complex structures.

C. They relied heavily on Roman architecture.

D. They were strongly influenced by the Renaissance.

PEOPLE
A: 7.1

7.   The Renaissance marked a rebirth of culture. How were Renaissance humanists influenced by the writings of ancient Greece and Rome?

    A.   Renaissance humanists stressed the power of human reason.

    B.   Renaissance humanists promoted the religious beliefs of the Catholic Church.

    C.   Renaissance humanists showed little interest in worldly affairs.

    D.   Renaissance humanists produced few new scientific ideas.

> HIST
> C: 7.5

8.   How did feudalism benefit both Europe and Japan?

    A.   It provided social stability.

    B.   It fostered the growth of religion.

    C.   It eliminated warfare.

    D.   It encouraged formal education.

> HIST
> C: 7.3

9.   What common belief do Judaism, Islam, and Christianity share?

    A.   The Pope is supreme in matters of religion.

    B.   The Koran reflects the commands of God.

    C.   People's souls are reincarnated after their deaths.

    D.   There is only one God.

> PEOPLE
> A: 6.2

10. Which statement **best** describes a belief held by mercantilists?

    A.   Universal suffrage leads to educated citizens.

    B.   Controlling trade is the key to increasing power.

    C.   Only the strongest deserve to survive.

    D.   Strict social control prevents revolutions.

> HIST
> D: 7.7

11. What was an important similarity between the Mongols of Central Asia and the Incas of South America?

    A.   They developed cash-crop farming.

    B.   They based their wealth on the ownership of slaves.

    C.   They adapted to difficult physical environments.

    D.   They practiced monotheistic religions.

> GEOG
> C: 6.5

12. Which statement accurately describes an important impact of the "Columbian Exchange" on the lives of Europeans?

> ECO
> B: 7.2

    A.   New foods and an influx of gold and silver promoted economic growth.

    B.   Native Americans emigrated to Europe and competed with Europeans for jobs.

    C.   Millions of Europeans were killed by new Native American diseases.

    D.   The introduction of Native American religions shattered the unity of the Catholic Church.

13. The picture to the right is taken from an old Aztec text of the 1530s, showing the fall of the Aztec capital in 1521.

   Which explanation for the defeat of the Aztec Empire is **best** supported by this illustration?

   A. Aztec religious beliefs encouraged surrender over resistance.
   B. European countries joined together to defeat the Aztecs.
   C. Spaniards fought hard to defend their homeland.
   D. Spanish technology played a major role in the defeat of the Aztecs.

   > HIST
   > D: 7.7

Look at the partial outline below.

> I. Kingdoms of Ghana, Mali, and Songhay
>   A. _____
>   B. Spread of Islam
>   C. Development of centers of learning

14. Which phrase **best** completes the partial outline above?

   A. Use of gunpowder
   B. Control of gold and salt trade
   C. Renaissance achievements
   D. Invention of the printing press

   > HIST
   > C: 7.7

15. "Just as a man casts off old garments and puts on new ones, so does the dead soul cast off his old body and take on a new one." Which belief is expressed in this quotation?

   A. Seven Pillars of Wisdom   C. monotheism
   B. reincarnation   D. Eightfold Path

   > PEOPLE
   > A: 6.2

16. During the Crusades, Christians from Europe fought Muslims in the Middle East for control of the Holy Land. What was a direct effect of the Crusades?

   A. Protestants separated from the Catholic Church.
   B. European demand for goods from the East increased.
   C. Christians gained permanent control of the Holy Land.
   D. Nobles gained power over their monarchs.

   > HIST
   > C: 7.4

17. Starting in the 800s, a series of kingdoms in Africa enjoyed great wealth. Which statement **best** explains the economic prosperity of the kingdoms of Ghana, Mali, and Songhay?

> HIST
> D: 7.6

   A. They controlled oases used by caravans crossing the desert.
   B. They profited from the trade routes across West Africa.
   C. They maintained stability through their feudal systems.
   D. They rejected Islam in favor of tribal religions.

18. What kind of society is represented in the diagram to right?

> PEOPLE
> A: 6.1

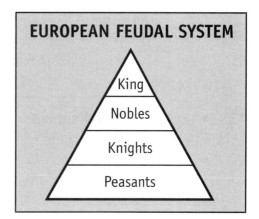

   A. a society with rigid, hereditary social classes
   B. a society based on educational achievement
   C. a society that rewards monetary wealth
   D. a society that values democracy

19. Jacqueline's class has completed a study of the Maya, Aztec and Inca civilizations. What should this study show about their agricultural practices?

   A. They adapted to their environments with creative farming techniques.
   B. They relied on agricultural machinery.
   C. They carried on an extensive trade in food with other groups.
   D. They grew only a few crops to export overseas.

> HIST
> D: 6.5

Look at the events in the box below.

1. Crusades	3. Golden Age of Greece
2. Fall of the Roman Empire	4. Renaissance

20. Which sequence places these events in the correct chronological order?

   A. 1 → 2 → 3 → 4   C. 4 → 3 → 2 → 1
   B. 3 → 2 → 1 → 4   D. 3 → 4 → 2 → 1

> HIST
> A: 6.2

21. Historians use multiple-tier timelines to see events taking place in two different areas. In your **Answer Document**, make a multiple-tier timeline showing two events from the history of Europe and two events from the history of the Americas or West Africa. (4 points).

> HIST
> A: 6.1

Look at the following two statements.

> "On my manor, I am the noble lord. I have total authority over everyone but my king and the Church. I collect rents from my serfs and administer justice in disputes between my knights."
>
> *Lord Thomas Lyon,*
> *1100 A.D.*

> "I work very hard. I am up at dawn to yoke my oxen to the plow. However hard the winter, I dare not stay home for fear of displeasing my master. I have to plow a whole acre or more of my lord's land."
>
> *Aelfric, a serf,*
> *1005 A.D.*

22. In your **Answer Document**, compare how the lifestyles of these two authors differed under feudalism. (2 points)

HIST
C: 7.3

_____

_____

Painting: Middle Ages

Painting: Renaissance

23. The Renaissance greatly altered the way that artists painted.

In your **Answer Document**, describe two characteristics of each painting above showing how it represents the time period in which it was created. (4 points)

HIST
C: 7.5

_____

_____

_____

UNIT 4

ECONOMICS AND GOVERNMENT

In this unit, you will learn about the social sciences. **Economists** study how people earn and spend money. **Political scientists** study how people are governed. In this unit, you will study both economics and government.

◆ **Chapter 17. Specialization and Trade.** In this chapter, you will learn how the unequal distribution of resources causes different regions to specialize in what they produce. Then they exchange their products through trade. You will also learn how this exchange of goods and services has led to the growth of cities, the establishment of trade routes, and the interdependence of regions from ancient times to the present.

◆ **Chapter 18. Types of Government.** In this chapter, you will examine what governments do. You will learn how governments protect lives and property, and how they provide services and public goods. You will also learn about three different types of governments — *monarchy*, *democracy* and *dictatorship*. Lastly, you will compare the rights and responsibilities of citizens under each form of government.

◆ **Chapter 19. How Governments Interact.** In this chapter, you will learn how the world is divided into different countries with their own sovereign governments. You will also learn how these governments interact through conflict and diplomacy.

KEY TERMS YOU WILL LEARN ABOUT IN THIS UNIT

- Scarcity
- Goods and Services
- Opportunity Cost
- Entrepreneurship
- Specialization
- Trade-offs
- Supply / Demand
- Imports / Exports

- Interdependence
- Government
- Sovereignty
- Monarchy
- Democracy
- Dictatorship
- Representative Democracy
- Productive Resources

- City-State
- Kingdom
- Empire
- Participation
- Diplomacy
- Treaties
- International Meetings
- Political Process

LOOKING AT ECONOMICS

Economics is the study of how people meet their needs by making, distributing, and using goods and services. Economists study how people work and earn money, how they save and invest money, and how they use their time, energy, and money to satisfy their needs.

THE PROBLEM OF SCARCITY

One of the basic principles of economics is the problem of scarcity. Most people have **unlimited wants** — things that they would like to have or do. We can never be wholly satisfied because we have **limited resources** at our disposal to meet these

unlimited wants. We have only so much time, energy, and other resources to satisfy our many wants. Economists refer to the inability of our existing resources to meet our unlimited wants as the **problem of scarcity**. For example, everyone in Ohio may want a new home, but there are simply not enough materials, land, or labor available to build new homes for everyone.

What stops everyone in Ohio from having a new home like this?

OPPORTUNITY COST

Because we have only limited resources at our disposal, whenever we choose to use our resources to satisfy a particular need, we give up the chance to use those same resources to satisfy other needs. A "**trade-off**" occurs whenever we give up one thing for another. Every economic decision using resources actually involves a trade-off, known as the **opportunity cost** of that decision. Economists define the opportunity cost of a decision as the *next best choice* that was given up. For example, if you use money to buy a stereo, you lose the opportunity to use that same money to buy a computer. This is your opportunity cost. Economists use the concept of opportunity cost to determine the true cost of a decision.

Not only individuals, but also entire societies have opportunity costs when they make economic decisions. For example, if a government spends its resources to equip its army, it has fewer resources available for other purposes.

APPLYING WHAT YOU HAVE LEARNED

▼ Select one economic decision you recently made and its opportunity cost.

- Decision: _____

- Opportunity Cost: _____

A place where people meet to exchange goods freely is known as a market. Even in earliest times, people met at market places to exchange goods. Seeing new goods from other places increased people's desires to own that item. Thus, trade was further encouraged.

THE THREE BASIC ECONOMIC QUESTIONS

Every society has **scarce resources** to meet the **unlimited wants** of its members. Therefore, every society has three basic economic questions it must answer:

What should be produced?   **How should it be produced?**   **Who should get it?**

In other words, each society must decide **what** things to produce, with the limited resources it possesses. It cannot satisfy all of its members' unlimited wants. **Which** wants and needs should it try to satisfy? **What** should it produce to satisfy these wants? **Who** should have control of those goods and services? Finally, who should receive the goods and services that are produced?

Societies answer these basic economic questions in different ways. In some societies, people follow tradition to answer these questions. They produce whatever their ancestors produced, using the same traditional methods, and then divide it as their ancestors did. In other societies, a ruler tells everyone what to do and decides who gets what. Finally, in some societies, people are free to do what they want. In these societies, individuals produce what they think they can sell to others, while others are free to buy whatever they can afford. This is known as a **market economy.**

CHAPTER 17

SPECIALIZATION AND TRADE

In this chapter, you will learn why different regions specialize and trade their products. You will also learn how the forces of supply and demand help to set prices. Finally, you will see how the exchange of goods has encouraged the growth of cities, the establishment of trade routes and the interdependence of regions.

MAJOR IDEAS

ECONOMICS, BENCHMARKS A AND B

A. Each region of the world has different **natural resources** and **human resources**. The **uneven distribution of resources** makes it easier for regions to produce some goods and services and harder to produce others.

B. Regions **specialize** in producing what they can at the lowest opportunity cost. Then they trade to obtain those things they do not make.

C. **Trade** is an exchange of goods and services. **Exports** are the goods that producers in a country sell outside their country. **Imports** are the goods and services produced outside a country that are brought into the country.

D. **Supply** is how much of a product is available; **demand** is how much of the product people want. The interaction of the forces of **supply and demand** generally establish the **prices** of goods sold on world markets.

E. The desire for certain goods, such as spices and special foods, encouraged the growth of trade, the rise of cities, and the establishment of trade routes.

WHAT ARE GOODS AND SERVICES?

Producers make goods or provide services for **consumers** — those who use goods and services.

GOODS AND SERVICES

Goods are objects that people make and use. Goods include such things as foods and clothing.

Services are activities people do for others. A plumber provides a service by unclogging a drain. Teachers and doctors also provide services.

The foods we buy are examples of goods.

WHAT ARE PRODUCTIVE RESOURCES?

In order to make a cake, a baker must bring together several ingredients. The ingredients that go into making goods or providing services are known as **productive resources** or **factors of production**. Productive resources include *natural resources, human resources, capital goods* and *entrepreneurship*.

NATURAL RESOURCES. Natural resources are the resources provided by nature that people use to create goods and services. They include air, water, plants, and minerals. Lumber, cotton, iron ore, and fresh water are all natural resources.

HUMAN RESOURCES. Human resources include all the human labor that is required to produce something. Human resources include all the planning, studying, and training as well as the work that was required to produce the good or service.

PRODUCTIVE RESOURCES

CAPITAL GOODS. Capital goods are goods made, not to consume, but to make other goods and services. Machines and tools are capital goods. For example, a hammer is a capital good used by a builder. It is used to help make houses.

ENTREPRENEURSHIP. People who bring together and organize all the other productive resources are called entrepreneurs. Often they are the owners or managers of a business. Entrepreneurs risk their money bringing these resources together in order to make a **profit** — money left after all expenses are paid.

APPLYING WHAT YOU HAVE LEARNED

1. List two natural resources that might be used to build a house.

   • _____   • _____

2. Why are natural resources important for producing goods and services?

   _____

   _____

THE UNEVEN DISTRIBUTION OF PRODUCTIVE RESOURCES

Productive resources — *natural resources, human resources, capital goods* and *entrepreneurship* — are not spread evenly around the world.

Different parts of the world have different climates, different soils and landforms, different bodies of water, and different mineral resources. These differences are not limited to natural resources. Different areas also have people with different training, education, and experience as well.

Ancient Egypt, for example, had many important mineral resources. These resources included copper, tin, gold, and iron. Egypt's copper and tin were used to make bronze. Later, Egyptians used their iron ore to make iron tools and weapons. Gold was used for decoration and became a form of wealth. Other places in the Mediterranean region did not have the same mineral resources that Egypt possessed.

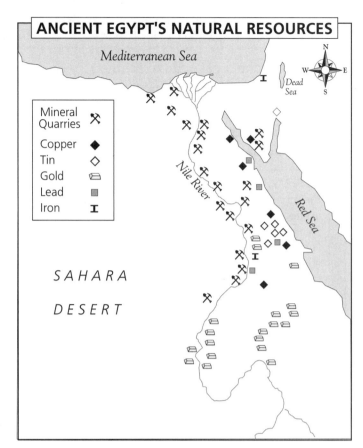

SPECIALIZATION

Even in ancient times, the uneven distribution of both natural and human resources around the world encouraged specialization. **Specialization** is the making of only some types of goods or services. Each region began making more of certain types of goods based on the productive resources it had available. These specialized products were then traded with others to obtain other goods.

For example, the ancient Greeks lived on rocky hillsides that received plenty of sunshine. They could grow grapes and olive trees, but not much wheat. They crushed their olives to produce olive oil for cooking, eating, and using as a skin lotion; they crushed their grapes and turned the juice into wine. The Greeks also became skilled at making clay pottery. The ancient Egyptians, on the other hand, lived along the banks of the Nile. They were able to grow wheat on the flat, fertile lands alongside the river.

A Greek clay pot depicting olive harvesting.

ADVANTAGES TO SPECIALIZATION

Economists see several important advantages to such specialization. Each region can take advantage of its own productive resources. A region may have fertile soil and a mild climate that is suitable for growing particular crops. By specializing in the production of these crops, farmers take advantage of these local characteristics.

As a result, each region tends to produce those goods and services it can make at the *lowest opportunity cost*. It sacrifices less labor and time to make those goods than it would to make their other goods. By providing just a few kinds of goods or services, producers in a region become more skilled at making them. Producers also learn how to make these goods faster and more efficiently. For example, producers in a region might invest in special tools and training to produce these goods. This helps to lower production costs even further.

HOW SPECIALIZATION ENCOURAGES TRADE

Because regions specialize, they rarely produce everything they need. Instead, different regions depend on one another to supply many goods and services. They exchange these goods through trade. **Merchants** bring goods from one place to another, and then sell them in **markets**. Countries and regions thus **export** products they make and **import** products from others.

Imports	Exports
Goods from foreign countries brought into a country for use or sale.	Goods and services sold from one country to other countries.

There are many examples in history that illustrate how specialization leads to trade between regions.

THE MAYA

The ancient Maya, for example, inhabited the Yucatan Peninsula in Mexico. The salt beds that lined the coast of the Yucatan provided salt to the Maya. Salt is an important ingredient in the human diet. The need for salt and its abundance in the Yucatan gave the Maya something to trade with others. In addition to salt, the Maya had obsidian (*volcanic glass*), cacao, seashells and pottery. They exported these goods to their neighbors in the central lowlands of Guatemala. The city-states of Tikal and Copan served as major trading centers. In return, these Guatemalan city-states gave the Mayan their turquoise, jade, and quetzal (*bird*) feathers — goods greatly valued by the Maya as symbols of wealth and status.

ANCIENT EGYPT AND GREECE

Because the Egyptians could grow large amounts of wheat, they could exchange their surplus grain with other Mediterranean peoples, such as the Greeks, for olives, wine, and pottery. It was easier for the Greeks to exchange their olives, wine and pottery for Egyptian grain than it was for them to grow their own wheat on the rocky hillsides of Greece. It was also possible for these peoples to ship their products easily, since they could be carried by boat across the Mediterranean Sea.

ROMAN EMPIRE

The ancient Romans also engaged in extensive trade. Like the Greeks, the Romans shipped goods across the Mediterranean. They exported olive oil and wine from the hillsides of Italy. Sicily and North Africa grew wheat, which was shipped to Rome. Romans also obtained marble from Greece, gold and silver from Spain, and iron ore from Britain. The Romans even traded along overland routes across the steppes, deserts, and mountains of Central Asia in order to obtain cotton and spices from India and silk from Han China.

CASE STUDY: TRADE ALONG THE SILK ROAD

China's climate and soil were well suited to the planting of mulberry trees and the raising of silkworms. The discovery of how to unwind a silkworm's cocoon to make silk cloth was a well-guarded secret in China. When the Romans obtained samples of this wondrous new material, it quickly became prized for its texture, strength and appearance. Wealthy Romans were eager to obtain silk, which came to symbolize wealth and status. Merchants used caravans of camels to cross Syria, Persia, and Central Asia. Other goods traded along this "Silk Road" included gold, furs, porcelain, bamboo wares, ivory and exotic animals and plants.

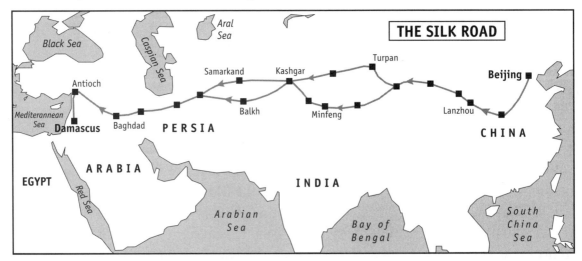

APPLYING WHAT YOU HAVE LEARNED

▼ You have just learned about examples of specialization and trade in Europe, Asia, and the Americas. How did the uneven distribution of resources and specialization also encourage trade between regions in West Africa?

_____

_____

HOW SUPPLY AND DEMAND HELP SET PRICES

When merchants from different regions meet, no central authority sets prices for them. To decide what price something should cost, the buyer and seller usually must bargain with each other. Their bargaining will be influenced by the forces of **supply and demand**.

◆ **Demand** refers to how much people want or need a product. Many factors influence demand. How well does the product satisfy people's needs? Are there alternative products that satisfy the same needs? Is the product something that people must have, or can they do without it? People are also influenced by fashion and taste. Is this product something that everyone else has? Will having this product give the owner more power or status? The stronger the demand for a product, the more expensive it becomes. Buyers are willing to pay more for a product that is useful and valuable.

◆ **Supply** refers to how much of a product is available for sale. If only a small supply of a product is available, it may become very expensive. People will compete to buy it. Ancient Romans, for example, could not make their own silk. They could only buy silk from merchants who brought it across the Silk Road from China. Because silk was so rare, its price was high.

HOW PRICES ARE SET

The **interaction of supply and demand** helps set the price for goods. When the demand for a good is high and only a limited supply is available, its price will be quite high. On the other hand, if there is little demand for a product and a large supply, its price will be low. The interaction of these forces affects the price that a buyer is willing to pay and what a merchant is willing to accept.

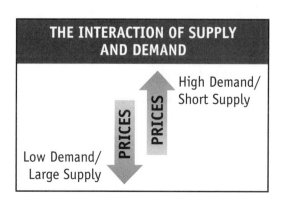

THE INTERACTION OF SUPPLY AND DEMAND

High Demand/ Short Supply

PRICES

PRICES

Low Demand/ Large Supply

APPLYING WHAT YOU HAVE LEARNED

▼ How are prices established in a marketplace if no one tells a seller how much to charge for a good and no one tells the buyer how much to pay?

_____

_____

_____

_____

THE EFFECTS OF WORLD TRADE

The need to exchange goods led to the development of trade and distinct trade patterns between peoples very early in human history.

TRADE ROUTES

Because of geographical factors, trade has often proceeded along certain fixed routes — usually along rivers, across seas, and through valleys and plains. In contrast, mountains, deserts, and dense forests often act as barriers to trade. Trade routes usually connect places with different resources or centers of population. The Mediterranean Sea and the Silk Road across Central Asia are two examples of trade routes. Later, the Atlantic Ocean provided routes linking Europe, Africa, and the Americas. **Merchants** are people who buy goods to sell to others at a higher price. They risk their money to order goods they think others may want. Merchants often pay to ship goods along trade routes from one place to another in order to sell these goods at a higher price.

THE GROWTH OF CITIES

The establishment of specific trade routes has often led to the growth and development of cities. Cities arise where goods are sold or where goods are unloaded to be placed onto a different type of transportation. Here are some examples:

◆ **Alexandria.** The city of Alexandria, located where the Nile River flows into the Mediterranean Sea, became an important Egyptian port. Merchants gathered in Alexandria to trade goods with merchants arriving from other places around the Mediterranean. They traded spices, textiles (*cloth and clothing*), silver, gold and foods. Because merchants living in Alexandria needed food, clothing, homes and other goods, they provided work to local craftsmen. This encouraged the city to grow.

◆ **Constantinople** was another famous city that developed along trade routes. Located on the Black Sea where Europe meets Asia, traders between these two continents crossed through this city. Here, merchants exchanged European goods for Chinese silks and Asian spices.

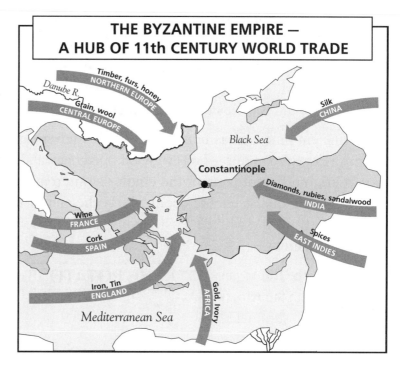

THE BYZANTINE EMPIRE —
A HUB OF 11th CENTURY WORLD TRADE

◆ **Venice** and other cities in Italy were also situated along major trade routes for East-West trade. During the Crusades, merchants in Venice built large fleets to carry Crusaders to the Holy Land. These same fleets were later used to open new markets in the Middle East.

◆ **Timbuktu** arose in West Africa north of the Niger River, on the southern edge of the Sahara. The city was an important center for the gold-salt trade. Arab traders crossed the desert to bring salt, cloth and horses. In exchange, they received gold and slaves. Under Mansa Musa, the city became a center of learning.

◆ **European Colonial Empires and Trade.** After the European conquest of the Americas, trade routes shifted and cities closer to the Atlantic Ocean grew. Several countries established colonies in the "New World." Spain, Portugal, Holland, France and Britain are located at the western end of Europe and benefited from the rise in Atlantic trade. Cities like Lisbon in Portugal, Seville in Spain, and Amsterdam in Holland grew quickly. Merchants exchanged slaves from Africa, **precious metals** (*silver and gold*) from Mexico, sugar cane, fur, tobacco, rice, and indigo (*a blue dye*), from the Americas, and furniture, clothes, and foodstuffs from Europe.

APPLYING WHAT YOU HAVE LEARNED

▼ How does trade react with geographic factors to encourage the growth of cities?

_____

_____

_____

THE INTERDEPENDENCE OF REGIONS

Over time, specialization and trade have made different regions of the world increasingly **interdependent**. Regions become interdependent when they depend on each other to obtain goods and services to meet their economic needs.

In ancient times, areas bordering the Mediterranean Sea grew interdependent through trade. Under Roman rule, goods were shipped back and forth across the Mediterranean Sea or carried to different parts of the empire along roads built by the Romans. After the fall of Rome, long-distance trade declined. By the end of the Middle Ages, trade had revived and goods from the Middle East, India, and China found their way into the fairs and markets of Europe.

In 1492, the European encounter with the Americas greatly stimulated the rise of long-distance trade, specialization, and the interdependence of regions. New food products like the potato spread from its origins in the Andes Mountains across the ocean to Portugal and Spain. From there, the potato spread to other countries in Europe, and finally, to all regions and continents.

Sugar provides another important example of the interdependence of regions. Most sugar is produced from sugar cane

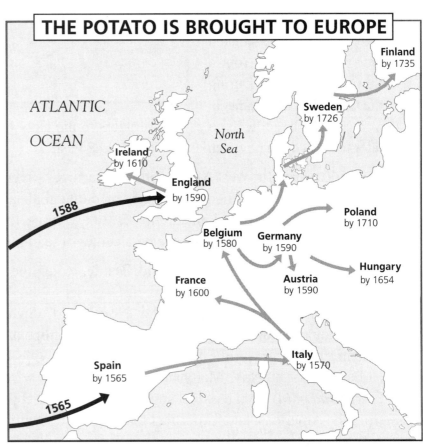

THE POTATO IS BROUGHT TO EUROPE

ATLANTIC OCEAN

North Sea

Finland by 1735

Sweden by 1726

Ireland by 1610

England by 1590

Poland by 1710

Belgium by 1580

Germany by 1590

Hungary by 1654

France by 1600

Austria by 1590

Italy by 1570

Spain by 1565

1588

1565

— a plant that only grows in warm, humid climates. Sugar cane was first grown in India. From there, it spread to the Mediterranean. After the conquest of the Americas, Europeans set up sugar plantations in the West Indies and South America. Enslaved Africans were sent to the Americas to work on these plantations. In the 1500s, sugar was still a luxury good consumed only by kings. By 1700, it had become a widespread household good, sold in street markets. The production of such large quantities of sugar only became possible because of specialization and trade.

Plantations in the Caribbean grew sugar cane for export. European ships carried this sugar to Europe. Meanwhile, foods from the English colonies in North America were sent to feed workers on the plantations. Enslaved Africans were shipped across the Atlantic to provide an unending supply of labor. The plantation owners imported furniture and clothes from Europe in exchange for the sugar. To produce large quantities of sugar, these different regions of the world had thus grown highly interdependent.

WHAT YOU SHOULD KNOW

☐ You should know that each region of the world has different natural resources and human resources. The uneven distribution of productive resources makes it easier for regions to produce some goods and services rather than others.

☐ You should know that regions specialize in what they can produce at the lowest opportunity cost. As a result, regions must trade to obtain those goods and services they do not make.

☐ You should know that trade is an exchange of goods and services. Exports are goods that producers sell outside their country. Imports are the goods and services produced outside a country that are brought inside it.

☐ You should know that supply is how much of a product is available; demand is how much people want it. The interaction of the forces of supply and demand generally establish the prices of goods sold on world markets.

☐ You should know that the need for goods led to the growth of trade, the rise of cities, the establishment of trade routes, and regional interdependence.

CHAPTER STUDY CARDS

Effects of Uneven Distribution of Productive Resources
★ **Regions and Countries.** These have different natural resources, human resources, capital goods, and entrepreneurship.
★ **Specialization.** Countries have the lowest opportunity cost when they specialize in making those things that they can best produce.
★ **Trade.** To obtain other products, countries must exchange the goods they make with other countries through trade.

Specialization and Trade in History
★ Since ancient times, different areas of the world have traded with other parts of the world. For example, trade between Han China and the Roman Empire was conducted across the **Silk Road.**
★ Throughout history, cities have emerged along key trade routes. Such cities include Alexandria, Seville, Constantinople, Venice, Timbuktu, Lisbon, and Amsterdam.

CHECKING YOUR UNDERSTANDING

Look at the boxes below.

Ancient Greece Wine, olive oil	**Ancient Egypt** Gold, wheat

1. What was one important result of the specialization shown in the boxes?

   A. Greeks copied Egyptian farming techniques.

   B. Greeks and Egyptians traded products with each other.

   C. Egyptians stopped drinking Greek wine.

   D. Egyptians sent explorers across the Sahara Desert in search of olive oil.

   ECO
   B: 6.3

*First, **examine** the question. This question tests your understanding of the factors that lead to trade. You should **recall** that ancient Egypt and ancient Greece each had different productive resources. This led them to specialize in making different products. To meet their other needs, they traded goods. It was less advantageous for Greeks to grow wheat or for Egyptians to produce wine. Now, **apply** this information to the answer choices. **Choice B** is clearly the best answer.*

Now try answering some additional questions on your own.

2. Which statement identifies an important reason why countries and regions specialize in their production?

   A. The region becomes more self-sufficient.

   B. Producers in the region have lower opportunity costs.

   C. Producers in the region require fewer capital goods.

   D. The region is less affected by its share of productive resources.

   ECO
   A: 7.1

3. The merchants of Renaissance Italy prospered through control of which trade?

   A. the Trans-Atlantic slave trade

   B. the trans-Saharan trade in gold and salt

   C. the East-West trade between Asia and Europe

   D. trade between Italy and North Africa across the Mediterranean

   ECO
   B: 7.2

4. Which is the **best** example of a "trade-off"?

    A. Sarah has a disagreement with her best friend.
    B. Jamal enjoys listening to both classical and rap music.
    C. Samuel wants more things than he can afford.
    D. Keisha gives up her lunch money to make a donation to UNICEF.

    ECO
    A: 6.2

Look at the flow chart below:

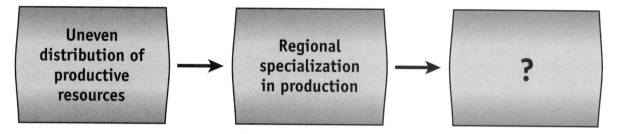

5. Which phrase **best** completes the flow chart?

    A. decreased consumption   C. political conflicts
    B. interdependence of regions   D. higher opportunity costs

    ECO
    A: 7.1

Look at the incomplete outline below.

I. _____
   A. Natural Resources
   B. Human Resources
   C. Capital Goods
   D. Entrepreneurship

6. Which heading belongs in blank line of the outline?

    A. Types of Economic Systems
    B. Opportunity Costs
    C. Productive Resources
    D. Public Goods and Services

    ECO
    A: 6.1

7. The uneven distribution of productive resources around the world has led to specialization, trade and interdependence.

    In your **Answer Document**, identify and describe one example from ancient times in which the uneven distribution of resources led to specialization, trade or interdependence. (2 points)

    ECO
    B: 6.2

_____

_____

LOOKING AT GOVERNMENT

The Greek philosopher Aristotle once wrote that people are social beings. They need to live in groups or combinations to obtain food and shelter, to raise their children, and to protect themselves from hostile outsiders.

Every community makes some rules about how its members should behave. Each community also needs some authority to resolve disagreements, to enforce community rules, and to protect the community from attacks from outsiders.

WHAT IS GOVERNMENT?

The organization set up to protect the community and enforce its rules is called the **government**. Just as a pilot guides a ship, a government guides the members of a community in their dealings with themselves and outsiders. In general, governments are created for two purposes. First, governments protect the lives, liberty, and property of members of the com-

Building roads is one of those services for which we depend on government.

munity. Second, governments provide services, like educating children and building roads, that individuals usually cannot do for themselves.

THE POWERS OF GOVERNMENT

All governments are given special powers to carry out their decisions over the members of society. These powers include:

- a *legislative* power to make the laws

- an *executive* power to carry out the laws

- a *judicial* power to interpret and apply the laws

Think about how your own school is governed. It has its own unique form of government. The school board acts as a *legislature*, making important rules for the school. Your school principal acts as an *executive* with authority to carry out the rules set by the school board. The principal is assisted by teachers and other staff members. Finally, your local school may have special committees to decide disagreements and interpret school rules.

PUBLIC GOODS AND SERVICES

Some goods and services needed by a community are too expensive to be provided by individuals. For example, every community needs roads, schools, police and defense. These goods and services are generally provided by the government. Goods and services that the government provides are known as **public goods and services**. A key characteristic of a public good is that many individuals can use it.

A person cannot be prevented from using a public good even though he or she has not individually paid for it. For example, a public park and the national defense are public goods. On the other hand, your radio, DVD player, or notebook are goods owned by a private individual. They are not public goods: they are private property.

The U.S. Army provides a public service — our national defense.

APPLYING WHAT YOU HAVE LEARNED

▼ What would a society be like if there were no government? _____

_____

_____

▼ Give one example of a public good or service and one example of a private good or service:

• Public Good or Service: _____

• Private Good or Service: _____

TYPES OF GOVERNMENT

In this chapter, you will examine what governments do — how they protect people's lives, liberty, and property, and how they provide services and public goods. You will learn about the three major types of government: monarchy democracy and dictatorship. You will also examine the rights and responsibilities citizens enjoy under each type of government.

MAJOR IDEAS

GOVERNMENT, BENCHMARKS A, B AND C
CITIZENSHIP, BENCHMARK A

A. The organization that people set up to protect the community and to enforce its rules is called **government**. The role of government in a society is to protect the lives, liberties and property of members of the community, and to provide services that individuals cannot provide on their own.

B. There are three main types of government:
  - In a **monarchy**, a hereditary ruler controls the government and decides what to do.
  - In a **democracy**, ordinary citizens hold supreme power, and all decisions stem from those citizens.
  - In a **dictatorship**, power rests in the hands of an individual or a small group that tells everyone else what to do.

C. The rights and responsibilities of citizens vary from one type of government to another.
  - In a **democracy**, people participate in government decision-making by voting and running for office. They also enjoy many basic individual rights.
  - In a **monarchy**, a few people participate by advising the monarch.
  - In a **dictatorship**, people have no right to criticize or oppose government actions; however, they can participate in activities organized by the government.

TYPES OF GOVERNMENTS

Today, the world consists of a large number of sovereign, independent nation states. Their governments generally fall into three types, *monarchy*, *democracy*, or *dictatorship*.

MONARCHY

Monarchy is the oldest of these three forms of government. It probably first emerged when one strong leader seized control. The pharaoh of Egypt, for example, was a powerful monarch. The main characteristic of a monarchy is that the ruler *inherits* power. When the ruler dies, power automatically passes to one of the monarch's children or close relatives. There are two main types of monarchies:

◆ In older forms of monarchy, the king or queen claimed absolute power over his or her subjects. Rulers often claimed to hold their power by "**divine right**" — or the will of God. Ordinary people had no rights or freedoms, except those the monarch allowed.

◆ In England in 1215, King John signed the **Magna Carta**. This document limited the king's power in England. It gave citizens freedom from prison and protection of their property, except after a trial by a jury or according to the laws of the land. It also limited the king's right to raise new taxes.

◆ In more recent times, many monarchs have shared power with an elected legislature. Subjects of the monarch enjoy many traditional, protected rights. This system is known as **constitutional monarchy**. Great

King Henry VIII of England was a monarch.

Britain provides an example of a constitutional monarchy. Today, Britain has a hereditary monarch and an elected Parliament. The monarch serves as a symbolic head of state, while elected officials in Parliament govern the country.

DEMOCRACY

In a **democracy**, government authority is based on the people's consent. People either vote on issues directly, or they elect representatives who make government decisions for them.

Athens: The First Democracy. The first democracy arose in ancient Athens in the fifth century B.C. In fact, the very word **democracy** is Greek for "people-power." Citizens of Athens assembled to make important decisions facing their city-state. They voted on issues directly. This system is sometimes referred to as a **direct democracy**.

The Romans developed the first **representative democracy**. Different social groups elected their own representatives, who met in assemblies like the **Senate**. These representatives elected **Consuls** to act as executives, running the government and enforcing the law.

Later in history, various countries developed their own national assemblies of elected representatives. In England, landowners elected representatives to the **House of Commons**, one of the two houses in the English Parliament. When the English set up colonies in North America, each colony had its own colonial legislature. After the United States became independent, it created an elected national assembly known as **Congress**.

In a democracy, people also enjoy certain basic individual rights, like free speech. This gives them the confidence to criticize the government freely.

Remains of the Roman Forum, where the Senate once met.

DICTATORSHIP

A **dictatorship** is a system of government in which a single person or a small group of people exercises complete power over others. The dictator does not inherit his authority like a king. He either seizes control by force, or is placed into a position of authority by others. Dictators are free to do as they please, while other citizens in a dictatorship have few rights. Ordinary citizens in a dictatorship have very little influence over government policies

The main advantage of a dictatorship is that decisions can be made quickly. In ancient times, the Romans appointed a dictator when they were at war and needed strong leadership. When the war was over, the dictator was supposed to give up his power.

Rome's Julius Caesar was a dictator.

In the twentieth century, modern dictators like **Adolf Hitler** in Germany, **Joseph Stalin** in the Soviet Union, and **Saddam Hussein** in Iraq seized power.

Each of these brutal dictators used modern technology to impose their will on fellow citizens. Radio and television, magazines and movies were controlled by the dictator and repeated the dictator's views. Other views were suppressed. Individuals had no rights and very little influence over the government. Those who spoke out against the dictator were sent to concentration camps or gulags, where they were severely punished or killed. The dictator was not limited by the rule of law or any other restraints.

Saddam Hussein was one of the world's most brutal dictators.

APPLYING WHAT YOU HAVE LEARNED

Compare the main characteristics of monarchy, democracy, and dictatorship.

Government Type	Main Characteristics	How Government Leaders Are Chosen	What Powers Government Have
Monarchy			
Democracy			
Dictatorship			

THE ROLE OF THE CITIZEN

Each of these three main forms of government has its own view of the citizen's proper role in the **political process** — the process through which decisions about government are made. In a dictatorship or traditional monarchy, for example, the ruler has complete control over all decisions. Even under these systems of government, however, citizens still have some role to play in the political process.

MONARCHY

Even in an **absolute monarchy**, where the ruler's will is supreme, the ruler to some degree depends on the cooperation of his or her subjects. Usually one social class, the nobility, command great wealth and influence. These nobles often form a council that advises the king. They serve as officers in the army and as judges on their country estates, where they help to keep order. Commoners (*non-nobles*) also have some role. They might express their views in petitions to the monarch. In **constitutional monarchies**, citizens have assemblies like the House of Commons in England. This body once advised the king and voted on new taxes, but now governs the country.

The British Parliament where the House of Lords and House of Commons meet.

DEMOCRACY

In a democracy, the entire political process is based on **civic participation**. Citizens stay informed on issues, write their representatives, join political parties, run for political office, vote in elections, and serve in government. They are also free to criticize government policy and can even form opposing political parties. In a democracy, civic participation is essential. A majority of ordinary citizens either elect officials or directly determine what the government does.

Civic participation in a democracy begins with its educational system. Civic learning teaches the fundamental ideas of democracy and prepares young people to exercise the rights and responsibilities of citizens in a democracy. Students are instructed in the procedures of government, and encouraged to become involved in the democratic process.

Voting is one important way in which citizens participate in a democracy. It is a right and a responsibility.

DICTATORSHIP

Although modern dictators wield absolute power, they also depend on the support of thousands, or even millions, of people to do so. Usually, a dictator rules with the help of a political party. Adolf Hitler, for example, was the leader of the Nazi Party. In the 1930s, millions of Germans participated in politics by joining the Nazi Party. They held mas-

sive rallies and demonstrations to show their support for Hitler. Nevertheless, a dictatorship usually allows only one party, which is controlled by the dictator. Citizens can only participate in support of the dictator. Opponents of the government have no way to participate. Protesters are severely punished. Dictators also depend on the support of the military. Usually they take swift action against any political opponents or military leaders who appear to be disloyal.

Massive demonstrations were held in Germany to show support for Hitler.

APPLYING WHAT YOU HAVE LEARNED

1. Why are some forms of civic participation necessary even in an absolute monarchy or dictatorship? _____

_____

2. Compare civic participation under the different forms of government by completing the chart below.

Form of Government	Civic Participation
Monarchy	
Democracy	
Dictatorship	

WHAT YOU SHOULD KNOW

☐ You should know that the organization that people set up to protect the community and to enforce its rules is called government.

☐ You should know that the role of government is to protect the lives, liberties and property of members of the community, and to provide services individuals cannot provide on their own.

☐ You should know that there are three main types of government. In a monarchy, a hereditary ruler controls the government and decides what to do. In a democracy, ordinary citizens hold supreme power. They elect representatives or vote on issues directly. In a dictatorship, power rests in the hands of an individual or a small group that tells everyone else what to do.

☐ You should know that the degree of participation in government varies from one type of government to another. In a democracy, people participate in government decision-making by voting and running for office. In a monarchy, some people participate by advising the monarch. In a dictatorship, people have no right to criticize or oppose government actions; however, they can participate in activities organized by the government.

CHAPTER STUDY CARDS

Types of Governments

★ **Monarchy.** Rule by a king, queen or emperor. The ruler inherits power. Many monarchs claimed to rule by "divine right."

★ **Dictatorship.** One leader or a small group seizes power. Common citizens have no individual rights. The dictator uses force against opponents; citizens can only participate in support of the government.

★ **Democracy.** Common citizens decide issues directly (*direct democracy*) or elect representatives to decide issues (*representative democracy*). There are many opportunities for civic participation.

Why Governments are Created

★ Governments help protect the lives, property, and liberty of the members of the community.

★ Governments provide services to the community that individuals cannot provide for themselves.

Public Services and Goods

Something produced or owned by the government that is provided free to all its citizens. Examples include:

★ **Public Services:** defense, police, public education, postal services, public television, and fire protection.

★ **Public Goods:** parks, roads, and schools.

CHECKING YOUR UNDERSTANDING

Look at the information in the boxes below.

Usually has a single ruler	**Ruler is not bound by law**	**People have no rights**

1. Which two types of government are most closely associated with these characteristics?

    A. dictatorship and representative democracy
    B. constitutional monarchy and democracy
    C. direct democracy and dictatorship
    D. absolute monarchy and dictatorship

    > GOVT
    > C: 6.4

> *Begin by carefully **examining** the question. This question tests your understanding of the three main types of government. You should **recall** what a monarchy, democracy, and dictatorship are. Both a monarchy and a dictatorship often have a strong ruler. **Applying** this information to the answer choices, you should realize that **Choice D** is the best answer.*

Now try answering some additional questions on your own.

2. What would a supporter of monarchy **most** likely favor?

    A. Control of government should be given to wealthy individuals.
    B. All important laws must be passed by the people.
    C. The government should be ruled by a king or queen.
    D. Citizens should be allowed to elect their rulers freely.

    > GOVT
    > C: 6.4

3. How does a dictatorship differ from a democracy?

    A. In a dictatorship, individuals have no basic rights.
    B. In a dictatorship, there are separate social classes.
    C. In a dictatorship, people always trust their leader.
    D. In a dictatorship, there is strong support for public education.

    > GOVT
    > C: 6.4

4. Which is an example of a public good?

   A. a pet dog that a man takes wherever he goes
   B. a road built and maintained by the local community
   C. a television set that a woman shares with her neighbors
   D. a roadside billboard advertising a new soup mix

   > ECO
   > C: 6.3

5. What kind of government is characterized by a ruler who inherits power and is free to do as he or she pleases, while citizens have few if any rights?

   A. a constitutional monarchy
   B. a democracy
   C. an absolute monarchy
   D. a dictatorship

   > GOVT
   > C: 6.4

6. Which correctly pairs an ancient society with its form of government?

   A. Athens — direct democracy
   B. Roman Republic — absolute monarchy
   C. Egypt — representative democracy
   D. Sparta — direct democracy

   > GOVT
   > C: 7.1

7. Which phrase identifies an important reason why people create a government?

   A. to provide any good or service needed by citizens
   B. to protect the lives, liberty, and property of people
   C. to maintain its people's standards of living
   D. to insure that every citizen has healthcare and a good job

   > GOVT
   > A: 6.1

8. In which form of government do citizens enjoy the right to assemble, to criticize the actions of government officials, and to elect the head of state?

   A. representative democracy
   B. constitutional monarchy
   C. dictatorship
   D. absolute monarchy

   > CITIZ
   > B: 6.2

9. Countries are governed by three main types of government — monarchy, dictatorship, and democracy.

   In your **Answer Document**, select one of these types and describe two of its characteristics. (2 points)

   > GOVT
   > C: 6.4

HOW GOVERNMENTS INTERACT

In this chapter, you will learn about countries and how their governments interact.

MAJOR IDEAS

GOVERNMENT, BENCHMARK A

A. The world is divided into **countries** with sovereign governments.

B. A **sovereign government** exercises supreme authority over its territory.

C. Countries are further divided into **states** or **provinces** and **cities** and **towns**.

D. Today, most countries are **nation-states**. However, there have been many other types of territories with sovereign governments. These include:

- A **city-state** is a small area under a single government. A city-state could be a monarchy, democracy or dictatorship.

- A **kingdom** consists of an entire country or people ruled by a monarch — a king or queen.

- An **empire** consists of one country ruling over one or more other nations, territories or peoples. An empire is often ruled by an emperor.

E. Sovereign governments interact in many ways. These interactions include **diplomacy**, signing **treaties**, participating in **international organizations**, and engaging in **military conflict**.

WHAT IS A COUNTRY?

A **country** is any place that has (1) borders (*boundaries*) separating it from its neighbors; and (2) its own **sovereign government**. A government is **sovereign** if there is no higher official authority within the area it controls. A sovereign government has supreme power.

States and Provinces. Most countries are further divided into smaller political units known as **states** or **provinces**. Both the United States and Mexico are divided into states. Canada is divided into provinces. States and provinces are **not** sovereign: they are subject to the authority of their national or central government.

Counties, Cities, and Towns. States and provinces are often further divided into smaller political units known as **counties**. These may be divided into even smaller governing units called **cities** and **towns**. Smaller government units are often better able to take care of local problems than larger units can.

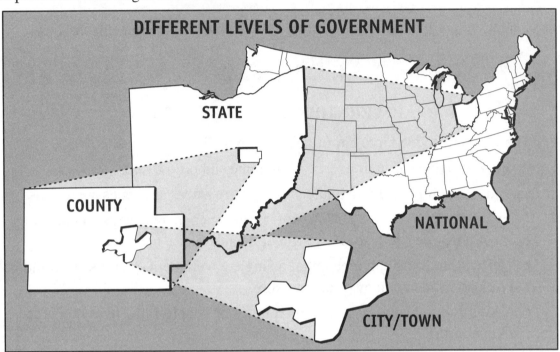

DIFFERENT LEVELS OF GOVERNMENT

STATE

COUNTY

NATIONAL

CITY/TOWN

APPLYING WHAT YOU HAVE LEARNED

▼ Give one example of a sovereign government in the world today.

_____

▼ Identify two characteristics that demonstrate that the example you named above is sovereign.

1. _____

2. _____

SOVEREIGN GOVERNMENTS IN HISTORY

Today, most countries are **nation-states**. Most countries have territory that is larger than a single city, but not as large as an empire. They consist of an entire people, or **nation**, with a common cultural heritage and identity. In the past, however, there was a much greater variety of sovereign territories. Among the most common forms of sovereign territories were *city-states*, *kingdoms*, and *empires*.

CITY-STATES

A **city-state** is the most ancient form of "country" with its own sovereign government. The earliest known city-states arose in Mesopotamia.

Mesopotamia. Archaeologists believe that after the Neolithic Revolution, people in the villages of Mesopotamia generally made decisions for themselves. As villages grew larger, residents found it necessary to select someone in times of trouble. At first this ruler was appointed only during times of crisis. Eventually the "king" made himself the permanent ruler over the city-state. Ancient cities like Sumer, Ur, Assyria, and Babylon in Mesopotamia were all ruled by powerful kings, who exercised control with their armies and the support of their priests. They collected grain and taxes from the surrounding countryside.

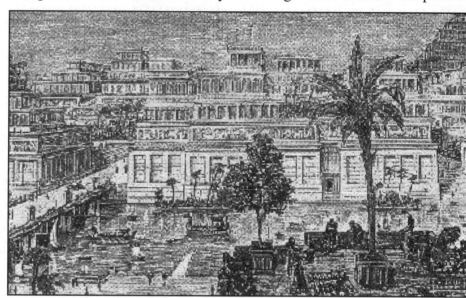
An artist's rendering of ancient Babylon

Ancient Greece. Centuries later, Greece was home to separate city-states like Athens and Sparta. These city-states were separated by mountains. Each city-state governed a single city and its surrounding countryside. Most Greek city-states were governed by kings. However, Athens developed the world's first democracy. This city-state was small enough for all adult male citizens to vote on issues directly. Most Athenians, however, were not citizens. After a series of devastating wars, the Greek city-states collapsed. Both Athens and Sparta were conquered by the neighboring kingdom of Macedonia.

Ancient Rome. Rome also began as a city-state. The city of Rome governed itself and the surrounding area. Gradually, Rome expanded to govern Italy and much of the Mediterranean world. Rome changed from a city-state to an empire.

Middle Ages. In the Middle Ages, there were many independent city-states, especially in Italy and Germany: examples include Florence and Venice. Some of these city-states were ruled by powerful noble families. Florence was governed by an alliance of wealthy merchants and nobles. Many of these city-states also developed representative institutions, such as elected town councils and officials.

A few city-states, like Singapore, still exist today.

APPLYING WHAT YOU HAVE LEARNED

▼ City-states might be called the world's first "countries." Explain this statement.

_____

_____

KINGDOMS

A **kingdom** is a country ruled by a king or queen. Usually a kingdom consists of more territory than a city-state. The king often claims the right to rule over an entire people — such as the English, French, or Scottish — and their traditional homeland. For most of history, kingdoms were the most common form of government. They existed not only in Europe, but in Africa, Asia, and the Americas. Because a king is a type of monarch, kingdoms are always monarchies. Nevertheless, some kings have granted limited rights to their subjects. In England, King John granted his subjects important rights in the Magna Carta. Later, the English king called together representatives from throughout England to form a Parliament. A kingdom with representative features and the rule of law is known as a **constitutional monarchy**.

EMPIRES

An **empire** is a country that rules over both itself and one or more foreign peoples. **Alexander the Great** created one of the greatest empires in history when he conquered Persia, Egypt and the Indus Valley. Rome became an empire when it conquered the Greeks, Egyptians, Persians, Gauls and Britons.

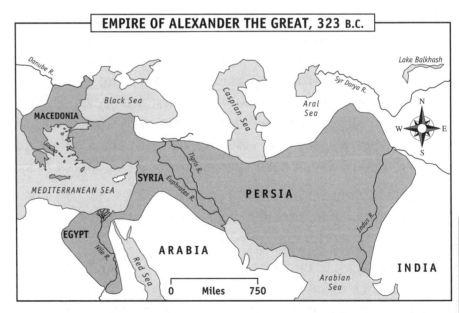

EMPIRE OF ALEXANDER THE GREAT, 323 B.C.

Shih Huang-ti conquered neighboring states to created the Ch'in Empire in China. Later, **Ghengis Khan** created an empire when the Mongols conquered Central Asia and parts of China and Russia.

An empire is usually ruled by an all-powerful monarch, known as the emperor. However, any country that conquers and governs foreign territories might be considered an empire. Spain created an empire when it conquered the Aztecs and Incas, even though the ruler of Spain remained known as the king. The word **imperialism** comes from empire.

APPLYING WHAT YOU HAVE LEARNED

The form of government that an area has can be influenced by the type of country it is. Show how this is true by completing the chart below.

	Example	Form of Government (for example, democracy or monarchy)
City-State		
Kingdom		
Empire		

HOW GOVERNMENTS INTERACT

Different types of sovereign territories — city-states, kingdoms, and empires — have existed side by side for most of history. Although each of these governments is sovereign within its own territory, it still must deal with other sovereign governments beyond its borders. These other governments often have common or conflicting goals. They might threaten the future existence of a country, or offer the possibility of helping it to prosper and grow. No world government exists to oversee relationships between countries. Instead, sovereign governments must rely on their own resources and skill to survive in a dangerous and often hostile world. To do so, sovereign governments interact in the following ways:

DIPLOMACY AND NEGOTIATION

In the Middle Ages, rulers sent envoys to other kingdoms when they had a message to convey. In Renaissance Italy, city-states began the practice of sending a permanent representative, known as the **ambassador**, to reside in a foreign city-state or kingdom. The ambassador watched out for his ruler's political and commercial interests. Other countries soon adopted this practice.

Diplomacy is based on the continuing practice of sending representatives to other countries. When there is a problem, these representatives discuss the issue in an attempt to find a solution. In **negotiations** between governments there is a general give-and-take. Each side usually gives up something to find a middle ground that is acceptable to all.

TREATIES

A **treaty** is a signed agreement between countries. Treaties are similar to contracts between individuals. In a treaty, each of the participating countries promises to do certain things. Sometimes, countries sign a treaty of **alliance**, promising to defend each other if attacked. Peace treaties are used to end wars. For example, the Thirty Years War in Germany ended when diplomats representing different countries met in Westphalia in 1648 and signed a peace treaty.

INTERNATIONAL MEETINGS AND ORGANIZATIONS

Governments also interact through meetings and by participation in international organizations. Before signing the peace treaty of 1648, diplomats representing France, Spain and other countries held long meetings at Westphalia. Today, the **European Union** is an organization of European governments that was formed to promote trade and unity, while the **United Nations** tries to promote international peace.

MILITARY CONFLICTS

Sometimes sovereign governments cannot agree on issues dividing them, even after negotiations or conferences. Then they may decide to pursue their interests through war. Military conflicts usually break out when one or both governments think they can win the conflict, and when they cannot see any other way of resolving their difficulty. Sometimes countries engage in war simply to conquer other countries and take their resources. Rome attacked its neighbors to add them to its empire. The Aztecs and Incas created large em-

Aztec warriors prepare to do battle with Spanish conquistadores.

pires by waging wars of conquest on their neighbors. Both empires later fell when Spain attacked them to seize their wealth. Governments may also engage in war for religious motives. Arab rulers waged war to expand Islam in the Middle East, and Christians and Muslims later fought one another during the Crusades.

APPLYING WHAT YOU HAVE LEARNED

▼ Identify two ways that governments of different countries interact. For each type of interaction you select, provide an example.

A. _____

_____

B. _____

_____

WHAT YOU SHOULD KNOW

☐ You should know that the world is divided into countries with sovereign governments. A sovereign government exercises supreme authority over its territory.

☐ You should know that countries are further divided into states or provinces and cities and towns. Most countries are nation-states. However, there have been many types of sovereign states, including city-states, kingdoms, and empires.

☐ You should know that sovereign governments interact in many ways. These interactions include diplomacy, signing treaties, participating in international organizations, and engaging in military conflicts.

CHAPTER STUDY CARDS

Types of Sovereign Territories

A **country** has a sovereign national government and well-defined borders. A **sovereign** government has supreme authority within its own territory.
★ **City-states** are small areas under a single government.
★ **Kingdoms** consist of an entire country ruled by a monarch — a king or queen.
★ **Empires** are countries that rule over one or more foreign nations, territories or peoples.

How Governments Interact

Sovereign governments interact with each other through the use of:
★ **Diplomacy.** The practice of conducting negotiations between countries
★ **Treaties.** These agreements are similar to contracts negotiated between countries.
★ **International Meetings and International Organizations.** Countries meet or join international organizations.
★ **Military Conflicts.** Governments unable to resolve their disputes enter into armed conflict with each other.

CHECKING YOUR UNDERSTANDING

1. Which example illustrates countries interacting in an international organization?

    A. France and the United States vote in the United Nations to impose sanctions against Iran.
    B. Japan launches an attack on American ships stationed at Pearl Harbor, Hawaii.
    C. The leaders of the United States and Russia meet in Iceland.
    D. Canada signs a commercial fishing treaty with Japan.

    GOVT
    A: 6.3

HINT

*First, **examine** the question. This question asks about the ways countries interact. Choice A describes the participation of France and the United States in the United Nations, an international organization. Choice B describes one country attacking another. Choice C shows international negotiations between two countries, while Choice D describes a treaty. Now, **apply** this information to the answer choices. The best answer is **Choice A**.*

Now try answering some additional questions on your own.

2. What do city-states, kingdoms and empires have in common?

    A. They are territories that are smaller than provinces.
    B. They are different forms of sovereign countries.
    C. They are the earliest known forms of dictatorship.
    D. They are forms of democratic government.

    GOVT
    C: 7.2

Look at the outline below.

> I. _____
>   A. Defined territory with borders
>   B. A settled population
>   C. No higher authority within its borders

3. Which heading **best** completes the outline?

    A. Characteristics of an Empire
    B. Government Interactions
    C. Characteristics of Cultural Regions
    D. Characteristics of a Sovereign Country

    GOVT
    A: 6.2

4. Sovereign governments interact in many ways. During the Renaissance, Italian city-states sent envoys to live in other city-states in order to keep an eye on their ruler's interests. Which type of interaction does this illustrate?

   A. participation in an international organization
   B. managing relations through diplomacy
   C. membership in an international meeting
   D. pursing a sovereign's interests by threatening military conflict

   GOVT
   A: 6.3

5. Governments often seek to resolve disputes through negotiations.

   Which form of government interaction is most likely to result if negotiations over a major issue concerning the vital security of both countries fail?

   A. a cultural exchange between the two countries
   B. a military conflict
   C. the conclusion of a new peace treaty
   D. the creation of a new international organization

   GOVT
   A: 6.3

Look at the Venn diagram below.

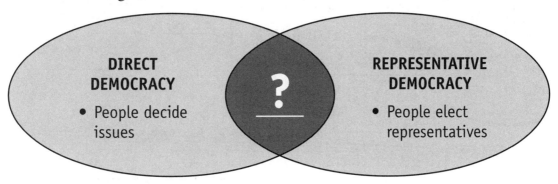

6. Which phrase **best** completes the Venn diagram?

   A. ruthless efficiency in times of danger
   B. political power rests with the people
   C. a lack of individual rights
   D. government by terror

   GOVT
   A: 6.4

7. Political regions are often divided into different types of governments.

   In your **Answer Document**, identify two ways that countries may be divided into smaller regions, and provide one example of each. (4 points)

   GOVT
   A: 6.2

_____

_____

_____

UNIT 4: ECONOMICS AND GOVERNMENT CONCEPT MAP

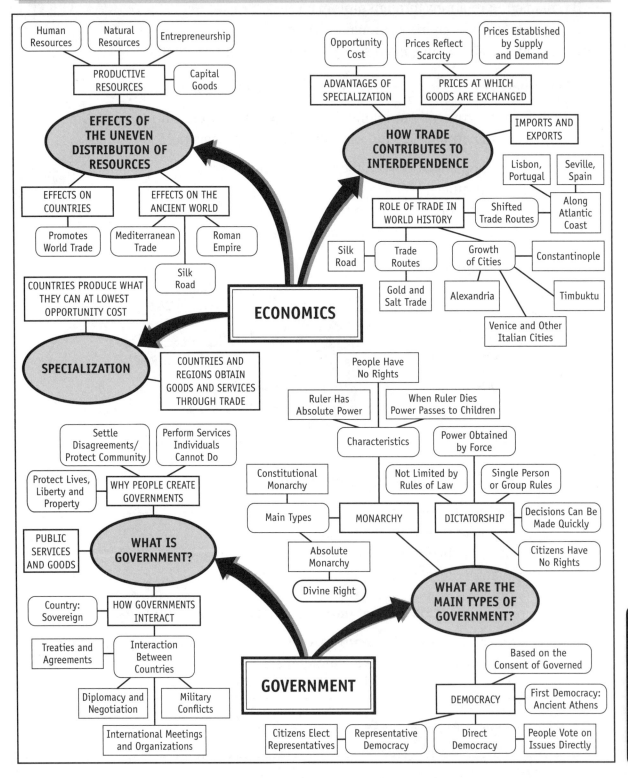

TESTING YOUR UNDERSTANDING

1. In Greece, the soil is quite rocky. However, the hillsides are excellent for growing grapes. The ancient Greeks excelled at making wine and pottery. It was easier for them to exchange their wine and pottery for Egyptian grain than it was for them to grow their own wheat.

   What does this example illustrate?

   ECO
   A: 7.1

   A. The Greeks grew the best olives in the Mediterranean region.
   B. By specializing in making certain products, people can take advantage of local characteristics.
   C. Although the soil in ancient Greece was rocky, an important civilization developed there.
   D. Ancient Greeks had special training in the production of wine and pottery.

2. Throughout the world, different regions produce different goods and services.

   What **best** explains why some regions produce more of certain goods and services than others?

   ECO
   A: 6.1

   A. the uneven distribution of productive resources
   B. the desire of some regions to become wealthier
   C. the interaction of supply and demand
   D. the attempts by rulers to attain self-sufficiency

Look at the information in the boxes below.

ROMAN EMPIRE	ANCIENT HAN CHINA
Wine, olive oil	Ceramics, silk, porcelain, bamboo wares, ivory

3. These boxes show some of the products that each society specialized in producing.

   Based on this information, what was an important outcome of this specialization?

   ECO
   B: 7.2

   A. Han China produced wine.
   B. Rome and China stopped all trading with each other.
   C. Merchants crossed Asia along the Silk Road.
   D. China sold most of its porcelain products in Africa.

4. Which is an example of civic participation permitted in a dictatorship?

   A. voting to elect critics of the dictator
   B. attending demonstrations to show support of the government
   C. writing letters to newspapers attacking government policies
   D. joining a political party opposed to the government

   <kbd>CITIZ A: 7.1</kbd>

5. Countries use a variety of methods to settle disputes. In what way do most developed nations today settle disputes with other countries?

   A. military conflict
   B. appeal to the International Court
   C. diplomacy and negotiation
   D. economic blockade

   <kbd>GOVT A: 6.3</kbd>

6. Which is the correct order of organization of these government units from smallest to largest?

   A. country, province, city   C. city, province, country
   B. province, city, country   D. country, city, province

   <kbd>GOVT A: 6.2</kbd>

Look at the map of the Western Mediterranean around 300 B.C.

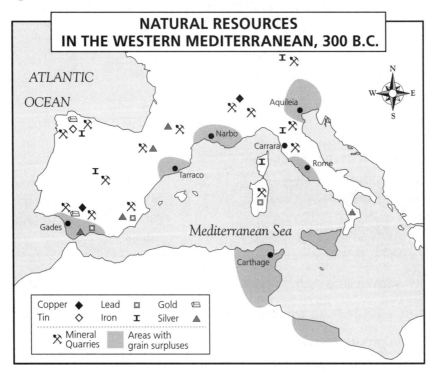

NATURAL RESOURCES IN THE WESTERN MEDITERRANEAN, 300 B.C.

7. Based on this map, what goods might have been traded at Tarraco?

   A. lead for gold   C. grain for silver
   B. copper for lead   D. tin for iron

   <kbd>ECO B: 7.2</kbd>

8. The Silk Road was a major trading route between Europe and Asia.

   What goods did the Roman Empire import from Han China along the Silk Road?

   A. sugar cane and rice
   B. clay pottery and olive oil
   C. tobacco and potatoes
   D. silks and porcelain

   ECO
   B: 7.2

9. After a severe drought, the number of oranges harvested from orange trees decreases. What effect will this most likely have on the price of orange juice?

   A. The price will decrease.
   B. The price will remain the same.
   C. The price will increase.
   D. The price will decrease, then increase.

   ECO
   B: 6.5

10. Which is an example of civic participation in a democracy?

    A. People have the freedom to choose their own goods and services.
    B. People have the responsibility to save for their retirement.
    C. People vote to elect their leaders.
    D. People can watch a variety of news programs.

    CITIZ
    A: 6.1

11. Which type of government was ruled by Louis XIV of France, Peter the Great of Russia, and George III of England?

    A. dictatorship   C. direct democracy
    B. representative democracy D. monarchy

    GOVT
    C: 6.4

12. In a democracy, the political process is based on civic participation.

    In your **Answer Document**, describe two ways that citizens participate in a democracy. (2 points)

    CITIZ
    A: 6.1

    _____

    _____

13. The uneven distribution of resources in the world has had important effects.

    In your **Answer Document**, explain how the uneven distribution of resources has affected two different societies. (4 points)

    ECO
    A: 7.1

    _____

    _____

    _____

14. Which type of government has an ability to act quickly in an emergency as one of its advantages, but also denies individual rights to its citizens?

    A. direct democracy
    B. constitutional monarchy

    C. representative democracy
    D. dictatorship

    GOVT
    C: 6.4

Look at the map of the Eastern Mediterranean about 300 B.C.

15. Based on this map, which goods did Egyptians most likely use for trade with other places in the region?

    A. grains and tin
    B. iron and copper
    C. timber and copper
    D. grains and iron

    ECO
    A: 7.1

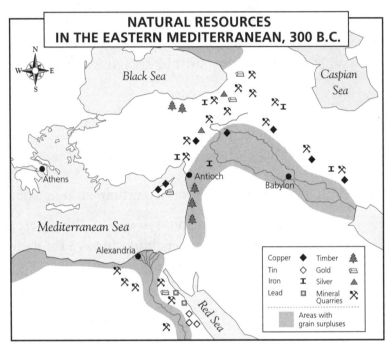

NATURAL RESOURCES IN THE EASTERN MEDITERRANEAN, 300 B.C.

16. The ancient Maya had a surplus of salt from salt beds lining the coast of the Yucatan Peninsula. The city-states of Tikal and Copan, in nearby Guatemala, had a large supply of turquoise, jade, and unusual bird feathers. These products were rare among the Maya.

    In your **Answer Document**, identify three goods that were imported or exported between these regions and explain how this trade made these regions interdependent. (4 points)

    ECO
    B: 6.4

    _____

    _____

    _____

17. In your **Answer Document**, identify and explain one way that citizens can participate in the political process in a monarchy, and identify and explain one way that citizens can participate in the political process in a direct democracy. (4 points)

    CITIZ
    A: 7.1

    _____

    _____

    _____

A FINAL
PRACTICE TEST

This chapter consists of a complete practice test just like the one you will take next year in eighth grade. Like the **Ohio Achievement Test**, this test includes of multiple-choice, short-answer, and extended-response questions. Before you begin, let's review a few hints for taking this test:

◆ **Answer All Questions.** Do not leave questions unanswered. There is no penalty for guessing. Blank answers are counted as wrong.

◆ **Use the "E-R-A Approach."** Be sure you are aware of what the question asks. Make sure to carefully **Examine** each question before you attempt to answer it. Then **Recall** what you know. Think about what you can remember about the main topic of the question. Finally, **Apply** what you know. Choose the response that best answers the question.

◆ **Use the Process of Elimination.** When answering a multiple-choice question, it should be clear that certain choices are wrong. They will be irrelevant, lack a connection to the question, or be inaccurate. After you eliminate incorrect choices, select the *best* response that remains. Often your first guess is correct.

◆ **Revisit Difficult Questions.** If you come across a difficult question, do not be discouraged. Circle or put a check mark (✓) next to any questions you are not sure how to answer. Answer these as best you can and move on to the next question. At the end of the test, go back and reread the questions you circled or checked. Sometimes the answer to a question might come to you on the second reading.

◆ **For Short-Answer and Extended-Response Questions.** Read the directions carefully. It may help to make an answer box before writing your answer. Be sure to address all parts of the question. If you have any time left, re-read your answer and correct any errors.

◆ **When You Finish.** When you finish, go back to the beginning. Review your work. Make sure you have answered all the questions. Don't disturb other students!

This final practice test indicates the *standard*, *benchmark* and *grade-level indicator* for every question being tested. This will help you and your teacher identify any areas that you might need to study further.

Good luck on this practice test!

A FINAL PRACTICE TEST

The box below should be used for writing your answers to both short-answer and extended-response questions. Fill in a copy of this box whenever a question asks you to write your response in your **Answer Document**. This box is similar in size to the space you will have for answering these questions on the actual **Ohio Achievement Test in Grade 8**. (*Your teacher has permission to photocopy this page if you or your school has purchased this book*).

Name _____ Date _____

Look at the map below.

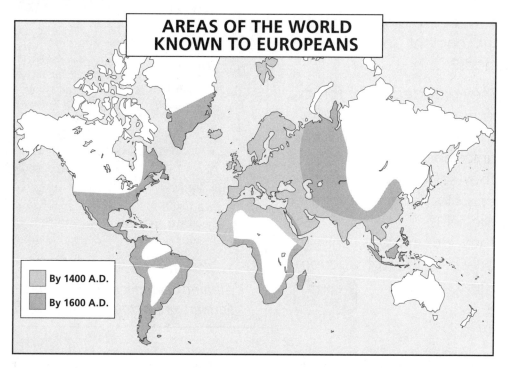

AREAS OF THE WORLD KNOWN TO EUROPEANS

By 1400 A.D.

By 1600 A.D.

1. Which statement **best** explains the changes from 1400 to 1600?

    A. European serfs began attending school after 1400.
    B. Chinese exploration awakened Europeans to new lands.
    C. New technologies led Europeans to engage in overseas exploration.
    D. European rulers sought an all-water route to West Africa.

    GEOG
    D: 7.2

2. "If a man destroyed the eye of a free man, his own eye shall be destroyed. If a man knocked out the teeth of a man of the same rank, his own teeth shall be knocked out." Which set of laws contains these rules?

    HIST
    B: 6.3

    A. the Code of Hammurabi   C. the Twelve Tables
    B. the Ten Commandments   D. rules made by the pharaoh

3. Why is it important to reflect on the performance of a classroom group in which one has participated?

    SKILLS
    D: 7.4

    A. It helps the group to manage conflict.
    B. It helps the group to establish goals and members' roles.
    C. It helps the group complete its project in an orderly and timely manner.
    D. It helps the group see if its goals were met and identify ways to improve.

Go to next page

SS Social Studies

Look at the illustration on the right.

4. What does this diagram reveal about ancient Inca farming methods?

    A. They provided crops for various groups in their society.
    B. They left much of their lands unfarmed.
    C. They set aside half of their crops for those who farmed the fields.
    D. They grew crops only for priests and high government officials.

    SKILLS
    B: 6.4

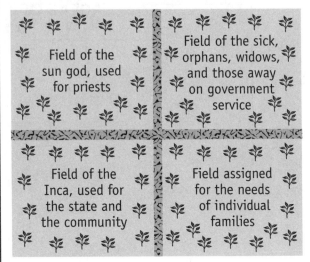

INCAN FARMING SYSTEM

Field of the sun god, used for priests

Field of the sick, orphans, widows, and those away on government service

Field of the Inca, used for the state and the community

Field assigned for the needs of individual families

All lands belonged to the community. Farmers grew crops in different fields.

5. A group of three students is assigned the task of giving an oral report to their class on the achievements of the Renaissance.

    In your **Answer Document**, identify two rules or guidelines for effective group work they should establish as they begin. (2 points)

    SKILLS
    D: 7.3

6. Early civilizations frequently specialized in producing particular goods based on the natural and human resources they had available.

    Which example correctly pairs an ancient civilization with a product that contributed to its economic growth?

    A. Ghana and lumber   C. Egypt and tea
    B. China and silk   D. India and furs

    ECO
    A: 7.1

7. What was the primary method used by Alexander the Great to spread Greek culture from North Africa to the Indus River Valley?

    A. economic opportunity
    B. military conflict
    C. technological innovation
    D. trade

    GEOG
    D: 7.5

UNLAWFUL TO PHOTOCOPY

Social Studies **SS**

8. Contact between the Aztecs and Europeans brought about many changes. How was Aztec society most affected by its contact with Spain?

    A. Aztecs adopted European weapons to defeat enemy tribes.
    B. Aztecs began eating corn as a part of their diet.
    C. Aztecs migrated to the Yucatan to escape Spanish rule.
    D. Aztecs died in great numbers after the introduction of new diseases.

    > HIST
    > D: 7.7

Look at the map below.

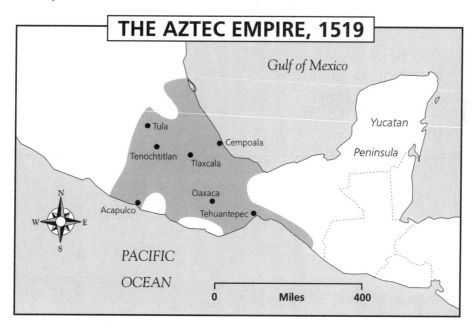

THE AZTEC EMPIRE, 1519

9. Which phrase characterizes the Aztec Empire in 1519?

    A. a physical region
    B. a trade route
    C. a human region
    D. a peninsula

    > GEOG
    > B: 6.4

10. A disagreement has arisen over the location of a common border between two countries. Which action would be **most** likely to prevent a war?

    A. The two countries agree to enter into diplomatic negotiations.
    B. Both countries reject offers from the United Nations to negotiate peace.
    C. One of the countries refuses to pull its troops out of the disputed area.
    D. One country withdraws its ambassador from the other country.

    > GOVT
    > A: 6.3

Go to next page

SS Social Studies

Look at the three historical events in the boxes below.

Tea drinking originates in China around 100 B.C.	In 1264, Marco Polo visits China and returns to Europe with tea and other goods.	Today, tea is the world's most widely consumed beverage, second only to water.

11. Which process do these events illustrate?

A. social mobility
B. cultural diffusion
C. human migration
D. Columbian Exchange

PEOPLE C: 7.3

Look at the map below.

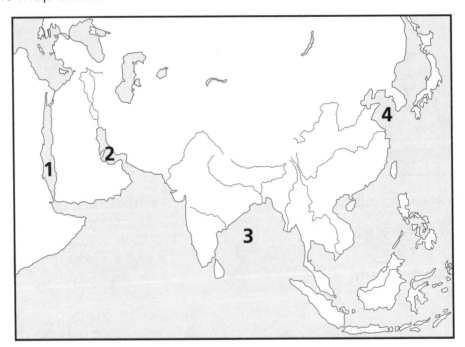

12. Which number on the map indicates where the Persian Gulf is located?

A. (1)
B. (2)
C. (3)
D. (4)

GEOG A: 6.1

Go to next page ➤

Social Studies SS

13. The achievements of early civilizations in India, China, Egypt, Greece, and Rome after 1000 B.C. still influence us today. Their accomplishments included the development of concepts of government, scientific and cultural advances, and the spread of religions.

    In your **Answer Document**, select two of these early civilizations and describe two achievements for each civilization. (4 points)

    > HIST
    > B: 7.2

Look at the map from 1000 A.D. on the right.

14. Which major world religion was practiced by most of the people living in the shaded region of the map?

    A. Buddhism
    B. Judaism
    C. Hinduism
    D. Islam

    > PEOPLE
    > A: 6.2

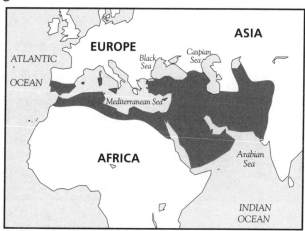

15. Which is the **best** definition of a government?

    A. A group of rules used by judges to interpret situations and settle disputes.
    B. A political organization exercising authority over the people living in a particular geographic area.
    C. An informal association of people who act to protect their neighbors from harm and discrimination.
    D. A collective effort by people from several nations acting to protect basic human rights.

    > GOVT
    > A: 6.1

16. Many religions describe their relationship with God in a sacred text.

    Which is the sacred book of Judaism?

    A. Koran
    B. Torah
    C. New Testament
    D. Upanishads

    > PEOPLE
    > A: 6.2

Go to next page

Social Studies

17. Which statement **best** explains why governments provide public goods and services for their citizens?

   A. It is not profitable for individuals or businesses to provide these necessary goods and services.

   ECO
   C: 6.6

   B. Governments do a better job of managing money than individuals and private businesses.

   C. The market system provides all the basic goods and services that people need, but government fulfills their additional wants.

   D. Governments provide these services to ensure that all household incomes are equal.

Look at the information in the boxes below.

The fertile soil of river valleys allowed the first civilizations to develop.	The Gupta Empire was separated from the north by the Himalayan and Hindu Kush Mountains.	Because Japan is mountainous, most of its people live in areas near the coast.

18. Which conclusion is **best** supported by these examples?

   A. Major urban centers are found only along rivers.

   GEOG
   C: 6.5

   B. Without mountains and rivers, people cannot become civilized.

   C. The physical geography of a region influences its human development.

   D. The spread of new ideas is often reduced by political conflict.

19. What do city-states, kingdoms, and empires have in common?

   A. All their citizens speak the same language.

   GOVT
   C: 7.2

   B. They are ruled by a king or queen with absolute authority.

   C. They have a sovereign government.

   D. They participate in some form of international organization.

20. Which economic activity was the basis for the wealth and power of the West African kingdoms of Ghana and Mali?

   A. overseas trade and exploration

   HIST
   D: 7.6

   B. farming along fertile river banks

   C. trade in salt and gold

   D. working in bronze and brass

Go to next page ➤

Social Studies

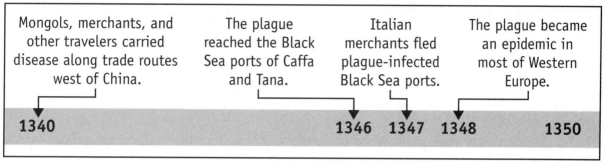

| Mongols, merchants, and other travelers carried disease along trade routes west of China. | The plague reached the Black Sea ports of Caffa and Tana. | Italian merchants fled plague-infected Black Sea ports. | The plague became an epidemic in most of Western Europe. |

1340 — 1346 — 1347 — 1348 — 1350

21. Which is a correct statement based on the timeline above?

   A. The plague primarily affected China.
   B. The interaction of people spread the plague.
   C. Most port cities remained untouched by the plague.
   D. The plague first began in Western Europe.

   SKILLS
   B: 6.2

22. Humanist scholars like Boccaccio examined worldly subjects and classical culture. Leonardo da Vinci and other painters used perspective and gradual shading to create life-like paintings.

   Which time period is directly associated with these achievements?

   A. Neolithic Revolution
   B. Middle Ages
   C. Renaissance
   D. Protestant Reformation

   HIST
   C: 7.5

23. What was the significance of the location of Constantinople?

   A. The city was able to conquer Russia.
   B. The city helped spread Christianity throughout Europe.
   C. The city controlled key trade routes between Europe and Asia.
   D. The city was able to unite Eastern Orthodox Christians and the Catholic Church.

   GEOG
   C: 7.2

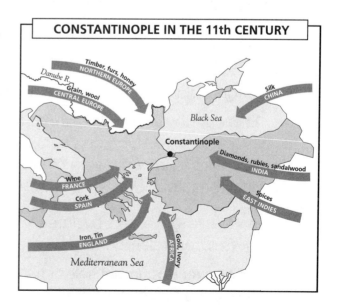

CONSTANTINOPLE IN THE 11th CENTURY

Social Studies

24. What was an important effect of the trade along the Silk Road?

   A. Roman leaders attempted to invade China.

   B   Farming methods in the steppes of Central Asia improved.

   C. Chinese religions became popular among Romans.

   D. An exchange of goods occurred between East Asia and Europe.

> PEOPLE
> A: 7.2

25. To protect themselves from the chaos and insecurity that arose after the fall of the Roman Empire, Europeans developed the system of feudalism.

   In your **Answer Document**, describe two characteristics of feudalism. (2 points)

> HIST
> C: 7.3

26. Military conflicts can sometimes bring unforeseen changes. Which military conflict led to a revival of trade and cultural interaction between Europe and the Islamic world?

   A. the Crusades

   B. the Spanish conquest of the Aztecs

   C. the Persian-Greek War

   D. the Mongol conquests

> HIST
> C: 7.4

Look at the table below.

FACTS ABOUT THE WEST AFRICAN KINGDOMS

The people of Ghana used iron to make tools and weapons.
The city of Timbuktu became known as a center of learning and trade.
Under Askia Mohammed, Songhay established a highly centralized government.

27. What conclusion can best be drawn from these facts?

   A. Religious beliefs were important to West African societies.

   B. People in West Africa and Europe had similar standards of living.

   C. West Africa and Asia were highly interdependent.

   D. West Africa achieved a high level of economic and cultural development.

> SKILLS
> B: 6.2

28. Countries are governed by three main types of government — monarchy, dictatorship, and democracy.

   In your **Answer Document**, select two of these types. For each type, describe two of its characteristics. (4 points)

> GOVT
> C: 6.4

Social Studies

Look at the statement below.

> "You have seen a great nation united under one man. You have seen his sacred power, caring and absolute. You have seen the image of God in kings. In the reflection of God's majesty lies the majesty of the Prince."
>
> — *Jacques-Benigne Bossuet*

29. Which type of government is described in this statement?

A. direct democracy
B. representative democracy
C. dictatorship
D. monarchy

GOVT
C: 6.4

Look at the illustration below.

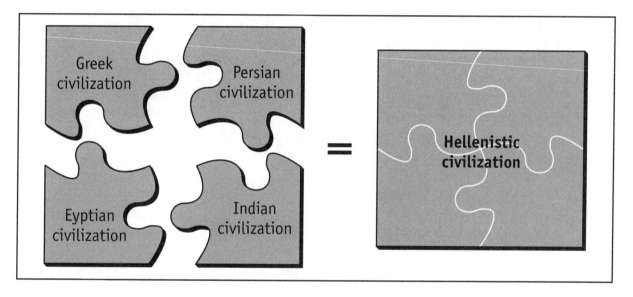

30. Which process is illustrated in this example?

A. human migration
B. military conflict
C. cultural diffusion
D. international negotiation

PEOPLE
A: 7.4

31. To obtain different perspectives on a topic, researchers often examine a variety of primary and secondary sources.

In your **Answer Document**, describe one primary and one secondary source that a researcher might use to obtain information about the spread of Buddhism in Asia. (2 points)

SKILLS
A: 6.1

Go to next page

SS Social Studies

32. Countries generally specialize in producing certain goods to lower their opportunity costs.

What is one result of such specialization?

   A. Production and consumption gradually decrease.
   B. Countries depend on trade to obtain other goods.
   C. Countries become less interdependent.
   D. Prices increase as many goods become more scarce.

ECO
B: 6.3

Look at the graphic organizer below.

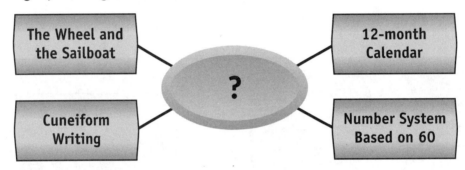

33. Which title would **best** complete this graphic organizer?

   A. Arab Accomplishments
   B. Achievements of Mesoamerican Civilizations
   C. Contributions of the Ancient Egyptians
   D. Mesopotamian Achievements

HIST
B: 6.4

34. A variety of factors can lead different cultural groups to cooperate or conflict. These factors include language, religion, economic interests, historical relationships, and forms of government.

In your **Answer Document**, identify and explain one example in which one or more of these factors caused different cultures or countries to cooperate or conflict. (2 points)

PEOPLE
B: 6.3

35. Which phrase describes Magna Carta (1215)?

   A. a journal about English feudal society
   B. an agreement establishing important individual rights
   C. a list of all the nobles in feudal England
   D. a statement of grievances by English serfs

CITIZ
B: 7.2

Go to next page ▶

UNLAWFUL TO PHOTOCOPY

Social Studies SS

Look at the multiple-tier timeline below.

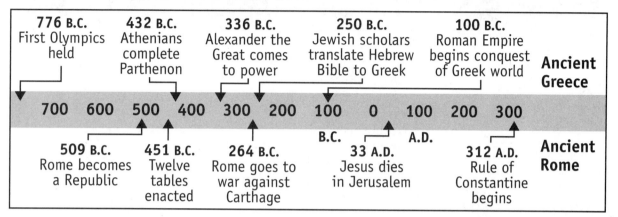

36. According to the timeline, which statement is most accurate?

    HIST A: 6.1

    A. Jesus died before Alexander the Great was crowned king.
    B. The first Olympics were held after Constantine assumed power.
    C. Rome became a republic before Alexander the Great came to power.
    D. The Twelve Tables and the Parthenon were completed at the same time.

"After we crossed this bridge, [the Aztec Emperor] Montezuma came to greet us. With him came two hundred lords, all barefoot and dressed in a different costumes, but also very rich... They came in two columns, pressed close to the walls of the street, which is wide and beautiful."

Hernán Cortés, Spanish Noble

"My people were devastated by diseases brought to our land by Cortés and his men. Entire villages were destroyed by small pox, whooping cough, malaria, and yellow fever. We have never seen such horrible diseases. My people lacked all resistance to them, and many people died."

— Montezuma, Aztec Ruler

37. Which best explains why these two accounts focus on different aspects of the same encounter?

    SKILLS C: 7.2

    A. Each author had different motives, concerns and perspectives.
    B. Montezuma was too proud to ask Cortés for help.
    C. Only one of the authors was telling the truth.
    D. Cortés deliberately brought new diseases with him to destroy the Aztecs.

38. Under which system of government do citizens participate by electing legislative representatives and other public officials?

    CITIZ A: 7.1

    A. monarchy   C. direct democracy
    B. representative democracy   D. dictatorship

STOP

INDEX